Aug. 24, 2009

Why Sh*t Happens

Why Sh*t Happens

THE SCIENCE OF
A REALLY BAD DAY

PETER J. BENTLEY, PhD

Rodale books may be purchased for business or promotional use or for special sales. For information, please write to:
Special Markets Department, Rodale Inc., 733 Third Avenue, New York, NY 10017

Printed in the United States of America
Rodale Inc. makes every effort to use acid-free ♾, recycled paper ♻.

Book design by Christina Gaugler
Interior illustrations by Hugh D'Andrade

The information in this book was previously published in the UK by Random House under the title *The Undercover Scientist*.

Library of Congress Cataloging-in-Publication Data

Bentley, P. J.
  Why sh*t happens : the science of a really bad day / Peter J. Bentley.
      p.   cm.
  Includes bibliographical references and index.
  ISBN-13 978–1–59486–956–3 hardcover
  ISBN-10 1–59486–956–1 hardcover
  1. Science—Humor.   2. Science—Miscellanea.   I. Title.
Q167.B46   2009
502'.07—dc22   2008043619

Distributed to the trade by Macmillan

2   4   6   8   10   9   7   5   3   1   hardcover

We inspire and enable people to improve their lives and the world around them

For more of our products visit **rodalestore.com** or call 800-848-4735

CONTENTS

PROLOGUE ix

INTRODUCTION xi

1 Oblivious Beginnings................................. 1

2 Bathroom Skating....................................... 8

3 Sword Fighting... 14

4 Dark Clouds 21

5 Flash in the Pan 27

6 Cheesy Grimace... 35

7 Drowning Out Noise 42

8 Warm Snow 49

9 Losing Track.. 56

10 Losing Grip... 64

11 Mixing Your Drinks.................................. 72

12 An Unpleasant Trip................................... 79

13 Coming Unstuck.. 87

14 Staying Afloat 93

15 Knowing Your Place 100

16 Pain in the Neck 107

17 Lost Underfoot 113

18 Crossed Connections 120

19 Hissy Fits.. 127

20 Mightier Than the Sword 134

21 Seeing Is Not Believing 143

22 Ripping Yarns.. 150

23 Infectious Messages 157

24 Tight Squeeze.. 164

25 Fading Memories 170

26 Shattered Hopes 177

27 That Sinking Feeling 185

28 Feel the Burn 192

29 Kitchen Fireworks 199

30 Finally Cracked 207

31 A Black Mark 214

32 Hot and Bothered 221

33 Taking It All In 228

34 Shocking... 236

35 Pus in Boots.. 244

36 Jumping Tunes 251

37 Chewing It Over 258

38 Patience and Pain... 266

39 Eureka! 273

SELECTED BIBLIOGRAPHY.. 281

ACKNOWLEDGMENTS 295

INDEX.. 297

PROLOGUE

When I watch television, I can't help but be puzzled. I live in a society built on science, but it is a society filled with contradictions in its attitudes. The painstaking efforts of scientists enable our technology to work, our medicines to save lives, our criminals to be identified. We know the nature of our world, the life that surrounds us, and the universe we share, all because of the work of scientists. Yet opinions have become confused. Science is respected, trusted, and largely misunderstood. Fewer and fewer children want to study sciences, thinking that such topics are incomprehensible or boring. Worse still, many adults seem to believe that science might even be the cause of new misfortunes in their lives. If scientists hadn't developed computers, we'd never have to worry about them getting viruses. If they hadn't invented superglue, we'd never accidentally adhere our fingers together. If they hadn't created the tiny MP3 player, we'd never be able to drop our entire music collection down the toilet. Perhaps, they think, without science our lives would be much simpler and we would all be happier. (Ignorant, starving, suffering from many medical conditions, and living in caves, but happier.)

In this book I'll try and show that this is entirely the wrong way to think about science. Blaming science for mishaps is like blaming the power of speech for all the arguments in the world. Should we abandon speech, or simply learn to exploit its power?

Turning your back on science is closing the door on curiosity. It means you have stopped wondering *why*. Science is nothing more or less than our best way of understanding the world around us. It's not a machine or technology. It's just a simple, cynical process followed by a human being: I will only believe something is true when I have enough evidence to support that belief. If I think a new medicine works better, I have to prove it. If I think a certain material interacts with heat in a specific way, I have to perform tests to show that it really does. Like a detective gathering evidence to prove the guilt or innocence of a suspect, scientists gather evidence to support or refute an idea. The more evidence that supports it, the more likely it is to be true. But when the evidence does not quite support the idea, then that idea is modified, updated, and improved, and then the testing begins again.

So if something goes wrong—if my car skids on the road, or my engine is damaged by filling its tank with diesel instead of regular gasoline—science is not to blame, but the results of science can provide me with explanations of what happened. What I do with that understanding is my own responsibility. In this book, I give you that responsibility. I'll open the door to curiosity and help you wonder again, by questioning those sometimes frustrating events that happen to you every day, and by explaining the best understandings science gives us to date. In the process, I'll show that science can be exciting and fascinating (and sometimes a little revolting), and helps us understand the true nature of our world.

INTRODUCTION

There are no sirens or flashing lights. No police tape securing the premises. No undercover scientists arriving in discreet vans with tinted windows and no clunk of the doors as they step out, wearing sunglasses and carrying impressive black bags filled with anonymous equipment. You are on your own. And you alone will have to solve the mess in front of you. Whether it's a new stain on the expensive rug, your favorite MP3 player rattling around inside the washing machine, or chewing gum entangled in your hair, this is *your* problem. So what are you going to do about it?

You could move your sofa over the stain, sorrowfully throw the soggy MP3 player in the kitchen drawer with all the other nonfunctioning junk, or snip out a chunk of your hair. You could tell yourself that it was Murphy's Law (if it can go wrong, it probably will). You could buy some chocolate ice cream, and try and tell yourself that it didn't matter anyway.

Or you could try to understand why. You could look through a magnifying glass and discover the science behind your mishaps. You could understand exactly what went wrong and how it happened. Soon an accident won't spoil your day any more than a crime spoils the day of a policeman, for you will know exactly what to do to clear up the mess.

Your first step is to understand why accidents happen. We're not talking about accidents that the police, firefighters, or EMTs have to deal with. No, our mishaps are much more common, everyday occurrences. They're the frustrating annoyances that trip up our day, that at the time may drive us nuts, but to which we later respond resignedly with a shrug of our shoulders and the phrase, "Sh*t happens." Even if it's not happening to you, somewhere nearby, it is happening to someone as you read these words. Each of these occurrences is caused by technology going wrong, or more commonly, us going wrong with our technology.

Our world is full of the most astonishing inventions, from MP3 players to stain-eating soaps. Each of these is the product of centuries of scientific and technological effort, resulting in an artifact that is designed to improve our lives in some small but significant way. But the technology that surrounds us is based on a set of assumptions about how it will be used. Shampoo works just fine in your hair, but spilled on the floor it suddenly becomes a slippery mishap waiting to happen. The objects that we use every day are only designed to operate in the right context. Put that object out of context (metal in a microwave, chewing gum in your hair, wine on a rug) and suddenly the science works against you. Now the dirt-removing soap acts as a lubricant on your feet—exactly the worst place for it. The metal in the microwave causes alarming sparks to zap and crackle inside. The chewing gum becomes an appalling adhesive impossible to untangle from your hair. The spilled wine is transformed into a dye that seems more permanent than the original pattern on the rug.

Sh*t, as they say, happens—and always will. But now you will know exactly *why*. Enter, if you dare, the world of everyday disaster. The superstitious among you know that accidents happen in 3s, and that 13 is the unluckiest number. So imagine, if you will, 13 triplets of catastrophe—yes, 39 mishaps—are about to hit you one after the other. Prepare yourself for the most accident-prone day of your life.

Oblivious Beginnings

A little snore emerges from the pile of bedding. You're fast asleep, and dreaming that you're lost in a busy city. You stop to cross the street and a car pulls up in front of you. The next thing you know, it becomes a truck backing toward you, making a reversing *beep, beep,* warning noise. You wait for it to stop and turn, thinking how familiar it sounds. Of course it sounds familiar, you realize—it's your father's truck that he uses to pick up the groceries. But he seems to be having trouble turning it, going forward, then backing up again. Finally he moves off, and you see that it wasn't a truck at all. Why would he use a truck for a box of cereal? It was a bicycle. You find yourself riding the bicycle with him, whizzing down a hill, the wind in your hair. There are lovely fields of flowers rushing by, faster and faster. You look down and see you're on roller skates. Surely this is a bit fast to be traveling on roller skates?

You groan and turn over, looking up at the ceiling. That was a weird dream, you begin to think, as it fades from your memory. You rub your eyes and look at the clock. You frown. The hands seem to be in the wrong places. You reach over and pick it up. That can't be right. Your watch, also on the bedside table, confirms that it is right. You're late! You've managed to sleep straight through the loudest alarm clock ever invented! But you're such a light sleeper—how could this possibly happen?

Sleep is not a simple activity. You may like to think of it as a bit of shut-eye or a little snooze, but your body and brain undergo some remarkable changes during sleep. If they didn't, you would literally lose your mind in a matter of days. We're all just 7 days from madness.

Going to sleep is not an on or off activity. We don't just "fall asleep" or "wake up"—it's actually much more complicated than that. We're also never "half asleep" as the common expression suggests, but we do slowly sink into different depths of sleep. These are called stages, and there are five different stages of sleep that we cycle through, several times every night.

When you settle down into bed and close your eyes, your first task is to move from wakefulness to stage 1 sleep. It's a gradual process in which your muscles relax, your brain slows down, and your eyes become more static. Your breathing becomes shallow and regular. If the electrical activity of your brain were being measured, we would see you moving from alpha waves to theta waves—your neurons are changing from a relaxed pulsing state to a slower, more synchronized state. But if you're disturbed during this stage, you probably won't even be aware that you'd been asleep. Stage 1 sleep lasts for 5 to 10 minutes, before you start to sink into stage 2.

Now your heart rate slows and your body temperature decreases. You may begin to snore, if you have a suitably floppy throat. Your muscles may occasionally twitch. Taking a look at the electrical activity of your brain, we would see spiky interruptions to your slow, pulsing theta waves, corresponding to those twitches. Your body is preparing for the deeper sleep of stages 3 and 4. Now your brain slows down even further, the neurons firing in relaxed pulses that become longer, slower delta waves. You're in stage 3 sleep and snoring at full volume. Stage 3 gradually becomes stage 4 when your brain produces the slower delta waves more than half of the time. This behavior of the brain is very different from the fast-changing, chaotic, and unsynchronized activity that takes place during wakefulness. Not surprisingly, you are the most disorientated when woken from a deep sleep.

Stage 4 is when sleep talking and sleepwalking occur. These behaviors have little to do with dreaming, because you are not yet dreaming. Movement and activity during deep sleep is driven more by primitive, instinctive emotions such as fear or anger. Astonishingly, people are capable of amazingly complex behavior while in this state. Those who suffer from severe sleep disorders may go to the kitchen and prepare and eat a meal, or, in more extreme cases, jump out of their bedroom window or drive a car. Somehow all the necessary parts of your brain are hijacked by this deeper, instinctive part of you, without your conscious mind ever waking up. Thankfully, severe sleep disorders are rare. Many of us may mumble a few words during deep sleep, but most of us are oblivious to the world, our brains in the most relaxed state possible.

The different stages of sleep each initially last around 10 minutes, and then go into reverse. After descending into the depths of stage 4, your brain then slowly wakes again, moving back to stage 3, then to stage 2. About 90 minutes after you first fall asleep your brain has almost risen back to wakefulness. But instead of moving to stage 1 and waking up, we move from stage 2 into a different kind of brain activity—dreaming. This is known as REM sleep (REM being an acronym for rapid eye movement). REM sleep is easy to detect, because the brain and body undergo profound changes. Your heart rate and breathing speed up, your body suddenly relaxes, and your eyes dart back and forth quickly behind your closed eyelids. Measuring your brain activity at this point would show your brain is closer to its state when awake, with a complicated mixture of asynchronous neuron firing. You are now in a dream world, though unaware, of course, that you are dreaming. You act out different roles in a virtual world made up by your own brain. Your moving eyes are following dream events as though they are real. To prevent your other muscles from doing the same, your brain has cut its own phone lines by blocking all messages from motor neurons to your major skeletal muscles. Your brain can no longer move any muscles except the ones controlling your eyes, and the involuntary muscles involved with your breathing and heart rate.

Dreaming is the best form of virtual reality there is. You genuinely believe you are experiencing the bizarre and often contradictory world unfolding around you. You may be exhilarated, saddened, angered, or even frightened by these experiences. They may be heavily influenced by very recent events in your waking life, or they may seem to have no clear relation to anything you've experienced. But they are all figments of your own imagination.

It may seem like a lost opportunity—each night we create entire worlds, memories, and experiences for ourselves, yet we have no control over them and little memory of them afterward.

If only we could control our dreams, we would be gods of our own virtual universes every night, able to dream whatever we wanted. Fascinatingly, there is a technique known as lucid dreaming that makes this possible. It can only occur during REM sleep, and it usually happens when your conscious mind becomes aware that your virtual world just doesn't make sense. Perhaps you've pinched your nose and found you can still breathe through it, or you keep trying to read some text that changes every time you look at it. Or perhaps you realize that there are no such things as cartoon monsters in the real world. Whatever the trigger, when you realize you are asleep, your conscious mind is suddenly able to control the dream. More than 50 percent of us have had moments of lucidity during dreaming. Frequently the realization will simply make us wake up and the moment is lost. But with practice, we actually can hone our ability to control our own dreams. For some, this becomes such a fun experience that they use gadgets that will slightly disturb them during REM sleep.

Initially, dreaming lasts for only about 10 minutes. Then you may briefly wake up and turn over, or you may just sink back down through the stages of sleep again. This cycle of descending into deep sleep, then rising up to dream, then descending down again, will happen several times every night. In each cycle you spend less time in deep sleep and more time in REM sleep, until by the end of the night you may have had dreams that lasted as long as an hour. A typical person may have about five cycles of deep sleep and REM sleep every night. These cycles are heavily affected by age. Babies and young children spend much more time in REM sleep than adults do. As we get older, we also sleep less deeply, so adults spend less time in stages 4 and 5 and are more likely to enter REM sleep sooner and remain in it longer during the first sleep cycle.

We're still not sure why the brain sleeps the way it does. We don't know why we dream, and we don't know why we yo-yo between deeper and lighter stages of sleep every night. Perhaps it is an old evolutionary trick to make sure we are able to become alert to danger during the night. Perhaps it's a way to enable us to sort through the experiences of the previous day and better understand them. It seems likely that we're not the only ones who use this trick, though: most mammals and birds also sleep and dream like we do.

By the end of the night, most of us are spending little time in deep sleep and most of the time in REM sleep. It's why we often wake with a dream fresh in our minds—we have just stepped from our dreams into reality. It also means that should we hear any familiar noises that we've heard many times before, we are more likely to incorporate them into our dreams than to wake up. Even if we do briefly wake (and hit the snooze button), we're able to roll over and start dreaming again almost immediately because we're mostly in REM sleep by the morning.

Oversleeping often becomes a problem if you have not had enough sleep, if you're depressed, or if you haven't been sleeping normally. People who snore badly (enough to affect their breathing or enough for their partners to wake them), or who suffer from insomnia, may have interrupted sleep cycles, making them tired and irritable during the day. But if you are unfortunate enough to be deprived of all sleep (requiring constant and probably life-threatening disturbances to you), it only takes three days before you start to hallucinate and lose the ability to think normally. Prolonged lack of sleep also has a dramatic and serious effect on the immune system, to such an extent that you may die if you have no sleep at all for more than 11 days. But if you are an insomniac, don't worry. During those long hours that you may lie in bed, wishing for sleep, you will slip into stage 1 and 2 sleep regularly without being aware of it. It's enormously hard to stop someone from sleeping, just as it's enormously hard to stop someone from going to the toilet. There are some things we just have to do.

Ironically, waking up at the right time in the morning is a real problem for those who suffer from insomnia, but sleeping late happens to all of us now and again. Oversleeping is so common that there are a huge number of clever alarm clocks for sale. Some try to stop you from getting used to their alarms by making a different noise each day. Others actually jump off your bedside table while making the noise, forcing you to get out of bed and find them.

In the end, the best solution is to simply establish a good routine: Make sure you go to bed at a similar time each night and give yourself enough time to sleep (8 hours is recommended). Then, whether the alarm clock has gone off or not, you'll find you naturally wake up at the right time.

BATHROOM SKATING

Steam fills the bathroom with a swirling haze made golden by the morning sun. Standing with your eyes shut, your face toward the water, the remnants of last night's dreams flit through your mind like the shadows of birds flying past the window. You grope blindly for the shampoo bottle. Popping the top open, you pour some shampoo into a wet hand. It feels cold against your skin. As you try to put the bottle back, it slips from your grasp and bounces to the middle of the bathroom floor, the noise echoing around the small space. A quick peek around the shower curtain reveals that the bottle has landed on its side and is oozing shampoo onto the tile floor. You sigh, and leaving the water running, step out to pick up the bottle before its contents are lost. Leaving a trail of steaming water, you grab the bottle and turn, your foot squelching into something cold. Suddenly the world spins upside down. The next thing you know you're staring at the dusty underside of your sink, freezing cold tiles against your back, head throbbing painfully.

We've all had times when a shower or bath seems more like an obstacle course than a relaxing wash. Surely in our modern world, such bathroom danger is unnecessary. Why don't we have nonslippery shampoo? It's not like we're choosing to wash our hair in a lubricant like car oil . . . is it?

Washing your hair with gloopy oil does not sound like any sensible way to clean it. Surely massaging a dollop of pig fat into your scalp must be a horribly messy experience. Yet the ancient Greeks and Romans mostly preferred oils when bathing—they massaged the oils into their skin and then scraped off the excess along with (at least some of) the dirt, like cleaning a window with a squeegee.

Oil and soap may seem very different; in fact they are both largely composed of the same ingredients: fatty oils. Some of the earliest recorded uses of soap date back nearly 5,000 years, and the sapindus tree (often called soapberry or soapnut) has been used even longer. We don't know who first discovered the recipe for soap, though some theories suggest that the gooey remains of animal sacrifices may have been involved. In reality, this is probably nothing more than a myth.

The recipe for soap is very simple. Just find some ashes and pour water through them until you have "lye water"—or water made alkaline by the addition of potassium hydroxide. Put an egg in the solution to test if it is ready. If the egg floats, the solution is done. Next, get some fat or oil. Animal fats were often used, but olive oil is perhaps a bit nicer. Then mix the two, being sure to add just the right amount of oil to the mixture (the precise mixture depends on the types of oils used). You can boil it or mix it cold; either way, the same chemical reaction will occur. It's called saponification and, although a similar reaction can happen with other ingredients, when making soap it involves an alkali (the lye water) reacting to fat or oil. If we were to zoom in a few million times, we'd see that the oil is made up of triplets of similar molecules, stuck together. The alkali breaks down those molecules, severing bonds between some atoms, and chopping off chunks of them. The pieces that are left rearrange themselves in a different way and what's left is no longer oil and alkali, but a form of sugar alcohol called glycerol, and soap.

Because this chemical reaction only needs a couple of simple ingredients, there have been a few rare cases where it has happened naturally to buried corpses. If the cemetery soil happens to be very alkaline and few worms or bacteria are present, then saponification can turn body fat into adipocere, or "grave wax," as it is often called. One of the most extreme cases of this phenomenon happened to a woman buried sometime in the 19th century, whose entire body slowly turned to soap. The "Soap Woman" is now on display in the Mütter Museum in Philadelphia. She wasn't alone—a "Soap Man" buried with her was also found; he is sometimes displayed in the Smithsonian Institution.

Thankfully, the soap we use today has nothing to do with dead bodies of any type and often uses plant oils such as palm or olive oil with a few extra ingredients to make it smell nice. The soap is carefully purified to remove unwanted compounds such as glycerol, and sometimes finely ground scouring powder such as pumice is added to help the soap scrub away dead skin cells.

Hopefully you are aware that soap is good at removing dirt (if not, go take a shower—you stink!). Soap has this property because of another chemical reaction. Soap molecules are like tiny snakes made of sodium or potassium fatty acid salts. When water comes into contact with these long salt molecules, the head of the snake becomes negatively charged. The head then attracts water to it (becomes hydrophilic) and the tail repels water molecules (becomes hydrophobic). When dropped into water, it's a bit of a dilemma for each soap molecule—one end wants to be in contact with the water, and the other wants to get as far away from the water as possible. Their clever solution is to join forces with their friends and form themselves into little spheres with all the heads pointing outward and all the tails tucked inside, away from the water. But drop soap into oil, and suddenly the tables are turned. Now the tails love the oil, and the heads want to hide away. So this time the little globules are inside out, with heads buried away from the oil and tails on the outside.

The strange behavior of soap molecules makes them a surface active agent, or surfactant—they are able to break down the normal resistance between liquids such as water and oil, and allow the two to mix in an emulsion. Soap does not allow oil to dissolve in water—it can't do that because the two liquids are so repelled by one another that they are unmixable (or to use the right word: immiscible). So it does the next best thing. When you lather your skin with soap, the oil-loving tails of the soap molecules attach themselves to the natural oils and grease. Then when you rinse the soap off, the soap forms itself into those little globules with the heads on the outside, and the tails—still holding on to the oils—on the inside. So the soap has wrapped the oil from your skin in little parcels, allowing dirt and oil to be dispersed in the water and washed away. Most dirt is soluble in either water or oil, so if you are removing oil and using water at the same time, then you're going to take away most of the dirt.

Although we've had soap for thousands of years, soap-based shampoo is a much newer invention. Primitive shampoos of various types were usually made from mixtures of herbs, water, or sometimes, oils. More recently, the success of modern soap led to the first soap-based shampoos. These were liquid soaps designed to clean and remove oils from the hair, made from soap flakes dissolved in water. Unfortunately, soap works too well—it removes all of your natural hair oil (called sebum), making the hair brittle and prone to damage. For this reason, in the 1930s, the first synthetic shampoo made from synthesized detergent (rather than soap) was invented. Since then, all shampoos have been made synthetically, carefully designed to strip away some, but not all, of the natural oils of the hair. They use slightly different compounds than those in ordinary soap to make the detergent a little less effective, but the underlying principles are identical—shampoo is a surfactant and its molecules grab the oils and dirt and wrap them in nice water-loving parcels, allowing you to wash the water-oil emulsion away.

Shampoos also have another thing in common with soaps. They are slippery. This property helps us apply the soap or shampoo, so it is useful. But we did not choose to make them slippery—it is a property that all soaps, shampoos, and indeed surfactants have. Even if we wanted a nonslippery shampoo, we would find it extremely hard to make. Soaps and shampoos are made from oils, and as such their molecular structure is similar enough to give them many of the same properties as oils. They also like to grab hold of oils and hold them in suspension, adding yet more slipperiness.

A substance is slippery because of friction, or the lack of it. Friction is the force that slows down the motion of two surfaces rubbing together. Even two surfaces that may seem perfectly smooth and shiny will contain countless little bumps when examined under a microscope. Sliding one past the other grinds the two surfaces together, causing all those rough bumps to slow down the motion and heat up the surfaces. (In fact, a lot of friction is caused by temporary chemical bonds forming between two surfaces, so they don't have to be rough to be high in friction.) Friction is great when moving around—tires wouldn't stick to the road without it, nor would our feet stick to the ground. But for anything that has moving parts (and that's most of our machines in the world), friction is a problem. Unwanted friction inside an engine will make it heat up, wear out, or seize up altogether—which is why we need a lot of oil in a car. Oil is a lubricant—a nice gloopy substance that gets between the two surfaces and stops them from rubbing together. Most lubricants are oil-based because oil coats surfaces and forms stable layers or films rather than being squeezed away, as water would be.

But the latest research in tribology (it has nothing to do with tribes; it's the study of interacting surfaces, friction, and lubrication) is pointing to a new type of lubricant—surfactants. Not traditionally considered suitable for lubrication (who wants an "oil" that is washed away by water?), it is only in the past few years that these compounds in shampoos and soaps have been investigated seriously. It turns out that they also have the same properties as oils—they are good at coating surfaces and forming films between surfaces. Although you and everyone you know may have been slipping on soap for decades, only recently have scientists and engineers begun to realize that these compounds would make great lubricants—perhaps in machines that already use water, such as hydraulic systems or drilling platforms that use water for cooling the drills.

So the next time you slip on shampoo, remember: It's not your fault. The stuff is literally as slippery as the oil that was used to make it in the first place.

- 3 -

SWORD FIGHTING

You stand in front of the mirror, razor in hand. It's an old one and you know you should replace the blades, but you're in a hurry, your head hurts, and you've still got to make an early meeting at work. After a squeaky wipe of the mirror to clear the fog, you apply some shaving cream and get to work. The razor feels smooth as you hurriedly pull it along your skin. Nice. You wash off the remaining foam and admire your handiwork. Just one little bit you missed, but that is easily remedied—ow! You stare in disbelief as a line of red blood pushes its way through a perfectly straight cut in your skin. You don't have time for this, so you wet a tissue and wipe away the blood. But the line of blood keeps reappearing, every time you wipe it. It doesn't hurt, but it's going to make a mess on your clothes if it keeps bleeding like this. Why doesn't it stop?

For more than 7,000 years, unwanted hair has been plucked, shaved, dissolved, and even burned from our bodies. In ancient Egypt, the upper classes shaved their faces and heads with razors, and Pharaohs had carefully trimmed beards. A thousand years later in Greece, Alexander the Great shaved himself so that his enemies could not grab his beard in battle (or so he told his generals) and influenced fashion around the world.

Greek women burned off leg hair with a lamp. (Don't try this at home unless you want a trip to the hospital!). Before long, the Romans were influenced by these new styles. A daily visit to the tonsor (barber) became part of normal life and a good place to chat with friends. Beards would be trimmed, hair styled, and faces shaved using iron razors. This was often a painful process because the razors did not stay sharp for long and no soap or cream was used. Eventually, the first shave for young Roman men even became a rite of passage into manhood, celebrated by a ceremony. Among women, unwanted hair was more likely to be plucked than shaved. For many centuries, a high forehead and thin eyebrows were seen as a sign of aristocracy, so women would pluck their hairlines back an inch or two and remove their eyelashes and all of their eyebrows. They painted on thin brows afterward.

The first safety razor was not invented and sold until the 20th century. A salesman called "King Camp Gillette" noticed that the traditional cut-throat razors became blunt and needed to be sharpened all the time. They were also dangerous and had a habit of cutting skin. Gillette thought that a disposable razor could solve both problems. He teamed up with an engineer from MIT and together they created the first razor with a wire in front of the blade to help prevent the skin from being cut. Gillette also created what is now known as the "razor and blades business model" when he decided to sell the razors at a loss and make up the profit by selling replacement blades that would fit into the holder. It was a cunning plan that launched a highly successful company. Gillette (and its other brands, including Braun and Duracell) was eventually sold to Procter & Gamble in

2005 for $57 billion, and it continues to be a market leader today.

Modern razors are safer than they have ever been, but they are not infallible. They always contain some of the sharpest blades we can make, so they are dangerous. Use one incorrectly—press too hard, use without proper lubrication, or shave across a bump or wrinkle—and you won't just slice the hair, you will also slice your skin.

Cutting hair is no problem. Hair is the extrusion of a kind of protein in a tubular shape, like a slow squirt of toothpaste solidifying from a tube. The toothpaste tube is a hair follicle—a group of cells that grow very rapidly, deep within the skin. These are fed by our blood supply to keep them alive. Nerves are wrapped around the follicle to allow us to feel the movement of each hair, and a tiny muscle allows the hair to be raised up (and cause a goose bump). Closer to the surface, a tiny gland produces sebum, the oil that coats the growing shaft of hair and keeps it supple. There's also sometimes another little gland to produce scent. The shaft of hair (the toothpaste) is made from keratin, and so the part of the shaft visible above the skin is not alive. When we cut it, we feel nothing, because all the nerves are deep within the skin and the hair follicle itself is unharmed. But plucking or waxing is another matter—you are ripping out the hair and taking some of the deep-seated follicle with it, as well as ripping away the nerve endings. It hurts!

Fascinatingly, we have every hair follicle we'll ever use by the time we are a 22-week-old fetus. The follicles may become more or less active depending on our age and hormones, but we will never lose them—even if we might hurt them now and again through plucking. (Even those of us who go bald still have all our follicles on our heads; they just work less well.)

Our skin is another matter altogether. Hair follicles, nerves, sebaceous glands, muscles, and scent glands are just a few of the extraordinarily diverse components of this organ (which is the largest and heaviest organ of the human body). The skin also helps us maintain our body temperature by excreting water from pores in the form of sweat, and even excreting a very dilute form of urea (the stuff you pee). That's why if you eat something particularly stinky, you may smell of it for a while. It's not only your breath that has the odor—it's your skin as well. Your skin is also packed full of sensory cells that allow you to feel temperature, pressure, surface contact, and pain. It has cells called melanocytes that create the melanin that gives your skin its pigment and helps protect you from the sun. It even has special enzymes that help cells repair damage caused by the sun to the DNA within skin cells, and to prevent them from becoming cancerous.

Your skin has a remarkable blood supply, which not only feeds all of these cells but also allows you to cool down further by dilating vessels close to the surface. It's why your face may be red after exercising and look rather pale on a cold day. When you're hot, blood moves closer to the skin's surface to help the heat radiate away; when you're cold, the warmth is kept more central, away from the chilly air.

One of the primary functions of the skin is to protect our internal organs from the outside world. There are countless viruses, bacteria, fungi, and parasites all doing their best to find a new home where they can raise their young. Our warm, wet bodies make lovely homes for them, if they can only get inside us. This is where our skin comes in. Not only does it form a tough, stretchy barrier, ideal for protecting us against bumps and bashes, but it also has its own built-in army ready and waiting to attack potential invaders. Some of the most important soldiers in the army are called Langerhans cells. These are a type of immune cell within the skin, designed to gobble up anything nearby and tell their friends what they have found. If one happens to eat something nasty like a no-good bacterium, it sends out an alert and will quickly attract other immune cells. This causes swelling and allows the main force of the immune system to attack any more invaders. It's a good strategy, since most of the nasties like bacteria and viruses reproduce exceedingly quickly.

But if they can enter through a pore, which is too small to see, then when we cut ourselves shaving we open up a Grand Canyon for them. Although a razor cut is usually not deep enough to cut beyond the dermis (the lowest layer of skin where the hair follicles live), it is still deep enough to hit the tiny blood vessels, and so you will see the leaking blood pushing through the cut like a burst water pipe in the ground. It may seem like a disaster for the security forces in the skin; a hole ripped in a wall is not good for keeping unwanted visitors out. But although razors are a relatively new invention, living creatures have been encountering sharp objects throughout their evolutionary history. Sharp rocks, sticks, or more often, sharp teeth have been injuring us for hundreds of millions of years. If we didn't have an effective way of surviving these wounds then we would not live very long, so life has evolved some very clever mechanisms to cope.

When our skin is punctured and blood oozes out, the very best thing that could happen would be for the blood itself to seal up the very hole it is escaping from. So that is exactly what it does. As soon as a blood vessel is damaged and blood meets air, a series of chemical reactions takes place. Little cells known as platelets that are present in the blood find themselves in this new chemical environment and they become activated, getting very excited and activating their friends around them. The platelets immediately become sticky and glue themselves to the edges of the wound, and even create a net of a protein called fibrin, which is glued across the wound and catches more platelets. Before you know it, the gap has been plugged. It may be a slightly messy plug, but it was done in a hurry and can be cleaned up later. This plug is a blood clot, and when it hardens in place, we call it a scab. An army of immune cells gathers in the area just in case anything nasty got through while the defenses were down, causing redness and swelling. Over the next few days your cells slowly regrow and repair the damage under the scab until after around a week there is fresh, clean skin again, and the scab is discarded.

One advantage of a nick by a razor blade is that it is a very clean cut. A blade that is more blunt would rip your skin and create more damage. A shallow and clean incision means less destruction to the skin, and so if you are quick and press on the cut for 20 minutes, you may find that the platelets manage to bind your skin together from within quite invisibly. However, one common mistake is to keep touching a bleeding area with wet tissue paper—or even tear a little dry piece of tissue off and stick it to the wound. It's a bad idea for several reasons: You're bringing a foreign object into contact with an open wound, giving all of the bacteria and viruses a free taxi ride straight to where they want to go. You're also wiping or pulling away the platelets that are doing their best to plug the hole, so you'll only make it bleed for longer. For something as minor as a nick by a razor, your body knows exactly how to repair itself, keeping you healthy and looking good.

Dark Clouds

The kitchen clock indicates that you have a whole half-hour before you need to leave. A wave of relief washes over you—there's plenty of time for breakfast. You grab a bagel and roughly cut it into two, pushing the uneven, bready surface into the toaster. While it toasts, you go back to the bedroom to iron the creased shirt you'd thrown on, thinking you were late. You turn on the radio. One of your favorite songs is playing and you do a little boogie as you iron. Just 3 or 4 minutes later and the shirt is perfectly pressed. Turning the iron off, you smell something burning. Is the iron overheating? It looks fine. Suddenly your smoke alarm starts shrieking and you realize something is amiss in the kitchen. You run back and are greeted by the sight of black smoke billowing from your toaster. Your bagel!

Toasters are dangerous things. If you take a look at one while it's in use, on each side of the toast you'll see a meandering wire that glows orange and emits heat. This wire carries live electricity straight from your wall outlet. If you were unfortunate enough to touch this wire with a metal knife, you'd be electrocuted as surely as if you'd stuck that knife into a live socket. A toaster simply pushes an electric charge through the wire to make it glow red hot, then it turns itself off after a certain amount of time. A lightbulb makes light and heat in the same way, except the little wire is called a filament and it's held inside a glass bulb filled with gas to make it shine brightly and have a long life. An electric iron also works using the same principle. Electricity is so commonly used to generate heat that we often take it for granted. Even a computer gets hot and requires little fans to cool itself down. But how exactly does electricity turn into heat?

The electrical current that flows in the wiring of your house or apartment is called alternating current, or AC for short. It's different from direct current (DC) that comes from batteries because it doesn't exactly flow. Alternating electrical current is a push-pull-push-pull current, a crazy tug-of-war with the rope going back and forth 50 or 60 times per second, depending on the country. (This is why "50 hertz" or "60 hertz" is written on the back of electrical appliances.) AC is used because it can be transformed to different voltages and currents very easily, which makes it a little simpler to transmit energy from the power stations to our homes.

If AC is like an oscillating tug-of-war rope, then the rope inside the wires is made from little tiny particles called electrons. These naturally orbit atoms like planets orbiting the sun. They orbit a long way from the neutrons and protons in the middle, and they zip around at different distances, just as Pluto orbits our sun from much farther away than does Earth. In metals, the outermost electrons are able to hop from one atom to another. The movement of these "free electrons" is what we call an electric current. The pressure exerted on those electrons in order to move them is the electric voltage. (That pressure is like an invisible electric field, such as magnetism.) So our AC tug-of-war is an in-out-in-out pressure produced by the generators of power stations that moves free electrons back and forth within the wiring of our homes. Power stations don't really make electricity. They act as giant pumps that push-pull-push-pull electrons that are already there. This transmits power, just as a hydraulic system transmits power by pushing water, but does not create the water.

If we then connect something like a toaster, we attach a little wire to the circuit that has more resistance to the flow of electrons. Now the free electrons find it harder to move through the metal of the wire, because impurities have been introduced and act as an obstacle course. The electrons are trying to move in-out-in-out, but there are other atoms in the way that have electrons that are not so free. Some of the moving electrons can't go where they want to go; they bounce off the others in their way (actually, they are repelled from one another, like magnets of the same polarity). The result is that fewer electrons can get through a wire that has higher resistance. The ones that can't get through are left bouncing around and jolting all of the other electrons in the metal. "Jolting electrons" doesn't sound very interesting, but the effect is useful: The wire heats up.

Heat is really all about the movement of atoms. For instance, at room temperature, the atoms in water move around freely. If you reduce the temperature, the movement slows down and eventually ceases—and you're left with solid water, or ice. When the water temperature is increased, movement speeds up until the atoms float free as a gas, or water vapor. This is true of all materials. To go from solid to liquid to gas, just add heat and watch those atoms dance. Most materials can also conduct heat in the same way: If I heat up one end of a piece of wood, its atoms move around at that end, and start to vibrate their neighbors, who vibrate their neighbors, and so on, until the other end starts to feel warm. But materials like metal are much better at conducting heat. They do it using those free electrons, which chaotically hop from one atom to another, bouncing off their friends and causing everything to vibrate.

So when an electric current tries to flow through a wire that has been designed to give some resistance, those frustrated electrons that can't go where they want to go bounce around and jolt everything nearby. Every time they bounce off something, they transfer more of the energy of their motion into the surrounding electrons and atoms, and in doing so, they create heat.

This process is ideal for a toaster. Just use the right kind of wire, shape it so that it meanders left and right to produce heat over a surface, and place a slice of bread in front of it. A little electricity and you have toasted bread. Unfortunately, the machine is sometimes not so reliable. Older toasters often fail because of the way they are switched on and off. Most have a little tray that lowers the bread down inside the machine; it's operated by a lever at the side. When the lever is pushed down, the tray is at the bottom, and the power is activated—the wire is connected to the electrical current. But if the bread is too thick, the tray might become stuck in the down position, and the power can get stuck on. Even worse, if the bread is uneven, it might come into contact with that glowing red-hot wire.

There's a certain chemical reaction that can occur under these conditions. It just requires oxygen, fuel, and heat. There's plenty of oxygen in the air, plenty of fuel in bread, and the toaster can provide the heat. If the fuel reaches a high enough temperature, known as the ignition temperature, then suddenly the chemical reaction can begin. The molecules of the fuel are broken apart, releasing volatile gases as smoke. If the gases get hot enough, their molecules are broken apart, and they recombine with the oxygen to make water, carbon dioxide, carbon monoxide, carbon, and nitrogen. What's left is known as char, and the carbon in this black stuff can also break down and combine with oxygen in another reaction. As the fuel reacts with oxygen, a large amount of heat is generated, which keeps the fuel and gases above the ignition temperature. Once started, the chemical reaction keeps itself going, making enough heat to enable it to consume all the fuel and oxygen nearby. The region where the gases are undergoing this reaction may be visible as a flickering, hot, bright flame. We call the whole reaction fire.

Fire is scary enough when it's out of control, but a fire that has been caused by electricity is even more frightening. The movement of electrons generates the heat, and electrons are quite happy to flow through water as well as metal. If water is put on an electrical fire it only serves to provide a new, exciting place for the electrical current to flow—such as into you. It's not great to be faced with a burning toaster and to be electrocuted at the same time. If possible, it's always best to turn off the power, either at the socket or at the main fuse box, and then deal with the fire.

Thankfully, modern toasters have built-in protection mechanisms to cut off the power after a certain period of time regardless of the position of the tray, so electrical fires involving toasters are quite rare. In fact, investigations of electrical fires have shown that one of the most common causes is an over-loaded extension socket, and one of the most common places for the fire to start is in the bedroom. Nevertheless, even the best toaster in the world can't protect you if you force an unevenly cut bagel against its wires.

Some people actually prefer their toast a little blackened, of course. Research on what happens when you eat burned food is still a little unclear. Some studies have suggested that burned toast might help soak up excess alcohol and prevent hangovers, but there is no real evidence that this works. Most of the results are not so optimistic. Benzopyrene, found in coal tar and charred foods, is one nasty compound that is known to increase the risk of cancer. In the 19th century it caused cancers in chimney sweeps and fuel industry personnel. It occurs in tobacco smoke and diesel exhaust fumes and is found in lower levels within char-grilled food and burned toast. Acrylamide is another sub-stance linked to higher cancer rates. It's a substance used by the construction industry in dam foundations and tunnels, and it can be generated in low levels when food is burned. Despite these findings, it's highly unlikely that a small amount of burned material on food every now and then will do us any harm at all. If you don't like the taste, you can always scrape off the charred parts. Or better yet, eat cereal, instead.

FLASH IN THE PAN

A cup of coffee is what you need. Instant coffee, because you're in a hurry. You pick up the kettle, fill it, and put it on the stove top. But when you turn the knob to light the gas, nothing happens. You could try again, but given the way the day is going, you don't want to try your luck with gas and a spark. Instead, you find your shiny new mug, bought the day before, and fill it with some bottled water. Good, clean healthy water. You can use the microwave to boil it, you realize, and have your coffee despite the kettle. You carefully place the cup inside and set the timer for 3 minutes. Even if it boils for a while, it's only water, so it won't matter. The morning paper passes the time until the microwave beeps. Retrieving the cup, you notice with a frown that it doesn't seem to be boiling. Not much you can do about it, so you drop a spoonful of instant coffee into the liquid. As if you've added some magic ingredient, the water suddenly explodes like a bubbling cauldron, coffee jumping out of the cup and overflowing a brown stain all over the paper. You jump back in alarm, barely avoiding being sprayed by the scalding liquid. How could coffee granules make water do that?

Explosions come in many shapes and sizes. Exploding water may not be one that seems very likely, but in fact it is perhaps the most common kind of explosion that happens in the home. It's known as a steam explosion, and it happens when a liquid become superheated beyond its normal boiling temperature.

Normally when a liquid is heated, the heat soaks through gradually, and the container has many imperfections in its surface. As the boiling point of the liquid is reached, the liquid is trying to transform from liquid to its gaseous form. Because the heat is conducted through the container, tiny bubbles form on the imperfections of the container; the bubbles slowly grow, in a process called nucleation and growth. The bubbles soon become larger and larger as the liquid boils and is transformed into gas.

However, there are some rare circumstances when the liquid cannot behave like this. Put a smooth and shiny container of a pure liquid into a microwave, and things are a little different. The microwave heats up the whole liquid at once, so it does not circulate in the container, and the lack of any imperfections in the liquid or on the container walls means that nucleation cannot happen. The liquid wants to become gas, but there is nothing for the initial gas bubbles to cling to. They just can't get going, so the liquid sits there, getting hotter and hotter. When you finally take the superheated water from the microwave and put something into it, the gas bubbles go crazy, immediately forming around the foreign object with such speed that the remaining liquid explodes from the container in a superheated frenzy.

It's why most microwaveable drinks, such as hot chocolate, have instructions that suggest you microwave the liquid in short bursts, stirring the contents frequently. If you don't, it is quite possible that the drink will silently explode within the microwave and you'll be left with a cup about one-third full, and a lot of mess. Or even worse, it will explode in your face and cause serious burns.

Steam explosions can be much more devastating than this, however. On April 26, 1986, in the early hours of the morning, a test of the cooling system of reactor 4 of the Chernobyl nuclear power station went horribly wrong. Ordinary water was used to cool and control the temperature of the nuclear core; during the test, they attempted to check whether backup systems could power the pumps that normally circulated the water. They disconnected the turbine that normally powered the pumps and, through a series of errors, the fuel rods were fractured and began a runaway meltdown reaction. The resulting sudden heat caused a devastating steam explosion in the water, which threw radioactive gases and fragments from the core into the sky. In the immediate aftermath, 237 people suffered acute radiation sickness, and 57 died. Two and a half square miles of pine forest around the plant turned brown and died, and 135,000 people were evacuated from their homes in the surrounding area, leaving everything behind, never to return. Many of the surrounding countries in Europe were affected by the resulting cloud of radioactive material, which was blown by the variable weather conditions. It is not known how many have died from cancer as a result of the disaster, but some estimate the numbers to be many thousands.

Thankfully, most steam explosions are nothing like as horrible as this. In fact, as strange as it sounds, sometimes steam isn't even hot. Not only can water be superheated without it boiling immediately, but it can also be boiled without heating it. The process of nucleation and growth of little bubbles of vapor in a boiling liquid depends on pressure as well as temperature. Go to the top of a mountain and the air pressure is much less compared to the pressure at sea level. There is literally far less air above you, pushing down on you. Try boiling some water up there and you'll find that it boils at much less than 212°F. It's actually a big problem for mountain climbers, who can't make the boiling water hot enough to cook food properly. The reason why pressure affects the boiling point of liquids is down to those jiggling molecules again. In a liquid, although the molecules are jiggling about quite freely, they are attracted to each other and so together form a big sloshy mass. When the pressure of the vapor (the gaseous state of the liquid) is enough to overcome that attractive force, then a bubble of vapor forms and the liquid starts to boil. The hotter the liquid, the more actively the molecules fly about, and so the easier it is for molecules to start flying free as a gas. Also, the lower the pressure, the less there is pushing the molecules together in the liquid and the easier it is for them to fly free as a gas. So if you want to boil cold water, just lower the air pressure around it, and eventually it will boil just as though it were in your kettle. This is called Henry's Law, after the English chemist who discovered the principle in 1803.

Some 32 years after Henry had figured it out, Charles Darwin encountered the phenomenon when on an expedition to the Andes. He wrote:

At the place where we slept water necessarily boiled, from the diminished pressure of the atmosphere, at a

lower temperature than it does in a less lofty country . . .
Hence the potatoes, after remaining for some hours in
the boiling water, were nearly as hard as ever. The pot
was left on the fire all night, and next morning it was
boiled again, but yet the potatoes were not cooked. I
found out this by overhearing my two companions
discussing the cause, they had come to the simple
conclusion "that the cursed pot (which was a new one)
did not choose to boil potatoes."

Darwin's potato problems are no more. The common trick used by mountaineers today is to use a pressure cooker. The very first pressure cooker was invented more than 300 years ago, but the idea only became popular in the 20th century. It is really nothing more than a sealed pot that doesn't let much escape while cooking. As the water inside becomes hot, it turns to vapor. There is still the same number of atoms in the pot, but now they are no longer sloshing about together as a liquid, they are flying around as a gas. At the same pressure, a gas needs more space than a liquid (and a liquid needs more space than a solid). If there is no more space, then as the liquid turns to a gas, the pressure inside the container rises. But if the pressure is going up, this means that the boiling point of the remaining liquid is now higher, so the liquid must get hotter before more of it can turn into gas.

The result is that a pressure cooker, which cooks at 15 pounds per square inch (the normal pressure for most pressure cookers), will allow water to reach 248°F, and so food cooks much faster, and more harmful bacteria are destroyed. Take a pressure cooker up on a mountain and you can use it to increase the boiling temperature back to what it is at sea level, and cook potatoes properly. The whole process of pressurized cooking is so effective that it has been used to cook food during the canning process (to prevent it from spoiling once canned) for nearly 100 years.

It's not just mountain climbers who have problems with Henry's Law. Divers and pilots can suffer serious health problems or even die because of it. The illness is called decompression sickness, and one of the first groups of people to show symptoms were miners. In 1841, pressurized air was pumped down into coal mines to stop them from filling up with water—it was easier than pumping water up and away all the time. But when miners came back to the surface, they started complaining of sore muscles and cramps. When the first deep-sea diving began, things were even worse. Divers would complain of sore joints and itchy skin; they would become confused, have headaches, and might even have seizures, fall unconscious, and die.

The problem is caused by the pressure. It's more of a problem in water, because water is heavy. You only need to dive 33 feet to double the pressure around you. If you want to be able to breathe, then the air in your air tank has to be pressurized to the same degree (otherwise your lungs will collapse as the pressure squishes them). Dive to 100 feet and you need to breathe air pressurized to around 60 psi—that's more pressure than many car tires are pumped to.

At that pressure, some of the gases in the air start to turn to liquids in your blood. Levels of nitrogen and helium increase.

This is no problem, until the pressure is reduced again. Now all that dissolved gas starts to form bubbles in the blood, like the bubbles of carbon dioxide in fizzy drinks that escape when you release the pressure by opening the bottle. If the diver rises too quickly, then the pressure change will be so sudden that bubbles will form in the muscles, joints, and brain, causing many nasty symptoms. The same thing can happen when a pilot in an unpressurized aircraft gains altitude too quickly—the sudden drop in air pressure will make the normal levels of nitrogen fizz in his blood. The cure for divers is to use a hyperbaric chamber, which compresses the air to push those nitrogen bubbles back into the blood. It then slowly, slowly lowers the pressure, allowing the excess nitrogen to be released through the lungs without bubbles forming. Today the principles are well understood and divers are trained to take "decompression stops" on the way back to the surface. It is also important not to fly at high altitude shortly after a deep dive, so don't dive while on holiday and fly home immediately afterward. The cabins of passenger aircraft are pressurized, but often at an air pressure equivalent to 8,000 feet above sea level so that unnecessary strain is not placed on the structure of the planes. It's why your ears pop when taking off and landing—you are feeling the pressure drop and increase. A rapid change from a high-pressure underwater environment to a low-pressure cabin environment can cause decompression sickness, or "the bends," to occur, even when the diver made his decompression stops coming to the surface.

People are made from a lot of water, so it's not surprising that we are affected just as a cup of water is affected. Babies are around 78 percent water, adult men are about 60 percent, and adult women about 55 percent. Thin people are made of more water than fat people. Whether you're a person or a cup of water, it's best not to have sudden and large temperature changes or sudden and large pressure changes. Take your time, keep stirring, and there should be no explosions.

CHEESY GRIMACE

The kitchen clock leers at you. Only 5 minutes before you need to leave and you still haven't had breakfast. If a hot drink is no good, what's left? You leave the soggy mess on the kitchen table and walk to the fridge. The radio continues to broadcast happy tunes, oblivious to your darkening mood. You open the fridge door, but all you see are bare shelves. Right. You need to get some food. No juice left, no eggs. But there is milk. You grab the carton and fill a glass with the cold creamy liquid. As you bring it to your lips, you anticipate a refreshing drink. A nice glass of milk—that's surely a great way to start the day. But instead of chilled refreshment, your mouth is filled with a lumpy sour porridge. Trying not to vomit, you run to the sink and spit it out, looking at the glass in disgust.

Milk is the source of many products: butter, cream, cheese, yogurt, and even soured milk. Many of these foods are simply milk with things growing in it—and they're not only edible, they're tasty, too. Yet spoiled milk tastes awful, can give you food poisoning, and could even kill you. It doesn't just turn into cheese automatically—as you may have noticed, there is a big difference between moldy milk and delicious dairy products, such as cheese. But why is spoiled milk so disgusting and cheese so tasty?

The origins of cheese predate recorded history, but we can make a pretty good guess about how the process of cheese making was first discovered. In the stomach of mammals there is a naturally occurring complex of enzymes (proteins that help begin chemical reactions) that enable us to digest the milk from our mothers. Rennet, as the enzymes are collectively known, breaks down milk, causing it to separate into solids, which we call curds, and liquids, which we call whey. We can then digest the results more easily. It seems likely that in ancient times, the stomachs of cattle were used as handy waterproof skin bags for carrying milk. The enzyme present in the stomach lining then curdled the milk, and by pressing together the curds and draining off the whey, the first cheeses were made.

It may sound nasty, but the traditional method of extracting the rennet to make cheese was worse: dried and cleaned stomachs from young calves (who were still at the age when they needed to digest their mothers' milk) were chopped up, soaked in wine or vinegar, filtered, and then used to curdle milk. This process is still used today in central Europe, but the rest of the world has moved on. Alternative sources for rennet naturally occur in plants such as fig tree bark or thistles, and in some molds and fungi. Remarkably, however, today a very large percentage of cheeses (80 to 90 percent of all hard cheeses in the United States) are made using rennin (the active ingredient in rennet) from genetically engineered fungus. The genes from calves that produced the appropriate proteins were transplanted into the DNA of the fungus and mass-produced in huge quantities.

Most modern cheeses are first coagulated by adding bacteria to change milk sugars into lactic acid. Then rennet is used to curdle the liquid into curds and whey. The curds are dried, salted, and treated in a variety of manners depending on the type of cheese that is desired as an end product. Cheeses can be dried, heated, washed, or stored for long periods, or pressed into molds, stretched, milled, or mixed with other, special varieties of mold. The leftover whey can also be used to make various foods, such as ricotta cheese, and as an ingredient in many baked goods and confections.

Clearly, cheese and spoiled milk are very different products, but what about butter? Butter is made by churning milk until something called "butterfat" starts to form. Whole milk is full of tiny globules of fat, which help a nursing infant grow quickly. But fat does not naturally dissolve in water, so each little globule is surrounded by special proteins that act as emulsifiers (just like the method used by soap that allows oil and water to form an emulsion). When the milk is churned, the emulsifiers coating each globule of fat are broken away, and the fat clumps together. Churn for long enough, drain away the water, and you have butter.

Yogurt is different yet again. To make yogurt, bacteria are added to the milk. These little single-celled bugs feed on the milk's natural sugars, turning them into lactic acid. The acid then interacts with protein and coagulates into a gloopy, lumpy mixture. It's likely that the first yogurts were discovered in a similar way to the first cheeses—milk was carried in goatskin bags and the natural bacteria turned the milk into a thick mixture that they did not want to waste. Today, sugars and jams are added to cut the bitterness of natural yogurt and to add flavor.

So spoiled milk is clearly very different than yogurt, butter, or cheese, even though they each begin life as the same stuff. So what's the difference? There are a lot of useful things in milk, but the main constituents are butterfat, lactose (milk sugar), and proteins, which are all suspended in 85 to 90 percent water. Naturally occurring bacteria find it an extremely tasty mix, especially at a warm temperature. When bacteria enters milk, the first part it eats is the lactose, and so the first thing that happens is the same process that occurs in yogurt and cheese making: The sugars are turned into acids, and the milk proteins start to cling together and turn the milk lumpy. The milk is now sour, but not spoiled. There are other types of bacteria that also like milk, but they prefer the proteins. These bacteria (called pseudomonads) break down proteins in a process called putrefaction. This process leaves the milk smelling bad, and if you were to drink it, the pseudomonads might just decide to try living in your warm, cozy gut for a while, which would make you very sick. Yet more nasty microbes may find the butterfat and break it down in a process called rancidification. Now the milk smells, well, *rancid*, and there are few nutrients left. Leave the milk even longer, and molds may discover the acids and remaining proteins and fats, and start feasting. None of these is good for you if you're unlucky enough to drink the foul, evil-smelling liquid that's left. And the same processes of natural decay will also happen to yogurt, soured milk, and cheese if they are left uneaten past their expiration dates.

One advantage we have over all these nasty bacteria is that they are very intolerant to low or high temperatures. It's why food and milk keep for a long time in the fridge—the bacteria have a lot of trouble growing in a cold environment. When the temperature reaches several degrees below freezing, bacteria can't grow at all, so food lasts even longer. Things can't go putrid or rancid when they're frozen. We know this is true, because scientists have found almost perfectly preserved woolly mammoths, frozen in the Siberian ice for 10,000 years.

The other thing that bacteria hate is high temperatures. In 1862, a French chemist named Louis Pasteur proved that heating milk would kill most of the germs present and dramatically slow the subsequent spoilage. The process became known as pasteurization, and today, almost without exception, all milk (including the milk that is used to make products such as butter, yogurt, and many cheeses) is pasteurized by heating it to 161°F for 15 to 20 seconds. This does not sterilize the milk—it does not kill all of the bacteria, which is why the milk and the products derived from it still need to be refrigerated and will still eventually spoil. But pasteurization kills those bacteria that might just decide to kill *us* if they made their way into our guts. There's a more extreme form of pasteurization known as UHT (ultra-high temperature) processing, which heats milk to 280°F for 2 seconds. This does kill all of the bacteria, and so UHT milk has a much longer shelf life and needs no refrigeration (like canned foods). But the more you heat milk, the more the proteins, vitamins, and friendly bacteria are affected, as well as the taste, so most of us prefer "ordinary pasteurized" milk.

In the United States, "raw milk cheeses" are prohibited by the FDA or are required to be aged for at least 60 days, in the hope that harmful bacteria will die in this time. Many well-known and popular European cheeses are still made from unpasteurized "raw milk," such as Swiss Gruyère, Emmental, and French

Roquefort. It turns out that very few people ever fall ill from eating properly made cheeses, whether made from raw or pasteurized milk. Since pasteurization does not kill all bacteria, and cheese tends to be aged for some time, some argue that pasteurization makes little difference for cheese, except that raw milk cheeses retain more vitamins and a stronger flavor. But the argument is not true for milk and other dairy products such as yogurt and butter. These foods can and will go putrid and rancid very quickly without pasteurization. Those expiration dates stamped onto the packaging are there for a reason.

Your own nose and taste buds are also there for a reason. It's no coincidence that we find decaying foods revolting. The reflex to vomit immediately after consuming something that is rancid is also no coincidence. It's much better to get it out of our stomachs before it has a chance to infect us.

But surprisingly, many of our responses to different smells and tastes are learned as we grow. There are plenty of cultures that happily eat evil-smelling cheeses or fermented fish or vegetables that many of us might consider to be worse than spoiled milk. They know these foods are safe because of the long history of preparing them in the right way to prevent harmful germs from being present, and so they appreciate the flavors we might find repugnant. We are programmed to associate feelings of heath or illness with the flavors of foods. Grow up in a culture like South Korea, where kimchi (spicy fermented cabbage) is one of the main dishes, and you will associate its smell with good food. Grow up in the United States, where eating rotten cabbage may have made you ill as a child, and you may find the smell of kimchi is enough to make you run in the other direction.

We tend to stick to the flavors and foods with which we are familiar and avoid those with radically different flavors. It's a strategy that makes sense: As humans evolved, we almost never experienced the foods of other cultures, so anything different from our norm meant it would probably make us ill. Luckily, the smell of rotting food is generally sufficiently distinctive and different that we can almost always distinguish it, and we quickly learn to avoid anything that smells unpleasant. If in doubt, throw it out!

DROWNING OUT NOISE

Stomach growling, you dump the laundry in the washing machine and figure that you better get going. Who knows what the traffic will be like this morning? On the way out, briefcase swinging from your arm, you decide to grab your MP3 player. You can plug it into the car stereo to help pass time on the commute. Now, where did you put it? A strange banging noise is coming from inside the washing machine. You frown. When you last saw the MP3 player it was . . . clipped to your sweatpants? You threw the sweatpants in with the dirty laundry. You put the dirty laundry into the . . . ! You run to the machine and discover your expensive digital music player banging and sloshing its way around and around. Its screen already looks strangely discolored, and the earphones are wrapping themselves around the sweatpants. You rip open the door and grab it, and try drying it with a kitchen towel, but you know it's too late when you try to switch it on. It's so infuriating! Why does water ruin electronic gadgets? And can you ever make them work again?

Water and electronics are not a good mixture. Without batteries, the plastic and metal components of an electronic device may well survive immersion for many hours or even days with no harmful effects. But if there are internal batteries producing electricity (whether the gadget is switched on or off), everything becomes less certain. Immerse certain kinds of batteries in water and the result may be dead batteries. With some types of batteries, you might even produce a small explosion. Yet other types of batteries will survive a washing machine and keep going without much of a problem.

An Italian physicist called Alessandro Volta invented the first battery around 1800. A contemporary of his, Luigi Galvani, had discovered that placing certain metals next to each other and then touching a disembodied frog's leg would make that leg twitch as though still attached to a living frog (although his explanation that the cause was "animal electricity" was incorrect). To find a better explanation, Volta refined the ideas and discovered that alternating layers of silver and zinc separated by blotting paper and placed in salty water would create electricity, although he did not understand why. What was happening was a faradaic reaction—a chemical reaction that made electrons flow from one metal to another. Metals and chemicals made electricity.

The same kind of reaction happens in all batteries, although the chemicals and metals are different in each type. For example, in a car battery, lead and lead dioxide are placed in sulfuric acid. When sulfuric acid meets the lead, it reacts with the metal, forming a new compound called lead sulfate, which has a spare electron for each new molecule. If you connect the lead plate and lead oxide plate into a circuit (perhaps connect one to each terminal of a lightbulb) then the spare electrons will flow from the lead, through the circuit (through the bulb), and combine with the lead dioxide. This causes another reaction, which transforms the lead dioxide into lead sulfate as well and produces molecules of water. The "push" given to the electrons by the chemical reaction, or the voltage of the electricity, is about 2 volts. So in a car battery, six of these lead–lead dioxide "cells" are joined together to increase the total "push" to 12 volts. Not all such chemical reactions are reversible, but in a car battery, it is. This means that when too much of the lead and lead dioxide plates have been turned to lead sulfate and the power is low, we just need to apply electricity at a higher voltage to the metal plates and the reaction reverses, giving us lead and lead dioxide again and recharging the battery.

Because batteries push electrons out of one battery terminal and back into the other, it is possible to short-circuit them. Instead of connecting them to a circuit that gives some resistance to the flow of electrons, such as a lightbulb or an electronic gadget, if a piece of metal or wire accidentally connects the two terminals directly, then the flow of electrons will have little to slow them down. Huge numbers will flow very quickly (a high current), which may generate so much heat that either the metal connected to the battery becomes red hot and melts, or the battery itself becomes too hot. Because batteries often contain chemicals (such as sulfuric acid in a car battery), it's not a good idea to get them very hot. In the worst-case scenario, the chemicals inside might boil, turning into rapidly expanding gases that explode the battery casing with a bang. Typically, the larger the battery, the more power it can produce, and so the more dangerous it is to short-circuit.

Car batteries are large, high-power batteries and are actually particularly prone to exploding. Not only can you make them go bang through short-circuiting, but as a side effect of its normal chemical reaction, highly flammable hydrogen gas can also be produced. If the battery is not well maintained and a naked flame or spark ignites a buildup of hydrogen gas, the explosion may ruin your whole engine. If you are working on the car at the time, you will be seriously hurt. People have lost their hearing from the bang, or been blinded by the acid that sprays out.

It's not a good idea to immerse batteries in water because water conducts electricity. The water shouldn't get inside the battery, because the metals and chemicals are sealed inside casings to protect them. But it will create a short circuit, a wet path from one terminal of the battery directly to the other. What happens next depends on the water, the power, and the type of battery.

The conductivity of water is very dependent on what's in it. Pure water is actually a very poor conductor of electricity, but add lots of salt (such as seawater) and it is able to conduct electricity much more effectively. It does this because salty water contains a lot of ions, or electrically charged atoms or molecules that have less or more than the normal number of electrons. A positively charged particle missing an electron is attracted to negatively charged particles, just as magnets are attracted to other magnets of opposite polarities. So the more salty the water is, the more free ions it contains, and the more the solution is able to conduct the flow of electrons via the movement of those ions. Substances that have this effect are known as electrolytes, and they are used in our bodies to help us maintain the right balance of fluids within our cells.

Even the most salty water is still a million times worse at

conducting electricity than metals are, however (and pure drinking water can be ten thousand times worse than that). Bring water into contact with a low-voltage electrical supply and not much happens. But spill water on a household supply of 120 volts (or 240 volts) and it will find its way through, just as it will find its way through you if you touch it (so don't). If you have enough voltage, electricity can even jump through the air. Lightning does exactly this because its voltage is more than a billion volts. The air molecules are exploded apart into free electrons and ions, making them much more conductive than normal air.

Batteries are a long way from lightning. Take a low-power, low-voltage watch battery and drop it into drinking water, and not very much happens. The battery may discharge quicker than usual, but the poor conductivity of water means that you'll probably be able to fish it out, dry it off, and still have a usable battery. Children sometimes swallow these batteries and have them pass through their systems without harm to child or battery. But take a modern lithium-ion battery designed to provide lots of power to a portable computer and dunk it in water, and something else happens.

Modern batteries like these are not just simple combinations of metals and chemicals. Many now also have little electronic brains that monitor the current state of the batteries. The little circuits inside the battery casing keep a close eye on the batteries as they are being charged, to stop them from becoming overcharged and becoming too hot. They also check to see how much current is being drawn from the battery. If you were stupid enough to try and short-circuit this kind of battery, the electronic brain would sense the excessive drain and would cut out the power. There's also a fail-safe internal fuse that is triggered by heat. If the battery somehow became overcharged, or was short-circuited, or indeed was put in a fire, then this fuse would blow, cutting all power from the battery permanently. When that fuse has gone, your battery will never work again, so all you can do is buy a replacement and recycle the old one.

So when a lithium-ion (or similar modern battery) is accidentally put in water, in the worst case (if the water is very salty), the short circuit may cause enough heating of the battery for its fuse to blow. In the best case (if it is fairly pure water), the battery may just cut its own power for a while, until it dries off and its terminals are no longer being connected by the water.

Older batteries (such as AA- or AAA-size batteries, whether rechargeable or not) and some of the smaller modern batteries do not have these safety features. Get them wet, and the short circuit may make them hot enough to burst and contaminate with their corrosive contents the gadget in which they are contained. Even worse, because there is no safety cutout and the batteries might be powering the gadget at the time it gets wet, the short circuit may happen in the electronics first, forcing a large amount of current through one of the chips and destroying it, thus rendering your gadget dead forever more. (And if you're very unlucky, this might happen even if your device is powered by a modern battery with a built-in fuse.)

Dropping an electronic device into water is actually a very common accident. The most common offenders are puddles, washing machines, and toilets. If your electronic gadget has explored a new underwater world, the first thing you should do is take out the batteries and dry everything off. If the batteries have leaked inside, carefully clean everything (including your hands afterward!). Do not attempt to charge it, power it from an adapter, or use it at all until it is completely dry. An expert will quickly dismantle the device and dry it by hand. If you don't want to do that, then a nice warm spot in the sun (indoors) for a couple of days should do the trick. The longer you wait, the better. If you can, replace the battery. Then, when all is dry again, insert the battery and press the on button—your gadget might spring back to life.

WARM SNOW

It's getting late. You dash out of the house and slam the front door with barely enough time to make the 10-mile drive to work. You press the remote on your keychain to unlock the doors, half expecting it not to work. But the locks make their reassuring "clunk," accompanied by the usual flash of the lights. It's a nice car, shiny black, kept clean with a wash each week, and your parking space is sheltered under a lovely old tree, so it's never too hot when you get in. As you open the door you feel a few wet drops land on your jacket, and hear a little pattering on the car. Is it raining? The sky is blue. Brushing the water from your jacket, you climb into the driver's seat, place your bag on the seat next to you, and close the door. Hand on the steering wheel, you insert the key in the ignition . . . and then stop. Your hand is white. Your car has a splattering of white all over its hood. Your jacket has a big streak of white down the sleeve, which has deposited yet more white into the fabric seat of the car. Every-where you turn, you see bird poop.

If you must have a creature defecate on you, then perhaps a bird is not a bad choice. Birds' droppings don't smell very much, you can see them very clearly, and they're not usually that large. Imagine dog turds falling from the sky. And what a good thing pigs can't fly!

What use is bird poop to anyone? It's easy enough to dismiss as just another of life's daily annoyances, but in fact birds' droppings are very valuable. Amazingly, the bird poop business is worth more than a billion dollars, and there's not enough of it to meet demand. Countries have even gone to war over who can keep the most bird poop. That white gloop contains something extremely useful.

Birds, like marsupials and lizards, do not have separate openings for urine and feces. Instead, they excrete all waste out of one opening, known as the cloaca, which is why the result is rather runny. There are three elements to any dropping: the urine, the urate, and the feces. The watery bit around the edge is the urine. It should be clear; if it's green, the bird may be suffering from liver disease; if red, the bird may have eaten a lot of red fruits or it might be suffering from lead poisoning. The white stuff is the urate; it's a useful adaptation that evolved to enable birds to continue to remove waste in arid environments, without losing too much water. If the urate is white, the bird is stressed; if it looks yellow, then the bird is malnourished or starving. Birds produce more urate than urine because most birds have no bladders—it's another useful adaptation to keep them light and able to fly more easily. (The exception is the ostrich, which, being a large flightless bird, loses nothing by having a bladder—but its bladder works slightly different from mammalian bladders.) Finally, the dark blobs in the middle of the urate are the feces. Their color really depends on what the bird just ate.

It's the urate that is valuable to people, because it contains ammonia, and uric, phosphoric, oxalic, and carbonic acids. From large quantities of bird poop, you can extract phosphorus, nitrogen, and potassium nitrate. These just happen to form some of the important ingredients for fertilizers and gunpowder. Plants are nourished by these substances because the fertilizer provides many of the raw materials needed for the plants to grow. Plant cell membranes are made from phospholipids (which are derived from phosphorus), and their internal chemical energy supplies also make use of phosphorus. And nitrogen is used to create the amino acids that help build proteins in plants. Gunpowder (black powder) relies on potassium nitrate for the explosion because it releases oxygen, which causes everything else to burn quickly.

You need a lot of bird poop to make an explosion or a flower. Luckily, birds like to poop a lot. A small bird the size of a parakeet will generally poop every 30 minutes or more. A larger bird the size of a robin may only poop every hour. They can't help it—they have efficient little intestines and no bladders, so their food may be digested and out the other end in anywhere from 10 to 45 minutes. (Flightless birds are able to take several hours to digest their food.) Because of this constant need, birds aren't so picky about where they go to the bathroom. They'd never get anything done in the day if they had to relieve themselves in specific locations. However, inevitably, areas in which birds roost for the night or nest to rear young do become somewhat covered in droppings. Park your car under a tree and you're almost asking for it to be pooped on. But there are places in the world where birds do more than a few droppings.

In some remote islands, originally undisturbed by man or any other predators, millions of seabirds made their homes. There are many examples, such as Nauru (in the South Pacific),

Juan de Nova Island (near Madagascar), and Navassa (in the Caribbean). Over hundreds of thousands of years, millions of birds would nest, rear their young, and poop many times a day on the islands. These were dry places with not much rain to wash it all away. The results were unimaginably huge deposits of dried droppings, or guano as it became known. Deposits 150 feet deep are quite common on some islands. In the case of Navassa, the island is 2 miles long, 1 mile wide, and solid guano.

The ingredients in guano are so useful for gunpowder and fertilizer that they were extensively mined. By 1879, Chilean mining companies were making such a high profit from the business of mining guano and other minerals from the Atacama Desert that Bolivia decided to increase the taxes on Chilean companies in the area. This led to a dispute between Chile and Bolivia that quickly deteriorated into a territorial conflict, and then a full-scale war. Bolivia demanded the assistance of Peru, which resulted in fierce fighting at sea, but the eventual occupation of Peru by Chile. The War of the Pacific lasted for 4 years and resulted in Chile gaining new territory and Bolivia becoming cut off from the coast as a landlocked country. Even to this day, tension remains high between the countries.

Similar sad stories exist about other guano islands. In Navassa, black slaves were forced to mine guano for very little pay and were tortured or killed if they complained. (Surprisingly, this was after the American Civil War, when Navassa was owned by the United States.) Eventually, the slaves revolted against their captors, chopping off their arms, legs, and heads, killing 15 and injuring many others. The island became known as "Devil's Island."

Amazingly, bird poop does more than create islands. Guano plays a significant role in the world's ecosystems. It has been estimated that seabird droppings transfer somewhere between 10,000 and 100,000 tons of phosphorus from the sea to the land each year. Waterfowl may transfer as much as 40 percent of the nitrogen and 75 percent of all phosphorus in wetland environments. Without these birds fertilizing the land, many environments may have remained too nutrient-poor and so may not have been colonized by plants. Without the plants, there would be no insects, no animals, and no ecosystem. Indeed, about 100 years ago, when arctic foxes were accidentally introduced to the Aleutian archipelago (volcanic islands extending westward from Alaska), the resulting reduction in seabirds (which the foxes found to be tasty) dramatically affected the nutrients in the soils, which transformed a landscape of lush grasslands into sparse dwarf shrubs.

But what is valuable in one place is a nuisance in another. Bird droppings aren't going to fertilize anything if they land on our clothes or our cars. In fact, they're more likely to do harm than good, as they're slightly acidic. Leave a dropping for a while on a nice shiny car and it will leave a mark even when you do clean it off. The acid in the dropping actually eats a layer of paint away, leaving a tiny dimple in the surface where the dropping landed. It's the result of another chemical reaction, the molecules of the substance reacting with water and the surface of the car, resulting in bonds being broken between molecules and their hydrogen ions (protons) or electrons from atoms, and then the formation of new substances instead. Both the acid (within the bird poop) and the base (the car paint) are slowly transformed and used in the reaction, leaving nonacidic poop and a ruined area of paint.

The effect of acid on cars is very noticeable, since most car surfaces are kept clean and polished. Often the only way to restore the shine after bird sh*t happens is to use a slightly abrasive polish, which removes a tiny layer of paint and allows you to even out the damage to make it less noticeable. The best way to avoid damage from droppings is to wax your car. A nice layer of wax between droppings and paint will prevent the acid from reaching the paint and will also make it easier to clean nasty substances from your car's surface. But take care when wiping it away: birds often eat small particles of grit to help break down and digest food in their stomachs—they have no teeth to perform this role in their mouths as we do. So most bird poop has enough grit in it to badly scratch your car if you carelessly brush it or wipe with a dry cloth.

Bird droppings can cause serious problems for many other man-made structures. Apart from being a nuisance and the acids causing damage to statues and buildings, sometimes droppings can cause serious safety problems. For example, the landing pads for helicopters (helidecks) are often the only way to reach normally unmanned structures out at sea. The droppings of seabirds can cover markings and lights used by the pilots for guidance, making landing very hazardous.

It pays to be careful around bird poop because it contains many kinds of bacteria that can cause infection and illness. Limping pigeons with swollen and deformed feet are actually suffering from a poop-borne infection. These birds commonly injure their feet on sharp edges and "anti-pigeon" spikes on buildings. The injuries frequently become infected from the droppings at their roosting sites, leading to swelling and a deformity known as "bumble foot." We can't catch bumble foot, but we can be affected in other ways because dried bird poop becomes quite powdery when disturbed. A chalky cloud may contain several nasty varieties of fungus, some of which can cause serious respiratory illnesses in humans. It may be great as a fertilizer, but you don't want to breathe that stuff in.

LOSING TRACK

You slam the front door and get back into the car. Your stained jacket is now in the washing machine. Having wiped the marks off the car, you're finally ready to go. As you begin driving, you start to relax. There's good music on the radio and the traffic is blissfully light. You've left your troubles behind you. You pull up at a red light, and frown. That reminded you of something. The light turns green and you continue. Only about 10 minutes before you reach the office now, which will give you just enough time to prepare the papers you have in your bag. You glance at the passenger seat to your right, where you'd put the bag. It's not there.

Your eyes widen in disbelief. How can it not be there? You remember putting it there! Was it stolen? No, you'd used tissues from the bag to wipe at the bird poop, so the bag was definitely in the car. But you'd put the bag on the roof of the car to open it and retrieve the tissues. Then you'd thrown away the tissues inside the house and put the jacket in the washing machine. And then you'd hurried back to the car with its door still open, got in, and shut the door and backed out and . . . driven off with the bag on the roof. You pull over and jump out of the car. The bag is no longer there.

Think of a number between 10 and 100. (No pens or paper—this is a memory test.) Without forgetting that number, think of the age of one of your parents or siblings. Without forgetting both those numbers, think of your height in inches. Keeping those three numbers in your mind, think of the number of a house or apartment you grew up in. Now add a fifth number to your mental list: the sum of the last two numbers multiplied by two (use a calculator if you need to, but clear it after getting the answer). Now add a sixth: the last two digits of your phone number. Finally, one more: the approximate number of minutes past the hour that you woke up this morning. Without rereading this text, write down your seven numbers.

How did you do? (You can judge your score by reading through the text again.) If you only got four or fewer correct, don't worry, that's quite normal. If you managed to remember all seven, then you have a superb short-term memory. The average person can only remember about four or five different things at a time (and the memory test above was full of distractions to make you less likely to remember them all). Some research suggests that the more you remember, the higher your IQ, but there are plenty of extremely bright people who have very poor short-term memories.

What is short-term memory, anyway? Memory, like everything else that the brain does, is not a straightforward process. Much of what our brain chooses to store depends on the time it occurs and its significance to us. For example, sensory memory is nothing more than a split-second snapshot of our perceptions. It's what happens when you glance at something and then recall what you saw less than a second later. The things that we find more relevant may then be pushed through to our short-term memories, which last no more than a minute. And a few details (but really not that many) that are important may then be pushed further into our long-term memories, which can sometimes, through a process of recall and refreshing, last for the rest of our lives.

Short-term memory is different from the shorter sensory memory because you don't actually remember what your senses detected. Instead, you're remembering what other parts of your brain registered about the things you saw or heard. Glance at a giant "M" on a billboard and a half-second later you can recall the shape that made up the letter. Thirty seconds later you remember that you saw a big letter "M," but not necessarily what it looked like. Long-term memory becomes even more vague—a week later you might remember that you saw a big letter of the alphabet, but not what the letter was. An awful lot of information is simply discarded; in fact, many of our sensory experiences never even make it to our short-term memory. If you perform the same action every day (putting sugar in your coffee, washing your hair, brushing your teeth), you can often execute your routine without remembering that you've done it. Later you may find yourself wondering: Did I put sugar in this coffee? Did I just rinse out shampoo or was that conditioner? Did I already brush my teeth?

Because we only remember useful information that our brain has already processed, we are able to house much more data in our heads. It's the difference between storing a continuous movie of everything we see and hear, and a set of crib notes about our experiences—and the notes need far less storage space. But our brains are also designed to fool us about our memories. When we recall something, we use the notes to reconstruct imaginary movies, pushing the information back through the vision centers of our brains as though we're seeing events as they really happened. Like dreams, this process makes our memories feel vivid and real, but most of it is simply reconstructed out of our imaginations. It's why we can enjoy novels so much—our brains are very good at extrapolating entire worlds from just a few pieces of information. Every time we recall an event we see a slightly different movie, and over time we may make new mental notes about that experience, or change the original notes. So our memories are fluid, changing slightly each time we access them, and sometimes becoming corrupted and wholly incorrect. It's a phenomenon well known to the police. When crime witnesses are questioned, even people who have paid close attention can misremember very significant details such as height, hair color, and clothing. If the same witnesses are interviewed 2 months later, the police may hear a substantially different description.

It's also very easy to produce false memories in people, especially when relaxation states such as those used by hypnosis are employed. It has been known for people to be "regressed" under the suggestive state of hypnosis and then, with the help of prompting from the therapist, construct entirely fictional past experiences (or even past lives). As you dwell in the fictional past, often acting out roles for the therapist, your brain follows its normal method of making notes of the experiences and storing them as memories. When you wake after such a session, you remember the experiences just as clearly as you remember any real experiences, and indeed you may firmly believe that your hypnosis-induced dream is real and you have "reawakened" a previously lost memory.

Memories rely on various regions of the brain. The temporal lobes on each side of the brain, at about the level of your ears, help you remember things that you see (on the right-hand side) and things you hear (on the left-hand side). The hippocampus (a pair of little regions shaped like seahorses that form part of the temporal lobes) also has something to do with memory, helping us retain memories as longer-term memories and providing us with spatial memory. Indeed, some studies have shown that London taxi drivers, who are obliged to learn the entire street map of London, have hippocampuses that are larger than normal.

The movie *Memento* provides an excellent portrayal of what happens when an individual has damage to these areas of the brain and can no longer convert short-term memories into long-term ones. Those with this condition (known as anterograde amnesia) may recall everything before the accident, but are unable to lay down new memories. When anterograde amnesia combines with retrograde amnesia (the loss of all memories before the accident), the person may have a perpetual feeling of just awakening, of never having existed or been conscious before that instant—and yet older skills such as playing the piano may be retained.

But our knowledge and understanding of exactly how the brain creates, stores, and manipulates memories is extremely limited. We look at many brains of different mammals, but most of what we know comes from three sources. We know what separate neurons look like and what they do on their own. We can see which parts of the brain seem to have the most active neurons when performing certain tasks (as measured by machines such as electroencephalograms [EEC], which measure electrical activity, and functional magnetic resonance imaging [fMRI], which measures bloodflow). We know what happens when chunks of brains are damaged because of an accident. But that's about it. It's equivalent to trying to understand how a country works by watching one person, and also identifying the areas in the landscape that use the most power, and examining countries that may have had a power outage in some places. You can identify the major towns and cities, but you have no idea how the people work together to keep a country healthy. So we can identify the major regions of the brain, but with a hundred billion neurons involved, each connected on average to 20,000 neighbors, we don't really understand how the separate neurons work together to do everything the brain does.

While the neuroscientists, neurologists, and neurobiologists continue to work on the problem, we do know a few useful things. We know that our brains get better at certain tasks with practice—the more you use it, the better it becomes. We know that old age does not mean an impaired ability to think—if you are still active mentally, you should be just as good as ever. (There are many professors who continue to do groundbreaking research in their 70s and 80s). And we know that short-term memory can be improved, or at least used more effectively. One simple way to change your ability to recall something is to change how the information is presented to you. Sound is a sequential input; we have to listen to one word after another in a specific order, or we would not be able to understand their combined meaning. Sight is a parallel input; we see many things at once. Research has shown that people are better at remembering a list of numbers when hearing the list, compared to when they see it. The parts of our brain designed to cope with sequential sound are good at coping with the sequential, one-at-a-time items in a list. This is especially true with music—the highly complex sequential arrangements of notes in melodies are often remembered with ease, even by people who think they have terrible memories.

Another way to improve short-term memory, beyond simple repetition of what you've seen, is to develop skills or memory techniques. There are many variations, but most rely on the fact that your short-term memory is not a perfect record of your senses, but rather a collection of meaningful aspects of your perception. So if you need to remember a list that may be quite uninteresting to you, the trick is to give it some meaning. The sequence of letters "BSCFBIBAABBC" may seem very hard to remember, but chunk it into triplets—BSC FBI BAA BBC—and it becomes much easier. Make it into a story (I was awarded my B.Sc. degree and joined the FBI; my last case involved British airports owned by BAA and was reported on BBC television), and it's even easier to recall. Other techniques involve mnemonics; for example, to spell the word *arithmetic*, you might make up this sentence: A Rat In The House May Eat The Ice Cream. Or you might learn to associate numbers and symbols with familiar objects in your life and then make up a story. For example, if "1" is banana, "2" is a pair of shoes, "3" is Trixie the cat, and the number is 322133, then the story could be: Trixie (3) chewed one pair of shoes (2), peed in another pair (2), slipped on a banana skin (1), and came face to face with himself in the mirror (33). Remember the story and you've remembered the number.

If you do have a problem remembering to do something or to take something, just use one of these tricks. Acronyms are used universally for exactly this reason. For example, when traveling in Europe don't forget your BIKE: Bag, ID card, Keys, Euros. A little effort spent on making something relevant and memorable may save an hour of running around screaming, "Where the hell have I put it?"

LOSING GRIP

You check your watch and realize you're going to be late. Despite retracing the drive from home to the spot where you pulled over, there is no sign of your bag. It must have come off and landed in a ditch at the side of the road somewhere. Without spending several hours checking, you'll never find it. All you can do now is try not to be too late, and perhaps print out the crucial papers in your office before running to the meeting. You reach an empty stretch of road, press the "sport" button on the car, and put your foot down. This stretch is a windy country road, just a few miles from the office. You know it well, and despite the corners being a little wet because of runoff from the banks on each side, you're confident your car can take the corners at this speed. Anyway, you're not above the speed limit, you try to justify to yourself. A particularly sharp bend approaches and you suddenly realize there's a cyclist just ahead. Time seems to slow down as you wrestle with the steering wheel, swerve around the bicycle, and then cut sharp right to take the corner, but you can feel that you're going too fast. The rear of the car loses its grip and the world spins sickenly to the left. After what seems like an eternity, the car slides to a halt and you look around, dazed. You're now facing the other direction, but still on the road. The cyclist pulls up and asks if you're okay. Thankfully you're fine, just feeling foolish.

It's actually very hard to spin a modern car, but you can do it if you try hard enough. More than 100 years of tire technology and 80 years of safety systems development mean that today's vehicles are designed to stay on the road and pointing in the direction you steer them. Some will even override the driver and reduce power or apply brakes to ensure that you are safe. But drive in a car with worn tires, on a very slippery road, or with the antilock brakes and traction control disabled by a "sport" setting (or not there), and it's quite possible to spin a car on a wet corner (and end up in a heap of trouble if you're unlucky). So what do all these components and gadgets in your car really do? How can they keep the car wheels from slipping and sliding?

The most effective way to make sure your car stays on the road is to have decent tires. Modern tires are made of vulcanized rubber. Ordinary rubber just oozes out in the sap of a tree called *Hevea brasiliensis* when you cut it. Rubber can also be derived from by-products of petroleum refinement; today, 70 percent of rubber is synthetically made in this way. But untreated rubber is not very useful for tires. It goes extremely soft and may completely melt in the sun, while in the winter it becomes hard and brittle. This was good enough if all you wanted was an eraser—which indeed was one early use of rubber—but not much good on a wheel.

The key lay in heating the stuff in the presence of sulfur. Rubber is made from a latex: a bunch of long spaghetti-like molecules called polymers that give it its oozing, stretchy quality. When heated with sulfur, the sulfur molecules act like glue, sticking the long polymers together at different points to form a springy, spongy structure. Once vulcanized, rubber becomes deformable and much more stable at different temperatures.

The American businessman and inventor Charles Goodyear invented the process of vulcanization in 1839. Sadly, Goodyear struggled with debt for many years and despite being honored by the French emperor for his work toward the end of his life, he never made any real money from his invention. The Goodyear company, formed several decades after his death, was named after him, but it had no ties to Charles or his family.

Early rubber tires were used on bicycles, but although the solid rubber produced good traction on the ground, it was uncomfortable. A Scotsman named John Boyd Dunlop came up with the solution—an air-filled or pneumatic rubber tire. These were not only good at making the ride more comfortable on wheeled vehicles, but they also had much less rolling resistance. A solid rubber tire would hit each bump and be slowed down by the collision, but a pneumatic tire allowed rough bumps to push into its surface without a collision, smoothing out the ride and creating a much more efficient motion. It turned out that Robert William Thomson (another Scotsman) had patented the idea before Dunlop, but nevertheless the Dunlop tire company soon grew to become one of the most important companies in the industry. Pneumatic tire technology quickly developed, and tires were reinforced with fabric and wire to prevent tearing and to reduce the number of punctures. Today, tires are ubiquitous for all road vehicles, with thousands of different types designed for different conditions, and clever patterns of tread designed to pump away surface water and keep the tire in contact with the road.

Even the best tire cannot always provide enough friction to avoid skidding. If the surface of the road is too slippery, or an excessive amount of acceleration (from an over-enthusiastic engine) or deceleration (from braking too hard) overcomes the friction, then the tire will skid over the road instead of gripping it. These conditions happen rarely, but so many people use our roads today that you don't have to drive far on a highway before you see the tell-tale black skid marks left behind from some-body's frightening skid.

Cars were not the first type of vehicle to suffer from this problem. Airplanes travel at much greater speeds than cars, and when they land their brakes have to cope with far more weight and pressure. Planes also use their main engines to power all movement, and the main form of steering they have on the ground is breaking a left wheel to turn left or a right wheel to turn right. When a plane lands, the pilot has to apply the brakes hard to slow down from traveling at a speed of more than 100 miles an hour before the plane reaches the end of the runway. If the wheels of an airplane locked up and skidded when slowing, the whole aircraft could veer to the left or the right and destroy itself in a fiery rollover. The problem is as old as the aircraft themselves, and so a braking system had to be invented to pre-vent such disasters. In 1920, one of the pioneers of aviation, Gabriel Voisin, developed a hydraulic system that helped prevent the wheels from locking.

It was many years before our technology became good enough for antilock brakes to be reliable and small enough to use on cars. Early systems were mechanical, detecting the too-sudden slowing of a wheel and releasing the pressure on the brakes momentarily to allow the wheel to roll and find more traction on the road. By the early 1970s, electronics and motion sensors were small enough for the first modern-style antilock braking system (ABS) to be placed in production cars. These systems use computers to monitor the speed of rotation of each wheel continuously. If brakes are applied and the speed of the wheels slows dramatically, then the brake pressure is momentarily released. It's a very noticeable effect for the driver: brake hard when traveling over slippery or graveled surfaces and you will feel the shudder of the antilock braking system as the brakes are applied-released-applied-released to give the tires more chance to find traction instead of just locking up and skidding out of control. Cars with ABS can still be steered even when braking hard. A car without ABS will skid and slide in the direction you were traveling, whether you move the steering wheel or not. But you must always continue to steer in the direction you want to go, whichever way your car is pointing, for you never know when your tires might start to grip the road again. Get it right, and after a minor slide you will just continue along the road under perfect control. Steer the wrong way and you may end your skid by driving into a ditch. The "race car driver" skill of controlling a sliding car is very hard to learn, which is why most modern cars use ABS to save you the trouble.

ABS has some significant effects on the performance of the car. Brake hard on a graveled or icy surface and the ABS will stop you quicker than a car without ABS. But brake hard on a clean and dry road and the ABS will actually bring you to a halt slower than a car without it, because the ABS is lifting the pressure from the brakes in a series of shudders and letting the wheels roll to stop them from skidding. Some drivers find the shuddering brake pedal frightening and lift their foot off, which is the worst thing they could do. The more the brakes shudder, the more you know they're working. Pumping conventional brakes produces a similar (slower) effect. You can always tell the cars that have ABS from those that don't by the black skid marks on the roads: the ABS produces pairs of dotted lines (= = = =), while the older cars just leave big black stripes.

Sometimes, even ABS is not enough. If you're going around a bend, brake, and lose traction with the road, then you may still spin around in a circle and end up facing the wrong way. If your car has a habit of "oversteering" (the rear of the car stepping out and rotating the car around), then a spin may not be hard to produce. Again, an expert driver would be able to correct the car under these conditions, while an inexperienced driver might overcorrect, steer too far in the opposite direction, and cause the car to fishtail, sliding left and right before spinning. This can be very dangerous if the spin happens on a busy road full of fast-moving vehicles. To overcome this problem, many newer cars have electronic stability control (ESC; sometimes called dynamic stability control or something similar). This is integrated with the ABS system, but also may have sensors connected to the steering. When you go around a corner and brake at the same time, the ESC will alter the pressure on the brakes, using the brakes to help you get around the bend just as a pilot uses his brakes to steer his aircraft. The more advanced systems will also adjust the power to the wheels at the same time. The result is that such cars almost never experience oversteer (or understeer) and remain fully controllable. Many studies have shown that

ABS and ESC have dramatically reduced the number of serious accidents since their introduction.

Even if you have new tires with decent treads, they can lose traction when under acceleration (if you've ever heard the screech of a wheel spin when pulling out, you know what this feels like). Having ABS is no help when you have your foot on the accelerator pedal—it only works when you brake. If you're cruising along a highway on a cold day and hit a patch of black ice (invisible to the naked eye), then your tires can lose all traction and you may start to slide out of control. Alternatively, if you have a car with a huge amount of power, it's possible for the engine to be so strong that the wheels just slip and slide rather than grip the road. One of the first solutions to this problem was invented for such performance cars. The limited slip differential is a clever system for applying power from the engine to the wheels. All modern cars need a differential—this is a clever set of gears that allow the wheels to turn at different speeds. (When a car goes around a corner, the inner wheels don't have to travel as far as the outer ones, so the inner ones need to travel slower.) But if one wheel loses traction altogether, the differential just transfers all the power to that wheel and it spins, with the result that the car goes nowhere, or goes out of control. A limited slip differential prevents one wheel from ever going substantially faster than any other, and avoids the whole problem.

Modern electronics now provide an even more advanced method. It's called traction control and often integrates with all the other electronic systems such as ABS and ESC. Traction control senses the movement of the wheels when under acceleration, and if one wheel suddenly starts to spin too quickly, the power to that wheel is reduced. It's a remarkable system that allows a car to drive on pure ice, with the electronics feeding power to whichever wheel has the best grip and making adjustments hundreds of times a second.

Cars with good tires and full of modern safety systems such as these are amazingly reliable and safe to drive. Some suggest that because modern cars almost "drive themselves" they encourage greater speed and careless driving, but there is no clear evidence for this. Nevertheless, there are drivers who still like to enjoy the feeling of oversteer and to learn the skills of handling their cars in extreme conditions. For this reason, certain cars have settings (such as a "sport" button) that make the suspension firmer and the steering more responsive, and may reduce the effectiveness or actively turn off the electronic support. If you have such a car (or if you have an older vehicle without these clever electronics), be careful. The electronic support systems are there to keep you safe; if the road conditions are not optimal or your tires are old, you may just be disabling the electronic brain that will keep you alive.

MIXING YOUR DRINKS

The car starts immediately; you turn in the road and continue your journey. You're still feeling shaken by the spin. Up ahead there's a gas station, so you decide to pull in and take 5 minutes to calm down, check the car, and maybe have a cup of coffee. You walk around the car and see nothing wrong—no dents or scrapes, and the tires are fine. Deciding that you may as well fill up the tank while you're there, you drive up to a pump and realize, in your flustered state, that you've parked on the wrong side of it. Luckily, the hose seems to reach around the car. You insert the nozzle and fill the tank, trying not to breathe the noxious fumes, which somehow seem worse than usual. It's an older pump that doesn't let you pay by card, so you go to the cashier and pay, buying your coffee at the same time and taking it back to the car. The rich, nutty smell of the coffee relaxes you. But time is of the essence! You can drink the coffee when you get to work. You start the engine and begin to drive away. Before you've even left the station, a horrible thought hits you like a sledgehammer. The gas had a funny smell when you put it into the car. It was also the wrong price. You hit the brakes and fumble for the fuel receipt. Diesel? You've just put diesel into your car!

Diesel and petroleum gas engines may often power identical-looking cars, but they are dissimilar in many ways. Their history, and more important, the way that they work, is very different. One clue to the difference is that petroleum gas engines have spark plugs, but diesel engines do not. Another clue is that putting the wrong kind of fuel in an engine may cause it serious damage. But why would two engines that both burn fuel to make vehicles move work so differently?

Engines have been around since about 1700, but in those days steam was the main source of power. Coal-powered furnaces would be used to heat water into steam. The steam required much more space than the water, so it produced a high pressure. This pressure was the key to making the wheels turn; the pressure forced pistons to move, and the pistons pushed the wheels around. An ordinary bicycle pump can give you an idea of how a piston works. If you were to pump a tire until its air reached a very high pressure, then the pressure would naturally push the handle of the pump open. It's exactly how a piston works—the pressure of the gas forces the internal piston out of the cylinder. The resulting linear (straight line) movement is converted into a rotary (circular) movement in just the same way that hoops are rolled along the ground by children. Each push on the rim is a linear motion, and that is converted into a rotary motion by the hoop. Connect a piston to a crankpin (often attached to a crankshaft) and the piston rotates the crankpin, pushing it around and around.

The origins of internal combustion engines lie in a modification to the steam engine. Instead of heating water to make the pressure, why not produce pressure by creating a little explosion inside the cylinder of the piston? Perhaps injecting some flammable liquid, such as oil, and then adding a spark would provide the pressure needed to move the piston and rotate the wheels. By

1863, Belgian Jean Joseph Étienne Lenoir had invented the first petroleum-powered internal combustion engine and managed a 50-mile round trip in his three-wheeled vehicle. His engine used a simple carburetor to mix air with the fuel to allow it to ignite in the enclosed space of the pistons. It employed electrical sparks to explode the fuel inside the cylinders. The design was refined considerably by other pioneers, such as Germans Gottlieb Daimler and Wilhelm Maybach, who manufactured the first four-wheeled automobile, and Karl Benz, who patented one of the earliest forms of petroleum-powered cars and also founded a successful automobile factory.

The designs of petroleum-powered engines have improved and become much more efficient in the 100 years of development since then. Today, for example, computers are commonly used to inject fuel (in fuel-injection systems) instead of relying on carburetors. Nevertheless, the principles of the engine remain exactly the same: Fuel and air are injected into the cylinders and ignited by sparks (produced by the spark plugs), the resulting pressure from the explosion moves the pistons, which push the crankshaft around and, through a series of gears, make the wheels turn.

Diesel engines are designed differently. At around the time that Benz and Daimler were creating their spark-ignited petroleum engines, other engineers were investigating alternative ways to move pistons. One idea was to use combustible vapor or gas (as opposed to liquid fuel) mixed with air. Another was to use coal dust, or oil. But all of these ideas used the same trick to ignite the mixture in the cylinders—compression.

Take any gas or liquid and increase its pressure, and that substance becomes hot. It's a simple principle—when you increase the pressure, you're packing more molecules of that substance into a smaller space. Like a crowd of people pushed into a smaller room, the molecules jostle against each other more. The more the molecules jiggle about, the hotter the substance becomes. (Use an old-style bicycle pump for a while and it gets warm for exactly this reason.) If you have a very hot substance in the presence of oxygen and that substance is flammable, then once the ignition temperature is reached, the substance will catch fire and burn. If the fuel is rich enough, the burning will occur so rapidly that an explosion will take place, creating a large amount of gas. So if your engine relies on burning fuel, there is no need to create a spark to ignite it. You just need to compress the fuel (or the air) until it heats up enough to ignite by itself. This is how diesel engines work, and it's why a diesel engine has no spark plugs.

The first reliable engines that used compression to trigger ignition were developed in the 1890s; German refrigerator engineer Rudolf Diesel obtained his patent in 1892 and this type of engine has borne his name ever since. (It's no coincidence that a refrigeration engineer should think of compression to heat a substance, because the external compression and internal depressurization of a liquid is how refrigerators and air conditioners transfer heat outside.) Modern diesel engines draw air into the pistons, which compress it by as much as 25:1, then fuel is injected into the hot gas to ignite it. Modern diesels also have "glow plugs," which help warm up a cold car to enable the compression of air to reach the right temperature. (They have nothing to do with spark plugs.)

Diesel engines have many advantages over their petroleum

gas cousins. The lack of extra ignition sources means that they tend to be more reliable and less fussy over types of fuel, and also more economical with fuel. They run at slower speeds and have better torque at lower speeds (they exert more force in order to move), making them ideal for trains, ships, buses, and trucks. But because their power is limited to a small band of low speeds, a truck may need 16 gears in order to allow it to travel faster. Diesel engines can also be rather noisy and may produce blue sooty smoke when they're cold and not all the fuel is being burned. This, combined with their small power band, led to an image problem that prevented them from being used in cars until quite recently. Today, modern diesels have performance almost identical to that of petroleum engines, and this, combined with their cheaper running costs, has led to a dramatic increase in the number of diesel engines in cars. In Europe, diesels have become as popular as petroleum engines (and in some countries, more popular). Here in the United States, the image problem persists and diesels are still uncommon in private vehicles. The increase in the use of diesel engines means that mistakenly putting diesel fuel in a petroleum gas engine, or petroleum in a diesel engine, is one of the most common errors made by thousands of drivers today. (In 2005, 120,000 drivers made this mistake in the United Kingdom alone.)

Diesel engines can handle a surprising range of fuels, especially because the older engines don't use carefully timed electronic fuel injection. A diesel can happily run on vegetable oil, peanut oil, or biodiesel—a plant-derived oil that may become increasingly popular as natural oil reserves dwindle and become expensive. The normal fuel for diesel engines is a product similar to kerosene derived from crude oil. This is different from petroleum gasoline. Diesel is oily and provides lubrication; petroleum gas actively strips away oil. Because older diesel engines (earlier than about 1996) are very forgiving, they will probably cope with a small amount of petroleum gas if you were to accidentally add it to your tank. But put too much petroleum gas in a diesel engine and run it and you are likely to destroy the injectors and the seals on the fuel pump. For modern cars, even unlocking the doors may activate the fuel pump, spreading the petroleum gas through the system. The solution is usually to drain the fuel from the car and bleed the fuel up to the pump, then refill with fresh diesel. If you accidentally fill an empty tank with petroleum gas, don't try to drive anywhere or you risk a sky-high mechanic's bill.

If you managed to put diesel in a petroleum gas engine, you are also likely to be in trouble. If the fuel is more than 10 percent diesel, the engine probably won't run at all, or if it does you will really hear, see, and smell the difference. There will be a strange plinking or pinging noise and lots of smelly black smoke, and you'll be lucky to get far. Too much diesel and the spark plugs simply can't ignite the fuel, so once the nasty mixture is drawn into the engine it will probably just stall. As with a diesel engine, the solution is not to drive anywhere, drain the tank and fuel lines, and refill with petroleum gas. If you do manage to run the car for a little while on this unfortunate mix, you will probably ruin your catalytic converter from the sooty mix coming out of the exhaust and you might even damage the pistons within the engine. (Putting leaded gas into a car designed for unleaded will also ruin the catalytic converter just as effectively.)

Here in the United States, diesel pumps are usually marked with green pump handles, but not always. Sometimes black, yellow, or red handles may be used for diesel or petroleum gas. In European countries such as the United Kingdom, some (but not all) fuel pump nozzles are different sizes: diesel large and petroleum gas smaller, preventing you from putting diesel into a petroleum gas engine. For those driving diesel engines, this does not prevent you from putting petroleum gas in and ruining your engine. Sadly, the mistake is so common that insurance companies often refuse to pay out. Unfortunately, car companies, garages, and even the gas stations only gain more sales when we make these mistakes, so very few automatic "wrong fuel" detectors exist in cars or pumps (although scientists have published and patented solutions to the problem). The only option is to check and double-check each time you fill your vehicle that you have the right fuel for the right engine.

An Unpleasant Trip

You're not happy about leaving the car, but the friendly staff at the gas station assured you that they'd handled such situations before and now you're in a real hurry, so you have to get moving. Clouds are starting to blow in from the west, hiding the sun and turning the bright morning into gloom. You walk briskly along the road you should have driven down 20 minutes ago. It's a good 4-mile walk, but you're on the outskirts of town now and you think there are buses that go in the right direction. In fact, you see a bus stop just ahead—and there's a bus coming! Your legs move with a burst of speed you didn't know you had. At least you don't have a bag to slow you down. Each foot hits the ground solidly, powering you along like an athlete in dress shoes. There's no way you're going to miss the bus. Without warning, your foot hits the edge of a curb and your ankle twists. The ground reaches up and hits you in the face. You land heavily, bruised and out of breath, feeling stupid. How hard can it be just to run?

Walking, running, and even standing still may not seem like very impressive feats, but all such actions actually require a surprising amount of computation by your brain. When you consider exactly how many joints there are between your head and your feet, it becomes easier to see why it's such a tricky task. Ankles, knees, hips, and more than 20 joints in your spine and your neck, not to mention the joints in your arms, help you maintain balance. All have to be at the right angles at the right times to prevent you from falling. It's like threading elastic through 30 pens, end to end, balancing each of them on top of the other, and then somehow being able to move the wobbly tower without it toppling over.

In engineering, computer science, and rocket science, a highly simplified version of the problem is known as the pole-balancing, or inverted-pendulum, problem. Imagine a pole standing vertically on a movable platform. The problem is to keep the pole balanced vertically by moving only the platform. In the real world, this problem is equivalent to keeping a rocket pointing upward as its engine fires beneath it. If the rocket starts to topple, then its engine may make it spiral into the ground—not an ideal way to launch a satellite into space. We can solve both problems by using fast and clever controllers, which sense the direction of the impending topple and move the base in the same direction to halt it. But moving from a basic pole-balancing problem to the double-pole-balancing problem (another pole balancing on the end of the first), or the triple-pole-balancing problem, and it becomes enormously difficult to make computer controllers that are fast and precise enough to keep them balancing vertically end-to-end. It's one reason why robots never quite move with the grace of living organisms. We have the technology to build bodies that mimic our own, make all the same joints, and have motors to move all of the joints in the right ways. We just haven't managed to create electronic brains that are flexible and responsive enough to use the robot bodies effectively. In a very real sense, we solve problems harder than those in rocket science every time we stand up.

There are many good reasons why living organisms are adept at moving themselves around without tripping or falling all the time. This was such a crucial skill for survival that early on in our evolutionary history, the primitive brains of our ancestors were primarily concerned with coordinating muscles and senses. Any creature that fell over too much was eaten by predators pretty quickly, creating a strong evolutionary pressure toward animals that could move reliably. Only the creatures able to sense the location of their limbs in relation to the ground, and put this knowledge to use in the form of movement, would survive long enough to reproduce. So generation after generation of better-moving animals resulted in animal brains that could instinctively move over rough ground. We still have this primitive brain buried deep inside our own. In the millions of years of evolution since then, we've added layers of new brain material around this brain stem. But we have an instinctive ability to stand on our limbs, walk, and cope with rough ground that is given to us by the unconscious reptilian brain inside us. Without it, we would be much like one of our robots—stumbling, clumsy, and prone to losing our balance.

Another reason why our robots move "robotically" is that they lack sensory feedback. We have a huge number of very precise sensors built in all over our bodies. Without the feedback of all these sensors—called kinesthesia—even the best brain in the world would never be able to keep a body standing upright.

To get a sense of how kinesthesia works, try the following

experiment: close your eyes and raise your left hand above your head. How do you know it's above your head? You can feel it is there, but how? It's not touching anything. If you're thinking that perhaps it's the feeling of weight changing on the joints in your arm as you reposition it, then try moving while floating in the bath or a swimming pool. You will still instinctively "know" where your limbs are. The sense of your own movement and position that you feel in your arm is kinesthesia. It works through specialized stretch sensors in our muscles that tell the brain that muscles are in use. It also uses sensors linked to tendons and joints to tell us that a joint is being repositioned. Our brains even integrate feelings of skin stretching and touch to help us fine-tune our awareness of where all our joints, muscles, and limbs are. The myriad tiny senses are all correlated to individual muscle and joint movements, enabling us to make microscopic adjustments to every muscle and joint, giving us extraordinary control and precision in our movements.

Of course, like all senses, sometimes they become confused. Drinking a lot of alcohol impairs our ability to make use of the information from these senses, and so a simple test of touching our noses with eyes shut, or walking along a straight line, becomes a real challenge. There are also simple sensory illusions that demonstrate the senses of kinesthesia. One example used to study how the brain processes these senses is the Pinocchio Illusion. Close your eyes, touch your nose, and apply a vibrating device (perhaps the handle of an electric toothbrush or razor) to the triceps (the outer) muscle of that arm. The vibration will fool your brain into thinking that the muscle is contracting more than the biceps, pulling your hand further from your nose. But because your brain can also still feel that the hand is still touching your nose, it assumes that your nose must be growing longer and longer.

In addition to these internal senses, we also have another hugely important sense: balance, or equilibrioception. In mammals, this sense is found in the inner ears in a mazelike network of tubes known as the labyrinth. The vestibular system is a set of circular tubes and little sacks filled with fluid. The circular tubes are called canals and we have three inside each ear: the horizontal, anterior, and posterior canals. Imagine taking a tire inner tube, somehow coating its interior surface with fur, and then pumping it full of viscous gloopy fluid. Rotate the tube and the fluid takes a little while to catch up. Because the tube moves faster than the fluid, the fur lining the inside is swept against the motion. Shrink the whole thing a few thousand times and that's how the canals work. Whenever the fur (hairs) are moved, nerves in the hairs tell our brain that a rotation is taking place. To make sure we can sense rotation in all directions, we have one for turning in a circle, one for forward rotation and one for sideways rotation. But we can do more than this. When we go up or down in an elevator, for instance, we feel the motion—and that's not a rotation. Or when we accelerate in a car, we can feel the change in speed. To enable this kind of linear (straight line) sense, we have two other little tubes, filled with fluid and little tiny particles called otoliths. One detects any change in vertical movement and the other detects a change in horizontal movement. They are also sensitive enough to detect that we're tilted at an angle. Fascinatingly, because these sensory organs work in a similar way to the way our inner ears detect sound (little hairs are disturbed by sound waves), some research has suggested that one of these tubes—the saccule—may even enable some people to hear ultrasonic speech (which is too high to hear using our normal hearing).

Our sense of balance is wired directly to the muscles of our eyes through just a few neurons. Every time our head or body moves, the change in balance makes our eyes move to compensate. It's exactly like the antishake mechanisms used in modern digital cameras (which move their internal light-sensitive chips to counter the effects of a shaking hand), and because the compensating eye movements happen so quickly, our vision is kept sharp and in focus. Amazingly, our eyes even do this when we tilt our heads to the side, the eyeballs rotating in the sockets (look in a mirror and try it)! But the direct wiring from balance to eyes has another side effect: If we spin around in a circle for a while, the fluid in those canals eventually catches up and starts spinning with us. Then when we stop spinning, the fluid takes a little while to slow down. So for a few seconds, there's a flow of fluid moving the little hairs, telling our brains that we are spinning in the other direction. Our automatic eye movements then constantly adjust to compensate for the imaginary motion and we become very disoriented. We call this effect dizziness.

Despite the occasional false readings from our senses, the detailed and precise information that they provide to our brains enables us to propel ourselves around with amazing proficiency. Standing upright by balancing on two legs is impressive enough, but walking is an extraordinary balancing act. We have to initiate a controlled topple, but before we fall flat on our face, we must move a leg to support us, shift our entire weight onto that leg, continue the topple, move the other leg to support us, and so on. A single mistake can result in injury. Running is an even more amazing feat—we actually make little jumps, pushing off the ground with one leg, landing on the other, transferring our weight to that leg, absorbing the impact, and pushing off for another little jump to land on the first leg again. Observe even our best humanoid robots walking and you'll see a careful, clumsy, and extremely slow zombie shuffle. We can't make robots that can run like us—they just fall over.

With our stabilized, antishake eyes and large mammalian brains with impressive vision-processing centers, we are also able to look ahead as we move and predict the height and texture of the ground before we reach it. This clever automatic computation compensates for unexpected circumstances, falls, trips, and shoves, without any conscious thought. Once we've had some practice, we can even look at the movement of other creatures around us and effortlessly predict where they will be in the future. The information from these higher layers of the brain is then fed down to the brain stem, which automatically adjusts the different muscles to change our pattern of foot placements. Watch any four-legged animals run together and you'll see that they make constant split-second adjustments to their gaits to ensure that each foot is placed on safe, steady ground, and no collisions take place. We all have this ability. It's so automatic that consciously controlling where we place our feet takes quite a lot of concentration. And while we don't have four legs or a tail to worry about, we do use our arms to help us keep balance. Again, the swinging, counterbalancing movement of our arms is entirely unconscious, and actively trying to control it while walking can be a real mental challenge.

But these amazing brains and senses are of no benefit if we don't use them properly. Run for a bus without looking where you are going and you will be unaware of any rough terrain ahead. Your brain stem will assume that the ground continues without change, and so when your foot encounters the unseen hazard, your gait will be wrong—too much weight will be placed onto a leg that has nothing to support it, and you will stumble and fall. Do your brain stem a favor. Pay attention to where you're walking, especially if you're in a hurry.

COMING UNSTUCK

You reach the bus stop just as the bus arrives. Thankfully, the fall did nothing except hurt your pride. You step aboard, squeeze past the standing passengers, and collapse into the only free seat with a grateful sigh. Before long, the passenger seated next to you rises to leave and you stand to let her out. As you get to your feet, you feel something strange on the back of your head. Your searching fingers find a blob of something warm and sticky in your hair. As you touch it, you smell a sugary minty fragrance. Your nose wrinkles in disgust. It's chewing gum! And worse, as you stood up, it must have stretched into a long sticky snake that has glued itself to the back of your head and onto your collar. You try to pull it off and bring nothing more than a string of minty-fresh sticky glue before your eyes, which is now also sticking fast to your fingers. You sit back down and obsessively try to pull away the horrible substance, but all you seem to do is make it stick more. Why won't the stupid stuff come off?

The problem of sticky chewing gum is an unpleasant one, and not just because it involves a substance that has spent a while inside somebody else's mouth. In fact, the problems caused by used chewing gum can be so severe that Singapore banned gum from their country in 1992. This may seem a little extreme, but in the 1980s, vandals were habitually disposing of gum in mailboxes, on elevator buttons, inside keyholes, on the door sensors of trains, and on floors, walls, and bus seats. The whole transport system of the country was suffering because of chewing gum. The ban solved the problem, but Singapore was not allowed to keep its prohibition for long. Wrigley, the giant chewing gum manufacturer (and producer of varieties including Big Red and Doublemint), managed to have gum listed on the Singapore-America Free Trade Agreement, and lobbied the country to accept gum. In 2004, the country was forced to allow chewing gum (but only for health reasons) once again. Whether a return to chewing gum nightmares for the inhabitants of Singapore is in the cards remains to be seen.

The problem is that chewing gum doesn't degrade or get broken down by bacteria and insects as most of our food waste does. It behaves like tar, coating whatever surface it is left on with its sticky, stretchy goo. So when it ends up somewhere it shouldn't be, that's exactly where it will stay, until it is removed. How many times have you sat at a desk or on a chair and found your fingers squelching in somebody's gum? There's a lot of old gum out there, and more being thoughtlessly left behind every minute.

Chewing gum is not a new invention, despite its modern use for vandalism. Archeologists recently found three wads of chewed birch resin in the remains of the floor of a hunter-gatherer hut on a Swedish island called Orust. The teeth imprints in the gum were those of a teenager. The gum was 9,000 years old.

Many early gums were formed from resins extracted from the mastic tree, which grew in Greece and Turkey. The ancient

Greeks used the gum to clean their teeth and sweeten their breath. This is also the source of the English word for chew, "masticate." The Greeks were not unique. Native Americans in New England used the resin from spruce trees, and early settlers learned to copy this practice and substituted other substances such as sweetened paraffin wax, rubber, or the milky juice of the chicle tree. All these sticky resins are natural latexes, or rubbers, but today most gums use a man-made latex, mixed with oils to retain moisture. Sweeteners and mint oils impart flavor, and a coating of sugar powder (for stick gums) or a sweet candy shell (for pellet-style gums) prevent the pieces from sticking to the packaging. Once you begin chewing, your mouth dissolves and removes the sugars, while also mixing the ingredients and warming them to a temperature optimal for creating a stretchy, sticky texture.

The composition of latex lends gum its stretchy property. Whether man-made or oozing from a cut in a tree, latex is a mixture of water and polymer molecules. A polymer is a long string of smaller molecules called monomers, all chained together to form a long, molecular conga line. When you tug on a piece of ABC (Already Been Chewed) gum, it's like pulling a fork through a bowl of spaghetti—all the long spaghetti molecules are pulled out into strings. The result is that the gum is pulled out into strings, instead of simply breaking. Although these polymers are very related to the rubbers used in car tires, balloons, and other products, in chewing gum they are not elastic. So when you stretch out a piece of gum, it stays stretched. (As we saw in an earlier chapter, rubber is made elastic by heating the long polymer molecules with sulfur until the separate spaghetti-like molecules attach to each other where they touch. Then when you pull them, they stretch out a little way and bounce back into their bowl-of-spaghetti shape again.)

Gum sticks to surfaces like hair for a similar reason. You may notice that when gum is wet, it is less sticky. That's because your saliva provides a thin barrier of liquid between the long polymer chains and the surface it's on. But leave gum outside for a few minutes and the water will dry up, leaving the bowl-of-spaghetti molecules ready to hook onto anything that catches them. Unfortunately, hair happens to be the ideal surface for gum to stick to.

Despite appearances, hair is not silky smooth. Look at a strand of hair through a microscope and you'll see it's as scaly as alligator skin. Hair conditioner will glue down some of the scales and make the hair smoother, and oils and moisturizers will coat the hair and make it more flexible, but all hair is naturally scaly—it's the way it grows from the hair follicles. These scales are jagged, forming countless little rough edges. So on a molecular scale, your hair is like a collection of trillions of little hooks, and the polymer molecules of the gum have been chewed into a messy ball of loops. Bring the two together and it's just like Velcro—they stick together beautifully. But because gum stretches rather than breaks, when you try to extract it from your hair by pulling it, the molecules stay stuck.

If you're not careful, the gum-in-hair scenario can quickly get worse. The warmth of your hands and oil on your fingers will keep the gum nice and supple. All of those long molecules will be eagerly waiting to catch onto anything nearby—especially your clothing. Cloth has many of the same properties as hair—

whether it is made from cotton or wool, it's just a bunch of tiny hairlike fibers, woven into threads that are woven into cloth. So the molecules of the gum will grab onto the scales of wool (sheep hair) just as nicely as they will to your own hair. It will even stick to the cells on your fingers, if they are too dry.

The stickiness and long life of gum is not always a disadvantage. Over the years, many emergency repairs have been made using ordinary chewing gum. Gas pipes have been repaired, as have radiators, musical instruments, car tires, and on one occasion, even the landing gear of a bomber! But none of this is much help if you're angrily reading this with a big lump of chewing gum dangling in front of your face.

So what should you do? First, stop pulling at it—you'll only make it more likely to stretch, exposing more polymer molecules ready to glue themselves to more things. If you must touch it at all, make sure your fingers are wet, so you form a liquid barrier between the cells of your skin and the long molecules. Secondly, don't cut your hair out—there's no need for that. Instead, a little knowledge about the composition of gum will tell you the answer. Recall that gum is composed of latex and oil to make it supple. Like any mixture, if you change its composition, you will change its properties. Because ABC gum has had its ingredients mixed by chewing to form a very viscous (thick and gloopy) liquid state, that means you can mix in other ingredients. If oil makes it more supple, then mixing in more oil will make it thinner and will help those long molecules slide around more. This is why people have a lot of success removing gum using oil or products containing oil, such as peanut butter, mayonnaise, or even perfume. By mixing in this oily substance, you are changing the composition of the gum and helping the long molecules slide off your hair or clothes.

There's also a second alternative. Like any liquid, if you apply heat, it will become runny (the heat provides energy, making the molecules jiggle around). If you cool it down, it will turn into a solid (the energy will be so low that the molecules just lock themselves together). Because gum is already very, well, gummy (not very liquid), it doesn't take much cooling to turn it into a solid. Just take a piece of ice and hold it against the gum, and you will find that the gum sets into a solid. Before it warms up again, you can then smash that solid, like breaking ice. Instead of sliding the long polymer molecules off, you're simply smashing them apart.

It's easier to remove gum once you understand its basic chemistry and composition. If you have a blob of chewing gum stuck in long hair, cooling it and smashing it may be the simplest approach. If the gum is too close to your skin or you can't reach it (perhaps because it's stuck to the back of your head), or if you've sat on the gum and embedded it into your clothes, an oil or oil-based product will liquefy the gum and get rid of it in no time.

STAYING AFLOAT

You suddenly realize that the bus has gone past your office. The sticky distraction has made you miss your stop. You jump off at the next one and discover that you're in a part of town you don't recognize. Hopefully if you walk back in the direction you came from you'll see something familiar soon. The light is now ominously dark. Large black clouds have gathered overhead and you feel a cold breeze blowing. Suddenly the wind drops and there is a moment of stillness before the air is filled with torrential rain. You run for the nearest shelter—a nearby bookstore. But it's on the other side of the street. By the time you've found a gap in the traffic and crossed, you're already soaked, cold water running down your neck, feet squelching in their shoes. You enter the air-conditioned store, dripping and bedraggled. There you stand, miserably looking out at the rain, shivering with cold.

Water covers 70 percent of the surface of our planet, so it's not surprising that we might become a little wet now and again, wherever we live. But there are deeper questions, often overlooked except by space scientists or astrobiologists: Where did all that water come from in the first place? Why is the Earth not as dry as its neighbor, Mars? Or if Earth had been colder, would we have seas of methane or ethane (as recently discovered on Titan, one of the moons of Saturn)?

Considerable research has gone into finding an answer to these tricky questions. The Earth, like the other planets and our sun, formed out of the swirling clouds of debris left over from the death of previous stars and solar systems. Gravity caused clumps to form, attracting more and more material until hot spheres began to rotate around each other. (A giant mass of molten rock held together by its own gravity naturally forms a sphere, just as a single drop of water held together by its surface tension also forms a sphere.) Most of the remains of the debris were then blown away by the solar winds as the sun ignited its hydrogen-bomb fires and began its current hot, fiery existence.

Because the birth of our planet was so hot, it was believed that water could not have formed among its aggregating particles. In contrast, in the more remote, colder regions where the giant planets formed, a great deal of ice was able to solidify (some of the moons of Jupiter are almost solid ice). So one solution to the mystery of Earth's water was that chunks of ice from this region hit the young Earth as comets. We know that there was a period of time called the heavy bombardment period (4.5 to 3.8 billion years ago) when comets did rain down on us—just look at the craters on the Moon to see what happened there. But when our space probes analyzed the mixture of compounds in the ice of comets, their composition was quite different. Earth didn't receive its water from comets. So another source of ice was proposed, this time from meteorites (which come from the much-closer asteroid belt, circling between the orbits of Mars and Jupiter). But there is still controversy over the issue. We do not know whether the ice combined with the Earth as it formed from its swirling mass of debris or whether the ice rained down in meteorites. We'd like to know, because water is hugely important for life on Earth, and if we can figure out just how lucky we were to receive our water, we could figure out how likely it would be for other planets to resemble ours, and possibly contain life. It may be that all solar systems like ours have huge amounts of ice floating around, just waiting to hit the right kind of planet that has the right temperature and atmosphere to hold on to it.

Earth turns out to be just perfect for holding on to water. It has colder regions at the poles that receive such diluted sunlight that water remains in its solid state as ice. On most of its surface, it is warm enough for water to pool in the lower areas in its liquid form, as seas. In the tropical regions, the sun's heat is strong enough to cause evaporation from the sea: without actually boiling, the molecules in the water manage now and again to move vigorously enough to leave their neighbors in the sloshy liquid and fly free into the air. Just 0.001 percent of the water makes it into the atmosphere, but this is still 10 times the amount of water in all the rivers and streams of the world.

The process of evaporation causes a cooling effect as the fastest-moving (hotter) molecules fly free from the liquid, leaving the slower (cooler) ones behind. It's why you feel cold when wet—your skin temperature helps evaporate the water, but those escaping water molecules are stealing your heat as they go. Without evaporation, the temperature of the Earth might be as hot as 150°F. Evaporation is also affected by the moisture content of the air, or the humidity. The warmer the air is, the more water vapor it can support. (Warm air means more energetically moving molecules, making it easier for water to stay in its gaseous state.) If the humidity is too high, then no more evaporation can take place. So you'll find that water will evaporate quickly in front of the dry air produced by an air conditioner, but in a steamy tropical country the water just doesn't want to evaporate.

When the humidity is so high that the air is saturated (the "dew point"), then all those water molecules start gluing themselves back together to form a liquid again and you have precipitation (rain or dew). In cold air, the dew point is lower, meaning a lower humidity, which is why after a warm day has sucked up moisture into the air, a cool night may create dew on the ground. It's also why water droplets form when rising hot air takes water vapor high into the thin, cold air. Clouds are just droplets of dew forming on dust in the air. When the droplets become large enough, they eventually fall as rain, hail, or snow, depending on the temperature. In fact, water vapor is lighter than air, so it will always tend to rise high into the cold heights until it has little choice but to fall down again as a liquid or solid.

Water vapor cannot escape from the Earth's atmosphere as it has from the Moon, Mars, and other planets because the Earth is massive enough to keep its cloak of gases wrapped around it by the pull of its gravity. The Moon has no atmosphere at all—anything it may have once had just evaporated into space. Its gravity is too weak to hold on to those gas molecules. Mars has a thin layer of carbon dioxide, but not much else. Like Earth, Venus is massive enough to keep all of its atmosphere, but Venus is much too hot to contain water.

So it's really no coincidence that Earth has kept all of its water, unlike the other planets in the solar system. Earth is the only planet with the right mass and the right distance from the sun to allow the water to stay. All the other planets may have originally had water, but lost most of it. In a similar way, Titan is exactly the right size and temperature for seas of methane and ethane to exist, producing weather and shorelines resembling those of the Earth. Some scientists suggest a different form of life, perhaps based on silicon, could exist there, relying on the methane just as we rely on water.

But if life on Earth relies on water so much, shouldn't we be singing in the rain every time it falls? One important reason why we don't enjoy being wet is the loss of heat. It's very easy for us to become chilled and weakened, allowing infections to take hold and make us ill. Humans are particularly susceptible to heat loss through evaporation because we have a habit of wearing cloth over most of our skin. When the cloth becomes saturated in water, which then slowly evaporates over many hours, we suffer tremendously more heat loss than an animal with no clothes does. The solution is either to go naked in the rain, which might cause a few comments from other people, or to wear waterproof clothes.

Most cloth is not waterproof. In fact, most cloth is the opposite—it actively attracts water to its surface and sucks it inside. One reason why this happens is called "capillary action." The molecules of water are sometimes more attracted to another surface than they are to themselves. Put water into an ordinary glass and instead of lying perfectly flat, you'll see that the water creeps up slightly at the edges, forming a concave surface, or "meniscus." The water likes the glass so much that all the molecules are doing their best to touch it, but the surface tension and mass of the bulk of the water prevents it from climbing the walls. Make the glass much, much smaller—in fact, use a tiny little glass tube—and the water will climb up inside. Propelled only by the desire of the water molecules to touch the glass, water can climb tiny vertical tubes. It's a principle exploited by plants, which grow tiny little tubes (roots) that suck water from the soil through capillary action and, in the case of trees, pump gallons of water many tens of feet into the sky. Most cloth is just as attractive to water, but instead of forming little tubes to suck water, cloth has trillions of fibers woven together. Just as the wick of an oil lamp absorbs the oil into its fibers, so the fibers of our clothing pull the water along their surfaces. Spill some water on fabric (or another fibrous material, such as paper) and you can watch it being absorbed before your eyes. The wick effect, using the capillary action of fibers, will happily pump all the water from rain into your clothes until they are nicely saturated.

The solution is to prevent this attractive force between water and fibers from taking place. Water may be attracted to some substances, but it is positively repelled by others. Look at water on a waxy surface and you'll see it forms into a convex droplet—the water is trying to keep away from the surface as much as possible. So all you need to do in order to prevent water from soaking into clothes is to wear something waxy or oily (or perhaps oil-derived, such as rubber, or artificial rubber, such as neoprene).

Nature discovered this principle a long time ago. We have oily skin for a good reason—the oil makes our skin waterproof. If you want to know what happens when the oil is washed off, then take a long shower for at least 30 minutes. Because much of the oil has been washed away by the soapy water, the outer layers of your skin start to attract the water and let it soak in. Your skin becomes wrinkled as the upper surface is swollen by the water, but the layers of skin and tissue beneath remain the same size. (Take a dry sponge, draw around it, then soak it in water and try to fit the swollen shape in the smaller outline—the only way to do it is by wrinkling it up.) Our skin quickly returns to normal as the excess water evaporates once we leave the shower.

Today, these principles are well understood, and so fabrics with special water-repellent coatings are common. Some of these materials are so clever that they use the wick effect to draw perspiration away from our skin on the inside, but have a water-repellent layer on the outside to prevent water from soaking in. And if you'd rather not wear waterproof clothing, then the fabric of umbrellas works in exactly the same way. If you do happen to get wet, though, try to change into dry clothes as soon as possible and stay warm. Leaving on wet clothes is like stepping into a giant refrigerator on a cold day.

KNOWING YOUR PLACE

As suddenly as the rain began, it's over. Barely believing your eyes, you look up at a blue sky again. Already steam is beginning to rise from the wet sidewalks as the sun heats them. You leave the bookshop and start walking briskly back the way the bus had come. Perhaps it's the bright reflections or the spray from the cars, but nothing seems familiar. You keep walking for 10 more minutes, becoming increasingly anxious. The shops are gone and you now realize you've entered a quiet, tree-lined residential street. There's no one around to ask for directions and you feel too foolish to knock on somebody's door. Somehow the trees seem menacing, their branches looming over you. You look back the way you came. It looks much the same as the direction you are walking. You're lost. Completely lost.

We've all experienced a few minutes of panic in our lives, caused by the simple realization that we don't know where we are. Nothing seems familiar. We feel a mixture of danger, alertness, and confusion as we anticipate unknown perils, try to understand our surroundings, and attempt to link what we're currently seeing with any kind of memory that might aid us. Why can't we figure out where we are?

Compared to other creatures, humans have traditionally not

traveled long distances. While many of us may have a short commute to work or travel farther away on a planned trip, we rarely have to navigate the route ourselves. Today we are pampered by the luxuries of electronic gadgets that tell us where to go, maps that describe where everything is, and tarmac paths that have signs all along their lengths to inform us of where we are. Imagine making a journey of several thousand miles with no gadgets, maps, roads, or signs to guide you, and no vehicle to propel you. Yet such journeys are successfully undertaken by an incredible variety of creatures. Mammals such as wildebeest migrate hundreds of miles across Africa to find seasonal water and food. Turtles swim thousands of miles across entire oceans to return to the exact beach on which they hatched, laying eggs in the same safe place where they were born. Salmon fight their way against the currents for hundreds of miles through the ocean and back up the rivers they came down after spawning. Birds regularly migrate thousands of miles, sometimes from one end of the planet to the other, to find warmer homes for the winter and longer days in the summer (in the Northern Hemisphere). Even butterflies are able to migrate across countries to find food, their journey so long that it takes several generations to complete. All these different creatures travel staggering distances and somehow safely find their way, perhaps to the same beach, or even the same nest, each time. When the average human can easily become lost in just a couple of square miles of unfamiliar landscape, these creatures put our large, supposedly intelligent brains to shame.

All migratory creatures share the same problem: navigation. They need to know where they are and where they want to be.

The methods they use are generally fairly similar. One basic trick is simply to follow everyone else, and learn the route from them. Many species of birds rely on being taught which way to go, for they must often pick complex and tortuous paths through mountain ranges and around oceans to reach their destinations. The trick they use is to memorize important landmarks: a mountain here, a lake there, and to use them as road signs, pointing the way ahead. Remarkably, honeybees don't even have to lead their companions to show them the way. Instead they communicate with their companions in the hive by performing a "waggle dance." The orientation of the bee performing the dance provides the direction relative to the sun, and the amount of time spent waggling indicates the distance to fly. The smell of the nectar on the bee also helps them follow the instructions and find the flowers and the new source of nectar. Different species of honeybees use slight variations on the dance, as though each has its own accent or dialect.

Creatures don't use only their eyes when migrating. Salmon imprint on the chemical content of the rivers they were born in, and they use this "smell" to guide them as they get closer to the source. Ants lay down pheromone trails from the nest to useful food sources, guiding their companions along their smelly paths. Turtles and many mammals may also rely on smell to help them recognize the places where they were born. Because their olfactory senses are so much better than ours, they create mental maps of smells using specific scents as landmarks just as other creatures use sights. Humpback whales migrate to the warm Hawaiian waters to rear their young, and return to Arctic waters for the rich food in the summer. In addition to sight and smell, they use their sonar to "listen to" the underwater landscapes, and also learn to recognize the feel of the oceanic currents.

But while these conventional senses provide the detailed information creatures use to fine-tune their routes, sight, hearing, and smell are not enough to enable them to travel thousands of miles. There's a big difference between finding the right house in a town and finding the right house on a continent. No bird could ever remember 500 landmarks, nor could a salmon remember 1,000 smells to follow. Instead, a more general sense of direction is needed by migratory creatures. They need to know in which overall direction they should fly, swim, or walk, and then use their more precise senses to keep themselves on track.

One obvious strategy is to use the position of the sun as a guide, and many organisms do exactly this. By automatically adjusting for the movement of the sun, birds, bees, and fish are able to figure out which way is north or south, and keep flying in the right direction. Some nighttime migratory birds (for example, the indigo bunting) use the patterns of stars to help them navigate. Bees and ants are even able to cope when it's cloudy by having eyes that can detect and analyze the polarization (direction) of sunlight.

But sunlight and starlight are not always visible enough to serve as reliable navigation aides, and when crossing the equator, having the sun directly overhead provides very little information about direction. What migratory creatures need is an internal compass that points them north, and then they can figure out where to go relative to that. Astonishingly, that's exactly what they have, built into their brains.

A compass works because the center of the Earth acts like a

giant magnet, producing a large magnetic field that sweeps around and beyond the planet for some distance. The cause of this field is not fully understood, but the current theory is that the molten iron outer core of the planet is swirled around by the Earth's rotation, producing huge electric currents. The electricity generates a magnetic field, which is thought to reinforce itself again and again, resulting in a reasonably stable polarity with the north pole of the magnet at one end of the planet and the south pole at the other end. The magnetic field is not entirely stable, however, and the magnetic poles constantly move around, somewhere between 6 and 24 miles per year. Scientists have also discovered that lava from volcanoes can "trap" the direction of the Earth's magnetic field when it cools, preserving a record of its changes. According to this evidence, the magnetic field may sometimes completely reverse itself (about every 300,000 years), with north becoming south and south becoming north.

Luckily, the magnetic fields are constant for such prolonged periods that they make excellent navigational aides. We use them by watching a little magnetic needle become attracted toward the north pole in a compass. Some mobile phones, watches, and cars contain solid-state compasses, which use two or three tiny magnetic field sensors in a chip to detect the strength of the field at that point and trigonometry to calculate the current orientation of the device they are within.

Birds, fish, some insects, amphibians, whales, and turtles also use the same trick. Somehow they are all able to sense the direction of the Earth's magnetic field. Scientists are still trying to figure out exactly how they do it—whether there are minute particles of iron in their brains that affect the firing of some neurons, or whether the receptors in their eyes contain some kind of chemical mixture that makes them slightly receptive to magnetic fields in addition to light. Many birds are known to have a well-defined sense of magnetic fields (indeed, migrating birds that fly over iron deposits can become very confused and disoriented). Research has shown that the areas of the brain that birds use for vision are also active when they are subjected to different magnetic fields, so perhaps birds can actually "see" the Earth's magnetism.

Some of the most controversial research also suggests that humans may have some very basic form of magnetic sense. Experiments have shown that some blindfolded people can remain aware of their orientation after traveling some distance, but this awareness can be disrupted by placing magnets near their heads. More compellingly, neuroscientists have measured changes in our brain activity that correspond to the presence of magnetic fields, suggesting that something in our brains is being affected by the fields whether we are aware of it or not. Some researchers believe the sense may originate in a tiny crystal of magnetite often found in the base of the nose, between the eyes.

Sadly, even if we do have some kind of "magnetic sense," we surround ourselves with so many metal and electrical devices, and transmit so many radio and microwaves for communication and entertainment, that it is probably hopelessly muddled most of the time. We do the same thing with odor, temperature, sound, and sights, filling our towns and cities with so many repeated experiences that all our other senses become overloaded and confused. Architects try to counter these effects using different ideas. In the United States, our popular solution to this is to plan cities in regular "grids" with numbers for each street, to make navigation more a process of plotting coordinates. Other architects try to turn understandability into a science, by measuring lines of sight in different street and building layouts, and showing that the more we can see from any given point, the more we can understand the space we're in.

Becoming lost is all too easy, so the best thing to do is copy migratory creatures: learn landmarks along the route so that you'll be able to find your way back, consciously pointing out unusual buildings or trees as you go. Try to understand the general direction in which you need to head, either from signs, the shadows cast by the sun, or even a compass in your cell phone. Remember, you have a brain considerably larger than the peanut-sized brain of a salmon, or the grain-of-rice-sized brain of a bee, so if you're really lost, ask for directions!

PAIN IN THE NECK

Having retraced your steps back to the bookshop, your mistake is obvious: you turned right instead of turning left when you walked out the door. On track once more, you walk briskly, swatting a bee as it hovers annoyingly around your face. Things are looking much more familiar and . . . that bee won't leave you alone. It's attracted to your hair or something. Perhaps it likes your shampoo. You walk quicker, waving your hands around to persuade the bee that you're not a flower. It follows you like some miniature evil demon, intent on mischief. Now your flailing hand hits the bee, sending it into a high-pitched buzzing frenzy, darting around you like a miniature dive-bomber. You continue to try and swipe the insect away, connecting with it again and again, until suddenly you hear a loud buzzing by your ear and feel a sharp pain. You've been stung just below your ear; you can feel the stinger embedded in your flesh. The intensity of the sharp pain keeps increasing as though someone is pushing the stinger deeper and deeper. How can one little insect cause so much pain?

There are between 1.5 and 1.8 million named species of living organisms on our planet, with estimates of the total number of species somewhere between 5 and 20 million. Half of all known species are insects. (There are 300,000 different species of beetle alone.) Of this vast number, very few insects use poisons or venoms to protect themselves. Some rely on poisonous hollow or glasslike hairs (as in the case of some caterpillars) or may use compounds injected during a bite to numb the skin of their prey and prevent the blood from clotting (as used by mosquitoes). Some ants will squirt formic acid at attacking predators to drive them away, or they may inject acid from their jaws as they bite. (Spiders also use venom to paralyze their prey, but they are not insects—they're arachnids and belong to the same family as scorpions, mites, and ticks.) Thankfully, the vast majority of insects do not sting or bite us in any way.

Insects belonging to the family (or more properly, the order) known as *Hymenoptera* are best known for their venom. Ants, sawflies, wasps, and bees all belong to the order, and we all learn from an early age that there is something special about wasps and bees. They sting!

The sting of bees is only used for defense. These insects live on nectar from flowers and gain no advantage from attacking mammals like us. They're not carnivorous, as some ants are, so they have no interest in eating us. Most of the time, stings are used against other bees or wasps trying to enter a hive and steal food. So most stings (for example, those of the bumblebee and wasps) are smooth little hollow spikes at the rear of the insect, designed to act like hypodermic needles to inject painful venom into the victim and then be withdrawn. Invaders are either killed outright or are so badly injured that they fly away as quickly as possible.

Unfortunately for honeybees, their personal food storage

system is very tasty. Field bees gather nectar, storing it in special pouch separate from their stomachs. They regurgitate it into the mouths of house bees, who then chew it for a while, adding enzymes and transforming the mixture into a sticky, oily, sweet, and slightly acidic goo that resists fungi and bacteria for years. They store the fluid in special waxy boxes, fan it with their wings to remove most of the water and prevent it from fermenting, and then seal it away to feed their larvae at a later date. The result is a hive full of honey—a supersweet fluid that is always fresh and tasty. It's so good that large mammals such as bears find it irresistible, and they happily smash their way into hives to lick out the sweet food.

Bears (and humans) have been stealing honey for so long that there are even species of birds known as honeyguides. Some 17 species of these birds exist, all with a fondness for eating the wax and larvae of the bees. These remarkable birds deliberately lead humans or large mammals to the hives of honeybees, feeding on the remains once the honey has been removed.

Under such concerted attack, the honeybee was forced to improve its defenses. It already had a good sting for keeping other insects away, so its sting was further improved upon. In the life-or-death situation of the hive being potentially destroyed, it became acceptable for bees to act as kamikazes—sacrificing their lives for the good of the hive. So the sting of the honeybee evolved to become a very nasty weapon. Instead of a smooth spike, the stinger developed barbs to make it harder to remove from the skin. When stinging another insect, the bee can still sting more than once. But the skin of a mammal or bird is more elastic, so once the barbed sting is forced through, it cannot be retracted and the bee is trapped. In its fight to escape, it tears the stinger from its own body. The dying bee then flies away, releasing pheromones (which smell a little like old socks) that turn all the other bees into angry attacking machines. Its stinger is left in the skin, along with the venom sack, muscles, and a nerve cell. Although the bee is now gone, the nerve cell continues to activate the muscles, pumping more and more of the venom from the sack into the skin to cause the maximum possible pain to the mammal. If the honey thief is still stupid enough to stay near the hive, more and more bees will sting and release attack pheromones until the whole hive is an angry swarming mass of attacking insects. This is more than enough to make most creatures run away as fast as they can.

The reason why bee stings hurt is because of their chemical composition. Bee venom, or apitoxin, contains a complex and acidic mixture of different proteins and compounds. The main constituent is melittin, a mixture of venom proteins. One of the most damaging of these is called phospholipase, which breaks down the cell walls, decreases blood pressure, and slows clotting. Another, called hyaluronidase, makes tissues more permeable, allowing bacteria to easily spread. The one that causes much of the pain is called apamin—a nerve toxin that interacts with our pain receptors, making them react violently, sending their own equivalent of a siren wailing to our brains.

Our bodies react immediately to this nasty cocktail of chemicals, producing swelling in an attempt to flush away the toxins. If the stinger stays in place for more than about 30 seconds, then the large amount of venom may remain in the tissue for 2 or 3 days, causing pain and discomfort. Bee stings are generally not fatal, unless the person is weak and receives a large number of stings. Recent statistics show that deaths from bee stings have mainly occurred when the victim is over 70 years old and has been stung between 50 and 150 times. The bees are also typically Africanized bees in Central and South America, descended from aggressive Tanzanian bees, which were artificially bred for honey production and are now loose in the wild.

There are far more cases of bee sting fatalities caused by allergies than by angry swarms. Often triggered by just a single sting, the body of a human who is allergic to bee stings enters anaphylactic shock. In these people, the venom interferes with special immune cells (called mast cells) which are found in tissues. Venom causes the cells to release too much histamine and other normally useful chemicals. Fluid from the blood then starts to leak into the surrounding tissues, causing a variety of symptoms, including low blood pressure, swelling, pain, and difficulty breathing. In a small number of cases, the symptoms are so severe that they lead to death if untreated. But thankfully, treatment is very straightforward: an injection of adrenalin reverses the symptoms almost immediately. Those who know they have this allergy may have to carry adrenalin with them at all times, just in case.

Bee venom is generally not a nice substance, but a surprising use for it has emerged in recent years. For centuries people with arthritis had noticed that their symptoms were improved after a bee sting. It turns out that melittin works as a potent anti-inflammatory drug and also kills off many harmful bacteria and yeasts (including the bacteria that cause Lyme disease). The first scientific studies of this phenomenon only began in 2004, so researchers have not fully uncovered how this works. However, patients suffering from rheumatoid arthritis saw noticeable improvements when treated with bee venom, so this may be the beginning of a new treatment regimen for those who suffer from the disease. In the meantime, there are plenty of "holistic" treatments that use the idea in perhaps one of the most painful kinds of alternative medicine you could imagine: combining acupuncture with bee venom. Ouch.

Bees die when they sting us, so in order to attack they have to be provoked until it literally becomes a matter of life or death. If you do accidentally provoke a bee or disturb a hive, the best advice is to stay as far away from the insect(s) as possible. If necessary, run! If you are stung, try to remove the stinger as soon as you can. It doesn't matter how you do it (pinching it out with thumb and forefinger will not inject any more venom than scraping it out will, because the stinger needs to pump its own venom through little one-way valves). Just try and remove the stinger within 5 seconds of being stung to minimize the amount of venom injected. If anyone in your family has an allergy to stings, or if you have experienced symptoms such as shortness of breath after a sting, get yourself tested to see whether you have the allergy. Luckily, bee sting allergies are far easier to manage than many food allergies. Bees are very clearly "labeled" with black and yellow warning stripes, and they'll give you plenty of chances to go away before they attack. They really don't want to sting you any more than you want to be stung.

LOST UNDERFOOT

The sun is now warm overhead; the wet sidewalk is mostly dry again. Even your squelching shoes seem to be drying out. Ignoring the throbbing pain by your ear, you make your way back toward the part of town where you should be attending this morning's meeting. The sunshine is turning your feeling of hopelessness into optimism, as though the rain has washed away this morning's disasters. Perhaps you can persuade your colleagues to wait 15 minutes. You take out your cell phone, standing to one side as you try and find the right number. As you search, you notice your right foot feeling colder than usual. You wiggle your toes in irritation. They only feel colder. Glancing down at your shoes, you see to your dismay that the right shoe is now gaping open at the front like a mouth, exposing your toes to the world. The sole has become separated from the rest of your shoe. You can't go to the meeting like this. However, this is a problem you can fix—you're outside a drugstore, so you quickly enter and purchase some superglue. Back outside, you place a couple of drops on the damaged shoe, press down for 30 seconds, and let go. At last, you're fighting back!

Or at least, you try to let go. Your hand doesn't move. You've just glued your thumb to your shoe.

Shoes are constructed from several different materials. We prefer them to be waterproof and comfortable on our feet, so the "upper" is usually made from soft leather or a man-made leather substitute. But most leather is not durable enough to be used for the sole, which is typically made of something tough and flexible that can provide good traction, such as rubber. This layer of rubber is generally thick enough to prevent the shoe from wearing out too quickly. Shoe manufacturers and designers are thus faced with the dilemma of how to affix the hard, thick rubber sole to the soft leather upper. Stitching the two together is a good, secure method, but often expensive and slow. Even if they are stitched, there's still the problem of keeping the inner sole (the part that your foot rests on) in contact with the outer sole. The solution, used in the majority of shoes today, is to use that strangely sticky substance: glue. But what makes glues so sticky? And why do some glues (such as superglue) adhere two things together so quickly?

Glues have been in use for millennia. Early glues, or adhesives, were based on naturally occurring sticky substances, such as the resins or gums from trees, or tar from the ground. But one of the most commonly used early glues was produced from animal products. We discovered a long time ago that boiling bones, skins, or fish leftovers would produce a sticky jelly. This could be diluted with water to make it spread more easily, and it could be left to dry, in which case it would become a sticky glue.

The sticky ooze is called gelatin and it's made from collagen, or connective tissue. When still a part of an animal such as you or me, collagen is a mass of fibrous protein molecules that are woven together to form a strong connective tissue. We use a lot of it in our bodies to keep all of our parts attached to each other; one-quarter of all protein within us is collagen. When the collagen starts to fail in our skin, we develop sags and wrinkles. Boiling animal remains melts and separates the protein fibers, which are torn apart like a rope being unwoven, leaving a tangle of curly, springlike proteins. These springy molecules are what give gelatin its bouncy quality (the characteristic Jell-O "wiggle"). When it dries out, the springs lock themselves together more tightly, and so become more solid and stable. If you put a layer of gelatin, or "animal glue," between, say, two pieces of leather and let it dry, then the molecules will work their way into all the little rough gaps and holes in the leather before locking solid. The result is a mechanical join just like the pieces of a jigsaw puzzle, and the leather becomes stuck together.

Today, we rarely use animal glues. Many modern glues are based on polymers (the stuff we make plastics from)—long chains of molecules that are in a solvent such as water to make them move around. When the solvent dries out, the molecules are locked in place and the glue is set. The trouble with drying adhesives is that they can be dissolved by their solvents again. In humid countries, this means that water-based glues simply don't stick. One solution invented to overcome this was hot glue. Electric hot glue guns heat sticks of thermoplastic glue. When melted, the molecules form random coils and little crystals, which together become both flexible and hard as the plastic cools and solidifies, locking itself to a surface.

Often it is not practical to use drying or hot glues on complicated shapes, such as shoes. The drying might take too long, meaning that clamps would be required to hold the pieces in place for many hours, or the heat of the glue might melt one of the surfaces being stuck together. A nice solution to these problems was created in the form of contact adhesive. Two substances are used, one placed on each surface separately and allowed to dry. When the surfaces are brought together, the two substances interact, chemically locking together very quickly to form a secure bond. It's a clever idea, combining the easy application of solvent-based glues with the fast adhesiveness of hot glue. Because of this, many manufacturers of shoes use contact adhesives to join the soles of shoes with the leather uppers.

The origins of many glues were accidental, as new substances were discovered or developed and found to be surprisingly sticky. One notable example was superglue. In 1942, a scientist named Dr. Harry Coover of Kodak Laboratories was trying to develop a new kind of clear plastic, based on a compound called cyanoacrylate. He wanted to make a superclear yet tough new substance to replace the glass in gun sights. His invention wasn't good enough, so he put it aside for several years. Later, he had a new project—making canopies for aircraft—and again he looked at the substance, this time putting it between two optical prisms to check its optical characteristics. To his surprise (and probably dismay), he found that one drop had glued the expensive prisms together with an enormously strong bond. This was the beginning of superglue.

Superglue is so effective, even in extremely small quantities, that it's clear that it must have some really clever way of working. Other glues rely on mechanical interlocking, or even chemically melting into the surfaces, such as some plastic glues. But we rarely use enough superglue to allow it to provide much interlocking, and it doesn't melt into most surfaces. Just a 1 square inch of superglue can support a ton—how can one drop of this glue stick so well?

The short answer is that we're not entirely sure how it works. A popular theory is that the glue exploits a type of intermolecular force known as van der Waals forces. Unlike chemical bonds (which work because electrons or protons may be moved or shared across molecules, transforming the substances and locking them together), van der Waals forces are more general forces between molecules, caused by the interaction of their polarities. Just as magnets attract each other, the "north" polarity attracting the "south" polarity, so do molecules. There are a lot of complicated forces at work, when you look closely enough. One type is the electrostatic force (which enables plastic wrap to cling). Another is polarization (caused by the separate atoms in a molecule sharing electrons unequally and producing slight differences in polarity). Yet another is called London dispersion forces (which allow certain gases to condense at low temperatures and are caused by some very complicated interactions between different molecules that can induce temporary polarities).

We're fairly sure that some or all of these forces are involved with superglue, and indeed many other types of glue. But because the molecules are so small and the forces occur over such tiny distances, it's extremely hard to measure them, so scientists will be working out this problem for some time to come.

However it works, we do know what happens when the glue comes into contact with water. It turns out that the molecules of superglue (or cyanoacrylate) work in the opposite way to water-based glues. When cyanoacrylate meets water molecules, its molecules all join up to form long chains that coil around each other and bond together to form a hard resin. Because most surfaces on Earth typically do have some water molecules on them, the glue works very well on a wide range of materials. Superglue is so reactive to water that it has another use, as discovered by forensic scientists. Put an open tube of superglue in an airtight container with any object that might have fingerprints on it and the vapor from the glue will react with the moisture (and other organic compounds) of the fingerprints, gluing itself to their patterns and making them more visible. It's another reason why these glues say "use in well-ventilated areas"—cyanoacrylate will happily do the same thing inside your lungs if you breathe it in. Although it won't kill you, and your body will produce mucus to help you cough it all out, the idea of having superglue setting inside you is not very appealing.

Skin also contains lots of water, which is why superglue is so effective at sticking fingers together if you're not careful. Indeed, it's so good at sticking to skin that American soldiers used it during the Vietnam War to close wounds and help prevent bleeding, saving many lives. It's not a good idea to use ordinary superglue for this purpose because it can irritate the skin, and if a lot is used (especially on materials such as cotton), it can become sufficiently hot as it reacts that it may burn. Today, there are less-toxic versions designed for medical use.

Superglue reacts with water, becoming a resin. This means that if you leave a tube of superglue uncapped for too long, the water in the air will make the whole tube solidify. It also means that the resin is waterproof, so if you do happen to stick your fingers together, you won't unstick them with water—in fact, you'll only make it worse. Luckily, there is a solvent for superglue: acetone (often found in nail polish remover) will dissolve the resin away nicely. Another good solvent is nitromethane, an explosive, high-performance fuel used by drag car racers, often known as "nitro" (but this is not recommended for your skin). If you don't have a solvent available and the accidental gluing is minor, you'll naturally become unstuck in time. The glue only sticks the outer layer of your skin, which is always in the process of shedding away. As the cells naturally detach, so will the glue. If you've managed to stick something a little more delicate or inconvenient than a finger, then a trip to the hospital emergency room may be necessary so that they can apply a solvent and free you again. Superglue has its name for a reason!

CROSSED CONNECTIONS

You walk past a police car, parked by the curb. The right shoe flaps annoyingly as you shuffle toward the office. It's even worse than before, and you now have a piece of leather stuck to your thumb. It makes operating your cell phone a little more tricky, but you finally locate the number for your boss, who'll have been at the meeting for over half an hour by now. Almost exactly as you press "dial," the siren of the police car behind you goes off, scaring you with its screaming wail. You cancel the call, giving the idiots inside an annoyed glance. The siren stops just as you press cancel. But there is no one inside the car. You look around, wondering whether this is a joke. Seeing nobody, you select the number again, and press "dial." Instantly the police siren wails again. As soon as your finger jabs the cancel button, the siren stops. You stare at the car. How can this be happening? You choose the number for the third time and press "dial," finger on the cancel button just in case. Again the siren wails, and falls quiet as soon as you cancel the call. Suddenly, two policemen burst out of the nearby shop and run toward you. What in the world is going on?

Cell phones are sophisticated radio transmitters and receivers. They broadcast our voices to receivers, which then pass on the signal to other receivers and move it to the right recipient.

They also listen to the signal from transmitters and decode it, so that we can hear the voice of the person we are calling.

Cell phones do not talk with each other directly. The range of a normal phone is not much more than 30 or 40 miles in completely flat terrain, or 5 to 8 miles in a hilly landscape, so we'd never be able to call anyone very far away if our phones worked like walkie-talkies. One solution would be to put enormously powerful transmitters in each phone and boost their ranges, but this is not a great idea for many reasons including that the phones would need huge antennas and giant batteries, and they would probably heat our heads like microwave ovens. Even if we could solve these problems, the billions of phones we use today would interfere with one another to such an extent that no one would ever hear anything. We'd fry our brains with white noise.

The solution used in cell phones is to make every call a local call. Radio masts are placed in "cells," each covering its own small area. Neighboring masts use slightly different frequencies so that their signals do not interfere with one another, just as radio stations use different frequencies for the same reason. Every cell phone, wherever it is in the world, talks only to its nearby radio mast, and listens only to that mast. The signal is then transferred to the telephone exchange "switches" (which are really computers designed to do the job very quickly), which then pass it on to other switches in the cell exchange, or into the public telephone network. So when you call my cell phone using your cell phone, your call will really be made to your local "cell site" and the voice I hear will come from my local cell site. The transmission in between is routed using the switching computers, often through other transmitters or down optical cables.

It's a neat idea and works brilliantly. Perhaps surprisingly, it continues to work even when we're traveling on a train. The size of each cell may have a radius of less than a mile in our cities (because of limitations of capacity), and up to 25 miles in the countryside. Travel 100 miles on a train and you may pass through 10 or more cells, and yet somehow the phones keep working (at least most of the time). This is achieved because each cell overlaps with its neighbors. At the border of two cells, your phone's transmissions will be visible to two cell sites at once. The computer figures out which signal is the strongest, and if necessary tells your phone to switch to the new frequency of the neighboring cell without a break in the transmission and reception. The transmission from the new cell is then pushed through to the same destination without the slightest pause.

Because modern communication is digital, phones often share frequencies, sending pulses of coded information and leaving time for other phones to use the same frequency. (Some use another method, by which each phone uses a unique code and transmits in its own distinct "language" to prevent confusion with other phones using the same frequency.) The switches, cell sites, and phones always know who is talking to whom, because they don't just send and receive our voices, text messages, and other data. Every phone sends and receives regular little messages to and from the nearby cell sites, identifying itself and being told which frequency and code it should use for transmittal. These little messages are sent every few seconds while your phone is on. In each message, the phone is saying, "Hello, I'm still here," giving its name (a bunch of codes), and explaining which carrier network it prefers to use. The cell site responds, telling your phone which frequency it should use and whether your phone might need to switch to the frequency of a neighboring cell site. Each company uses a slightly different frequency; if your phone cannot see its home carrier signal, then it will report "no signal" (even though there may be signals from other carriers). If you're in another country and your network has agreements with foreign providers, you may well be able to roam onto their networks, your phone registering itself on the new networks and using them as though you were at home.

Wherever you are, your phone needs to keep on chatting to the local cell sites so that it always knows which frequency to use, and it can always make or receive calls at any time. These little "chats" are so important that a little more power is used for them than is used for ordinary voice and data transmission. So use a radio microphone, or put your phone too close to audio electronics (perhaps the amplified speakers of your computer or your MP3 player), and once in a while you will hear the communication: *dit di-dit, dit di-dit, dit di-dit, dit di-dit*. The reason you hear this noise is the same reason antennas can pick up radio waves.

Radio waves are electromagnetic waves—the same as light and heat, except that radio waves have a longer wavelength. The length of each wave of the light we see is much, much smaller than 1 millimeter. The wavelength of a radio station broadcasting at 100 MHz is about 10 feet. The wavelength of a phone using a 900 MHz band is just under 1 foot. Electromagnetic waves have this name because they are composed of two parts: they have an electric field and a magnetic field. The electric field is produced by the charges of particles—for example, electrons are negatively charged. The magnetic field is produced when charges move—for example, in an electric current. These fields are as fundamental to our universe as gravitation is.

Because electric fields and magnetic fields are aspects of the same thing, we can generate magnetic fields using electricity, and we can generate electricity using magnetic fields. We do this all the time: an electric motor spins because the electricity creates a series of little magnetic fields that are repelled from internal fixed magnets and push the shaft around and around. An electricity generator spins a shaft, which passes coils of wire through magnetic fields, generating electricity in the coils.

An antenna works in much the same way. When an antenna of the right size is placed in a radio wave of the right frequency, its electrons are vibrated by that wave, and so the electromagnetic energy is converted into tiny amounts of electricity. It's a little like the effect sound can have on glass. Take a crystal glass and flick it with your fingernail. The *ding* noise is the sound of the glass resonating. Produce a pure noise at the same pitch (a sound wave of the same frequency) and the glass may resonate so much that it smashes. Just as glass will resonate at a particular frequency of sound—the sound waves matching the resonant frequency of the glass—so an antenna resonates at particular frequencies of electromagnetic waves. Instead of making a noise, its vibrating electrons produce electricity. That's why antennas all have to be designed very carefully to ensure their lengths match the wavelengths of the radio waves they need to receive.

But radio waves don't just affect audio electronics; they affect all electronic devices that happen to have wire or metal in them of the same length as (or some multiple of) their wavelength. Parts of metal casings, or wires that are designed to perform a different function, will accidentally behave as antennas. It may not be anything more than a nuisance in your MP3 player, but if the signal is picked up by the metal in your car's ABS electronics, the problem becomes a bit more serious. Interference introduces an electric current where it's not supposed to be, and that might cause an electronic circuit to do almost anything. In the early days of electronics, this is exactly what used to happen. The clever new antilock braking systems of cars would fail regularly when exposed to radio transmissions, causing many accidents. There was one curved stretch of autobahn in Germany near a radio transmitter that caused so many problems that a wire mesh fence had to be erected to absorb the radio waves and prevent them from causing cars to spin out of control.

Some vehicles rely on relatively high-powered radio transmitters within them for communication, such as those used by the police or taxi drivers. A huge variety of problems have occurred over the years, all caused by the interference from these internal radios. In addition to numerous reports of ABS electronics failing, other examples included a fireman's car having its sunroof constantly open, a police car having its siren sound "strangled," and a police motorcycle slowing down.

Modern vehicles are extensively tested and shielded to ensure that our cell phones do not affect their electronics, and there are many stringent regulations that limit the amount of electromagnetic radiation any device can produce. Nevertheless, computers are used extensively in our vehicles, from engine management systems that control the timing of the spark plugs, to ABS and other safety equipment. Some major car manufacturers have warned that cell phones could accidentally trigger a car's airbags.

Just as airlines tell us to switch off our cell phones for the duration of flights, so some car manufacturers and auto organizations now suggest we switch off the phones while driving. Remember that cell phones chat with their local cell sites every few seconds, so the only way to stop them from transmitting their signals is to turn them off (or put them into "airplane mode").

Thankfully, these kinds of interferences by cell phones are relatively rare and usually occur when the car has become faulty or its electronics are improperly installed. If you're nervous about it, just turn your phone off when driving.

In spite of all the effort that's made to keep all of our electronics running as they should, one form of interference is still common. The "radar detector" gadgets that some people use to detect speed traps happen to have internal electronics that resonate at very high frequencies. These gadgets produce so much interference that they scramble the signal being received by satellite television dishes or GPS gadgets. So if you notice that your TV loses its picture just as a certain car drives by, or your GPS gadget becomes very confused at certain times, that's why.

HISSY FITS

Leaving the bemused police officers to play with your phone, you decide that the best thing to do at this point is abandon your disintegrating dress shoes and quickly purchase some running shoes. You enter a sports shop and grab the nearest pair in your size. Three minutes later, you're jogging your way to work, carrying one of your old shoes in each hand. You've bought some bouncy, "air-filled" sneakers, making you feel as though each step is powering you forward with more speed and ease than usual; you're flying with each stride. The road curves to the left and suddenly you see your office. You're going to make it! But something is uneven about the new shoes: the left one is making a strange hissing noise each time you bring it down, and it no longer has the same bounce. Running has become a lopsided *thud-hiss*, *thud-hiss*, *thud-hiss*. You stop and look at the left shoe. There's a piece of a paper clip embedded in its sole. You've punctured one of your expensive new shoes.

The spring in our steps always used to be entirely natural. The combination of the fleshy pads under our feet and the yielding, deformable nature of most natural surfaces (soil, sand, or foliage) gave us organic cushioning when we walked or ran. But we no longer run around on natural surfaces—we now surround ourselves with hard stone or concrete. To protect our feet from such unkind floors, we wear shoes. And to replace the natural cushioning of our feet and the soil we once ran upon, most shoes designed for serious walking or running have springy soles. Run around barefoot on a concrete floor (or even worse, in solid wooden clogs on a concrete floor) and you'll notice the difference—the hard, jarring impact on your feet and legs will quickly cause you discomfort and prevent you from going any further. Springy cushioning in shoes is an essential part of modern life.

Springy shoes are just the latest example of cushioning, often called suspension, which protects us from unwanted jolts caused by moving around. Perhaps the first use of bouncy suspension was in early passenger vehicles. Back in the days of horse-drawn carriages, the roads weren't particularly smooth. Riding in a wheeled carriage—assuming your solid wood-and-metal wheels were connected to an axle, and the axle was slotted directly into the chassis of the carriage—every bump on the ground was transmitted directly to your backside. Ouch! Ouch! Ouch! Padded seats might cushion the ride a little, but a much more sensible idea is to put some kind of spring between the wheels and chassis of the carriage. Then if the wheel shudders over bumpy ground, the spring will absorb much of the violent movement, cushioning and smoothing the motion of the carriage. It's exactly the same idea as having a bouncy sole in a shoe to protect your feet and legs against the jolts of your own footsteps.

Springy suspension systems may seem like an obvious solution to the problem of being jolted around. But bouncy springs are not obvious devices at all. Why should a solid lump of metal ever be bouncy like rubber? Their molecules certainly don't have the same springy spaghetti-like structures. Even more mysteriously, why should a gas be bouncy? Clearly, some shoes use pockets of gas to provide an extra bounce, but how can a bunch of loose air molecules provide a better cushion than rubber?

The springy properties of metal and gases are caused by very tiny but very strong forces between their atoms. Take a piece of common household metal—perhaps a stainless steel spoon or knife from the kitchen drawer. You will find that if you try bending it, the piece of metal will flex slightly. If you apply too much force, it will suddenly bend and you'll ruin it. The metal flexes because its atoms are all clinging tightly to each other with very strong bonds, but the metal is thin enough that you are able to pull and compress the individual bonds between them, without actually breaking them. Like a crowd of commuters stuck in a train carriage, they can be pushed and moved a little, but they're stuck together too tightly to be able to move far, and they prefer to maintain a certain distance from each other, so once you've stopped pushing them they'll settle back to their comfortable positions. The metal becomes bent when so much force is applied that the bonds are broken between the atoms, forcing them to move around and heat up. (The doors of the commuter carriage are forced open and the commuters are free to move in that area, changing their relative positions.) So when you flex a piece of metal, you are effectively storing energy in it, often called "potential energy." (In the commuter train analogy we'd measure the energy in terms of grumpiness of commuters as they are pushed to where they don't want to be.) But when you bend the metal, the energy is transformed into heat as the molecules all move around, so the energy is lost.

The trick to making a metal spring is to ensure that the metal is allowed to flex but never bend. The original carriage springs used in early vehicle suspension systems were designed to do exactly that. They were made by laying strips of thin metal, one on top of each other, each smaller than the last. Imagine a pile of metal rules, each shorter than the last, placed on top of each other to make a little pyramid and loosely joined so that they are free to flex against each other. The ends of this spring are fixed to the chassis and the middle part is fixed to the wheel axle. The result is a pile of flexing metal. The longer strips have more leverage and so will flex more compared to the smaller strips. Flexibility is provided by the longer strips, and stiffness and support are provided by the smaller ones, ensuring that none is ever flexed so much that it becomes bent. Such carriage springs, or leaf springs, were enormously successful and used for many years, even in quite recent automobiles. But before long, somebody spotted that the same properties of a leaf spring could be obtained using much less metal, formed in a different shape. The result was a coil spring.

You can find coil springs almost everywhere you look. Take a ballpoint pen, for instance, and look inside—chances are, you'll see a coil spring inside, enabling the click-top to spring in and out. They work using exactly the same principles as the leaf spring. Imagine a stiff piece of wire—perhaps a straightened paper clip. The wire flexes a little before bending, just like the strips of metal in the leaf spring do. Bend the straight wire into a coil (wind your straightened paper clip around a pen), and compress (or stretch) the coil, and you see exactly the same flexing, only now because of the way the metal is wound around and around, the flexing is added together to provide a much greater movement. You can still bend the metal in a coiled spring by stretching it too much or by bending against the direction of the coils, but the shape of the coiled spring protects it from most types of damage. Try to compress it too much and the separate coils just touch, preventing you from bending the metal out of shape. Even the circular shape of the coil helps give it strength and resistance to bending.

Coil springs are everywhere, providing tough, lightweight, and extremely springy solutions wherever they are needed. Most modern vehicles use coiled springs in their suspensions. But coil springs are actually too good at being bouncy to be used on their own. Fit four big springs between the wheels of a car and its chassis and it would be like driving a pogo stick on wheels. Hit a bump and the car would bounce all over the road. The solution, as used by all vehicles, is to dampen down the springiness using shock absorbers.

Some shock absorbers use the movement of fluids, known as hydraulic systems. Imagine a pipe filled with water and a valve inside that controls how much water can flow through. If the valve only allows some of the water to get through, then when you use a piston to push or pull at the water, it will flow, but it will resist any effort you make to force it to flow fast. If we connect that piston parallel to a spring, whenever the spring tries to bounce too quickly, it will try to move the piston too quickly and the water will slow down and dampen its motion. That's exactly how a hydraulic-based shock absorber works.

Other types of shock absorbers use pneumatics, or compressed air. Instead of water being pushed and pulled by a piston, air is compressed by a piston. Compress the gas, and its molecules heat up, moving more quickly and placing more pressure on everything around them, including the piston. So the more you compress a gas, the more it pushes back at you, rather like a spring except that the pressure from the gas is a nice even, smooth force, not like the sudden jolting *sproing!* of a spring. Pneumatic shock absorbers are very common in vehicles, and so are their related cousins, air springs. Open the trunk of your car and you may well see an air spring in action, looking like a black bicycle pump as it smoothly raises the trunk. Just the carefully balanced pressure of air, exerting its smooth, even force, powers the lifting mechanism. Every time you close the trunk, you repressurize the air, compressing the air spring so it's ready for next time.

The smooth properties of liquid movement and gas compression were noticed by Citroën in the mid-1950s. The company broke with convention and took away all metal springs from its cars, using hydropneumatics (liquid and gas) for the complete suspension of its vehicles. Today, many vehicles use pneumatic suspensions. By adjusting the pressure of the air, the ride height and firmness of the vehicle can be altered to a desired level.

Vehicles aren't the only mechanisms that benefit from air suspension. In 1977, a former aerospace engineer teamed up with a certain shoe manufacturer and invented the idea of an "air-filled" sole that would use the smooth force produced by compressed gases to give a comfortable but not too springy bounce to sneakers. Nike Air cushioning hit the shelves in 1979 and has been a hit ever since.

Ironically, many "air-filled" soles are not filled with air. Each shoe has a capsule made of polyurethane plastic (or a polyester polyol-urethane composite) to hold the pressurized gas in its sole, and they are filled with a very dense gas, probably sulfur hexafluoride (which was listed in the patent for the technology). More recent designs may be able to use nitrogen. Dense gases are needed because otherwise the molecules slowly seep through the polyurethane capsules, making the sole go flat. With the use of these gases and capsule materials, it is possible for gases such as oxygen and nitrogen to seep into the capsule, so the pressure inside can actually increase as they slowly inflate themselves!

Some of the early patents for the technology expired in 1997, so other companies are now free to use air cushioning in their shoes. One more recent concern has been that the fluorinated gases used in some shoes are major contributors to global warming. In 2004, the European Union drafted legislation that would make the sale of shoes containing these gases illegal in all 25 nations. Perhaps because of these issues, most other manufacturers continue to use foam as the easy solution for providing cushioning and bounce. Foam is nothing more than millions of bubbles of air, each trapped inside a type of plastic, so although the plastic removes some of the bounce, it makes the shoes much easier to manufacture.

The other problem with air-cushioning is of course that it can be punctured. Accidentally step on something sharp and you may well pierce the internal capsule holding all that pressurized gas. Because the capsules are completely sealed within the soles, once they're punctured there's no way to repair the damage. Keeping a spring in your step is not always easy, but there's one consolation: A sharp object embedded in a shoe is always better than one in a bare foot.

MIGHTIER THAN THE SWORD

Somewhat out of breath, you change back into your disheveled office shoes and enter the main building, waving the security badge at the door to open it. The elevator opens as soon as you press the button. When the doors slide open, you begin to walk briskly along the corridor, but one of your colleagues appears ahead with a sheet of paper—can you sign the requisition form? Sidestepping him doesn't work. He's cornered you. Sighing, you feel in your shirt pocket for your favorite pen. The pocket is still wet from the rain earlier. Ever the professional, you bring out the pen ready to approve the form—and discover your hand has turned blue. The whole of the bottom of the pen is a gunky, sticky mess of ink. The shirt pocket now has a large blue stain spreading over most of its surface. Ballpoint pens aren't supposed to leak! Why has it picked this morning to empty itself all over your clothes?

E ven if your handwriting is impossible to read, it's unlikely you'll go more than a day or two without using a pen. Computers may rule the world, but pens don't need batteries, they fit into even the smallest pockets, and they don't require new software every 18 months. The humble ballpoint pen gives us the freedom to write almost anywhere, at any time.

It was not always this way. Thousands of years ago, writing was a big deal. It was a way to leave a message for posterity, a magical way to speak to others when you were gone. Cavemen learned the arts of grinding certain kinds of stones to make long-lasting pigments, which were sprayed from the mouth or painted using fingers. In later centuries, many cultures developed the art of stone carving, engraving their messages in rock for what must have seemed like eternity. These forms of writing were performed by the special few skilled enough to leave coherent marks and were understood only by those trained in the magical art of reading.

It's one thing to leave your mark on a cave wall or a big rock, but murals are not very helpful if you want to keep a record of everyday events, perhaps of who traded with you this morning. Something a little smaller and easier to use was needed. Book-size clay tablets were one convenient solution, allowing symbols to be pressed into the wet clay and then dried into a more permanent form. More than 7,000 years ago, the tablets were used to record pictograms (pictures that resembled the concepts they were supposed to represent). As the images were duplicated over and over again, they slowly turned from pictures into simplified symbols, which, by about 4,000 years ago, gradually became standardized into alphabets. Two and a half thousand years ago, alphabets that resembled the ones in use today had emerged. The ancient Greeks even developed their version of a laptop: two tablets hinged in the middle, coated with wax to allow symbols to be pressed into their surfaces using an ivory or metal stylus.

Although clay and wax were the mediums of choice for relatively quick writing, the fine art of recording those special words for posterity had also been developed. Parchment (stretched and dried animal skin) and papyrus (made from strips of the stems of the papyrus plant, which were hammered, pressed, and dried) provided excellent lightweight and clean surfaces for the words. Charcoal (burned sticks) would leave marks on these new surfaces, but in reality they did nothing more than leave a thick layer of black dust. With nothing but friction to adhere the black sooty particles to the tiny imperfections in the surfaces, the results were very temporary. Smudged text was unreadable, so an alternative was needed. The solution was ink—a dark, slightly viscous liquid that would stick and dry to the primitive papers, allowing permanent marks to be made.

Many varieties of inks were tried over thousands of years. It's likely that only those documents that remained readable were kept, so the examples of unsuccessful inks are lost forever. Perfecting ink was a real challenge. Make the color from plant or animal extracts alone, and the color fades after a few years as the organic substances decay (or the molecules are excited by the energy in the light and undergo a chemical reaction with the oxygen in the air, making their color fade away). Make the ink too watery, and it will soak into the page and form wet puddles. Make the ink too oily, and it will just wipe off the page. Make it too sticky, and all you'll have is a colored glue.

One of the earliest known inks was made in China, more than 4,500 years ago. The dark pigment was made from the soot of pine smoke. Lamp oil and gelatin from boiled donkey skins gave it the right oily, sticky texture. (We call such burned carbon-based inks "Indian inks" today, despite their Chinese origins.) The first use of the ink was to darken the surface of existing stone inscriptions, but before long it became popular for its ability to stick to parchment and papyrus, and then dry (just as animal glue dries) as a perfect dark stain exactly where it was deposited.

Other recipes continued to emerge over time. Iron salts mixed with tannin produce a dark bluish black color and so were common ingredients (and still form the basis of many inks today). One method was to mix ground nutgalls with iron salts. Nutgalls are the bulbous outgrowths of trees such as oaks, often formed by burrowing insects such as the larvae of wasps. The tree's growth mechanisms are hijacked by the substances produced by the wasps, and nutrient-rich cells grow, forming a gall, on which the wasp larvae feed. As a side effect of the strange parasitic process and possibly as a defense against being eaten, the nutgall becomes rich in tannin (a compound that can give animals and some insects indigestion). It's the same stuff used to help preserve skins when tanning them. Tannin from nutgalls mixed with iron salts produces a great black color in ink.

While inks became better and better, writers still needed effective tools to place the ink onto the parchment or papyrus. The ideal tool would have some kind of internal tube that would provide enough ink to write several characters before it needed to be refilled. The ink could trickle down under gravity to a pointy end, and by scratching the pointy end on the paper, a trail of ink would be left behind. There are many substances in nature that resemble this, and many of them were used as writing instruments. Hollow reeds, bamboo, or, most commonly, feathers were used, their ends carefully cut at an angle to enable a fine line to be drawn. They were dipped in ink, the capillary action of the liquid making it climb a little way inside the internal tube, and then dragged across the paper. Although enormously successful and used for centuries, quills and other simple pens had very short lives (perhaps only a week of use), and each needed careful crafting with a penknife before being ready for use. The other problem with quills was that they didn't hold much ink. The writer had to keep dipping the quill into the ink every few seconds to replenish the internal tube.

As writing became more common, the need for better writing instruments increased. One sensible solution was to have an instrument that could hold much more ink. The first fountain pen was created in 1702, and it (and its later cousins) seemed to be the solution. It had an internal reservoir that could hold enough ink to write many lines of text. Some were refilled by carefully using eyedroppers to fill them from the top. Most had little rubber bulbs that would be squeezed to remove air, then the nib would be dipped into the ink and the bulb released. As the bulb expanded, it reduced the pressure of the remaining internal air, allowing the higher-pressure air outside to push the liquid ink inside the bulb. Although we may call it suction, a lower pressure (fewer molecules) cannot "suck"; instead, a higher pressure (more molecules) must always push.

Later fountain pens used little levers to squeeze the internal rubber reservoir, or were designed to enable a coin or matchstick to do the same job. Nibs (the pointy bits at the end) were also refined, with air holes and grooves enabling an improved flow of ink to the paper with fewer messy mistakes. Eventually, selffilling fountain pens were replaced with cartridge pens, where disposable plastic ink cartridges could be easily swapped for new ones without needing messy inkwells at all.

Despite all the clever advances, the fountain pen still used the same principles as the quill. The writing instrument was a tube filled with ink that was designed to stain, with a pointy end that guided the ink where you wanted it. Leave the pen unused for too long and the ink dried up inside. Flick the pen and out came a spray of ink. Take the pen in an aircraft where the air pressure is lower and the ink would leak out everywhere (there is less pressure pushing against the liquid, so it expands). Increase the temperature and again the liquid expands (the molecules are moving about more quickly) and the ink leaks out.

What was needed was a magical kind of pen that contained its own ink, deposited the ink onto paper in a controlled and easy way, and didn't leak! The very first attempt at a radical solution was in 1888, when an American leather tanner created a new device for marking leathers. It was a pen with a little ball in the tip. The idea was that the ball prevented the air from getting to the ink so it didn't dry out, and its seal prevented ink from leaking out. But as the tip was rolled over a surface, the ball rolled the ink from the internal reservoir to the outside and onto the paper. If the ink had the right consistency, then it would even act like a lubricant and make the ball turn smoothly, making writing a smooth and easy experience. That was the theory, but unfortunately the early designs had ink of entirely the wrong consistency and so initial ballpoint pens would only write at one temperature. At any other temperature, either the ink was too runny and would leak around the ball, or it was too thick and would form lumpy, inky messes.

Some 50 years later a pair of brothers, one a chemist and the other a newspaper editor, decided to improve upon the design. Their names were Ladislas and Georg Biro, and their Biro pen eventually became the most successful ballpoint to date. In addition to improving the ink, perhaps their most important advance was to make the internal reservoirs into much thinner tubes. Instead of relying on gravity to push the ink to the ball (which meant you had to write with the pen held vertically), the thin tubes used capillary action to draw the ink to the tip. As the ink was deposited on the paper, the ink's clingy molecules pulled the remaining molecules toward the ball, meaning it could work at almost any angle. But even their invention was prone to regular leaks and failures. It took a Frenchman named Marcel Bich to develop the ideas further and produce a reliable and ultra-low-cost pen with a six-sided clear plastic body. He called it the "Ballpoint Bic" and it became one of the most successful mass-produced products of all time. It also uses the capillary action of the ink to pull it toward the tip. You can see the process for yourself in every Bic pen with a clear plastic body—the little tube that holds the ink is clearly visible, and its end is simply open to the air. The capillary action of the gloopy ink molecules in the tube as they cling to each other and the walls of the tube, is strong enough to keep them inside even when held upside down.

Today's pens are amazingly well-designed implements that use inks specially formulated to write well and not leak. Pen manufacturers still continue to try and improve the design—for example, the pressurized ink cartridge of the "space pens." (There's a common story that claims that in the space race between the United States and the Soviet Union, NASA spent millions on the amazing pressurized pen that writes upside down and the Russians simply used a pencil. In fact, it's a complete myth. NASA did not pay for the development of the space pen; they simply bought the product from Fisher, who developed it to withstand the high temperature and pressure differences in space. Both Russia and the United States initially used pencils, and even an ordinary cheap ballpoint can work in zero gravity because it relies on capillary action and not gravity.)

Sadly, though, even the most expensive ballpoint pen can suffer from leaks. The design is rather like a tiny version of a roll-on deodorant—when left for a while, the ink dries on the ball and seals the liquid within. Rotate the ball and the liquid is rotated outside. It's a great design and copes with differences in pressure and temperature very well. But make the ball wet and the seal of dried ink is broken. With no seal, ink is free to leak out, being sucked into clothes just as water from the rain soaks your garments. Alternatively, keep a pen in a pocket and lint may find its way onto the ball of the pen. The next time you use it, you may roll the dirt inside as you roll the ink outside. Now you're writing dirty ink onto paper and the result is usually messy. Even worse, it only takes the smallest speck of dirt to become wedged between the pen and the ball for the seal to be broken and for ink to leak out. Use a ballpoint in a dusty environment or on dirty surfaces too often, and you may even damage the surface of the ball or its tiny socket, making the pen prone to leaving frequent inky splotches.

When you understand how the ballpoint pen works, it's easy to prevent leaks. All you need to do is keep it clean and dry, and only write on clean and dry surfaces. Even if your pen leaks, don't worry—most inks are now designed to be washable. Modern pens are unbelievably reliable compared to the long leaky history of quills and fountain pens. They just have to be treated carefully.

SEEING IS NOT BELIEVING

The meeting door closes loudly. Everyone looks at you. There's somebody standing at the front of the room with a projected slide showing some kind of financial chart. Muttering apologies and trying to avoid their gazes, you make your way to the large table and find an empty chair. There are about 15 people in the darkened conference room—the usual gang seems to be present, although there are a few faces that seem unfamiliar. For some reason everyone continues to stare. Perhaps it's the blue stain on your shirt. Or simply your lateness. Turning to the financial manager, Dawn, you whisper conspiratorially to her, asking what you've missed. Her response is loud and clear, for the whole room to hear, "I'm sorry, who are you? And what are you doing here?"

It's the sound of her voice rather than the words that suddenly make you realize you've never seen this woman before in your life. In a panic you look around and realize that there are, in fact, no familiar faces here at all. You've just gate-crashed a meeting of complete strangers. Have you turned blind? No, your eyes are fine. How could you possibly make such a mistake?

We might all have sharp eyes and a good-size brain behind them, but we're not born with the ability to understand what we see. Instead, we are born with an amazing ability to *learn* how to see and understand many useful things—and learn very quickly. Before babies even have the ability to focus their eyes, they begin learning to recognize their world. Faces are often some of the first things they perceive clearly, and so babies of all ages are attracted to these strange patterns of eyes, nose, and mouth. By the time they are 7 months old, infants are able to understand the overall patterns of faces in much the same way that adults can.

Perception in all mammals is a very complex process. When we're first born, the neurons in our brains are highly connected, much more so than in adult brains. The first few months and years of our lives are spent pruning away unnecessary neurons and the connections between them, until we are left with coherent neural circuits that connect our eyes to our brains in ways that enable us to perceive our surroundings. It's a little like creating a computer by taking as many transistors as you can get (100 billion or so) and wiring as many together as possible, then carefully cutting all the unhelpful wires and removing the transistors that do nothing until you've sculpted your powerful computer.

The neural "sculpting" process relies on testing—we must constantly interact with our environment to ensure that our developing brain is doing something useful. This means that frequently occurring stimuli in our environment stimulate our brains, and that process helps our brains develop to better respond to those stimuli. The more faces we see, the better we become at seeing them. Humans spend so much time looking at faces that significant parts of our brains become dedicated to recognizing them. By the time we are adults, our face-recognition centers are so highly developed that they can pick up a face almost anywhere. We can spot a face even in our peripheral vision. We even mistakenly see faces in random patterns: peering from forest branches, clouds, or even the craters of the moon.

The reason we know so much about the development of perception is not because we understand how the brain works exactly. We're still like cavemen looking at a supercomputer in terms of our understanding of the details. We understand what we do because of the unfortunate results when brains do not develop normally. If you like kittens, look away now.

In the 1970s, biologists studying perception reared kittens in very carefully controlled conditions. These poor little cats grew up in rooms where all they could see were horizontal black and white stripes, vertical black and white stripes, or diagonal stripes. No balls of wool, birds, or mice to chase, no grass or trees or sky. All they saw from the moment they opened their eyes was stripes. When the grown cats were exposed to other environments (moved from the horizontal-striped room to the vertical-striped room), they behaved almost as though they were blind. The cats' brains had developed to perceive and understand their limited environments, and when presented with something new, they simply could not understand what they were looking at. Their eyes and brains were working, but the computer had been programmed incorrectly and could not work in the radically different environments.

Enough torturing poor kittens. That was an extreme example of effects that we have observed many, many times since. One fascinating case was recorded by an anthropologist working in the Congo in the 1950s, who took a Bambuti pygmy called

Kenge from his home in the dense forest out onto a large open plain for the first time:

> *And then he saw the buffalo, still grazing lazily several miles away, far down below. He turned to me and said, "What insects are those?"*
>
> *At first I hardly understood, then I realized that in the forest vision is so limited that there is no great need to make an automatic allowance for distance when judging size. Out here in the plains, Kenge was looking for the first time over apparently unending miles of unfamiliar grasslands, with not a tree worth the name to give him any basis for comparison . . .*
>
> *When I told Kenge that the insects were buffalo, he roared with laughter and told me not to tell such stupid lies.*

Even the notion of something being smaller because it is farther away must be learned. If you never see anything from a distance, you will never learn this trick and so you will not perceive your environment correctly. Another way to see the effects of environments is through optical illusions. For example, take a blank sheet of paper and draw an upside-down capital "T," making sure the vertical line is exactly the same length as the horizontal line. Now look at it. Research has shown that people who are used to wide-open spaces will perceive the vertical line to be longer than the horizontal line. When looking out over a large open space, the horizontal heights of trees and buildings give us more clues about distance, so we magnify these in our perceptions. Another example is the "arrows" optical illusion—two lines of the same length side by side, one with normal arrowheads pointing outward, the other with backward arrowheads perched like Vs on the ends of the line. The second line appears longer than the first because we are used to interpreting these angles as cues for depth and corners of straight-edged buildings. When the same illusion was presented to a tribe of Zulus, who all lived in South Africa in circular huts with circular doors and who had never seen straight-edged buildings, the optical illusion had no effect on them.

Clearly our environments play a tremendously important role in our ability to see. But so do our brains. Patients with damage to the occipital lobe and temporal lobes of their brains (the regions at the back of your head, behind your ears) can develop agnosia. Despite having perfect eyes, because of the malfunction in these important areas of the brain, they are unable to process what they see. There are many types of visual agnosia. Some can perceive the separate parts of an object but cannot put them together in order to make sense of the whole (form agnosia). Some can even copy pictures of an object like a spoon, and know exactly what a spoon is for, and yet still be unable to recognize it, confusing it with a fork (associative agnosia). Some cannot distinguish between the fingers of their own hands (finger agnosia) or recognize written words (alexia or visual aphasia). And some people lose the ability to recognize faces (prosopagnosia).

Patients with prosopagnosia provide us with some tantalizing clues about how our brains recognize faces. For many years scientists have debated whether faces are "special enough" to need their own region of the brain dedicated to recognizing them.

Some argue that faces are just other objects that we happen to see in our environments and they become significant because all our emotional and physical needs are initially met by "things with faces" (our parents or care providers). Other scientists argue that evolution has clearly designed faces to enable us to communicate our feelings and emotions through expressions, so we should have a matching region in the brain to recognize and interpret the complexities of faces. The truth may be somewhere between the two, but it is clear that faces are recognized in very distinct parts of the brain.

One man suffered a gunshot wound to his head and developed prosopagnosia. Suddenly he could see and recognize everything except faces. He found himself living in a world of strangers, for he was unable to recognize the face of any friends or family—or even his own face. However, patients with prosopagnosia sometimes show a second form of unconscious face recognition. Although they are not consciously aware that they know a face, their emotional state is affected. They feel more comfortable in the presence of friends and more stressed when among strangers. The reaction indicates that humans use more than one mechanism in the brain to recognize faces. Another condition, known as Capgras's syndrome, may be the reverse of prosopagnosia (when arising from brain injury). People suffering from this weird condition are able to see and recognize faces, but they no longer have the correct emotional response. They become convinced that everyone around them has been replaced by identical strangers—everyone looks and sounds the same, but the sufferer feels nothing when perceiving them, and so "knows" that they cannot be the same.

Thankfully, these conditions are very rare. Although there are different degrees of most conditions and some may be caused by genetic disorders, if you are poor at recognizing faces, the reason is much more likely to be environmental rather than neurological. Recent research has shown that most perception (including face perception) is not learned on its own. We often use other cues such as sound and smell to help guide us in our recognition. Indeed, scientists have shown that babies become more proficient at distinguishing between faces when they do not have the extra cues available to them. Like the hearing of a blind person becoming more sensitive because of the lack of help from vision, if we learn to perceive faces without the assistance of the sound of the voice, then the ability improves.

So if you have a knack for remembering faces, it may be because you were exposed to exactly the right kind of environment when growing up, and you might also have a good brain to help you. If you struggle—particularly when stressed—don't worry. This is exceedingly common. Chances are, you've developed other unconscious methods for recognizing people you frequently encounter, perhaps using their voices, body language, or even their smells as guides. Our brains are also highly adaptive organs, so it is quite possible to train yourself to become a better face recognizer. One handy method is to use your cell phone camera to take pictures of everyone in your address book, and then every time you look for a number you will see the person's face. You'll never forget a familiar face again!

RIPPING YARNS

Your face glows with embarrassment, but by the time you reach your own floor in the building your mood has changed to anger. The open-plan office makes it easy to spot a victim on which to vent your increasing frustration with this day. Unfortunately, mirth is the only response. Apparently everyone else knew the meeting had been canceled; an e-mail had been sent late yesterday. Feeling no better, you stalk to the bathroom in order to wash the blue stain from your shirt and hand. You take the opportunity to pull off the piece of shoe stuck to your thumb. A rough push on the bathroom door makes you feel slightly better, although you'd prefer to kick it a few times. As if sensing your anger, the sleeve of your shirt catches on the closing door latch. You pull roughly at it, in no mood to be tangled up. It stubbornly stays hooked. You give it another tug. It makes a horrible ripping sound. With a sinking heart, you carefully unhook the material. There's now a large hole in your sleeve.

We're all so used to clothing that we never stop to marvel at its remarkable properties. But just imagine trying to get through the day wearing nothing but raw cotton balls for trousers and tissue paper for a shirt—within 20 minutes our clothes would be nothing but tatters. Our clothing is not made from anything particularly different from these substances, yet somehow it is enormously strong, able to withstand normal wear and tear for years. But if the strength of cloth does not only come from its material, where *does* it come from?

The answer is the twist. It's a trick that's very easy to see today: Take a piece of tissue paper and tear off a long strip, about 1 inch wide. Try pulling it apart. It should be clear that tissue paper has very little strength. Now tear another long strip off, 1 inch wide, the same as the first. Turn one end one way and the other end the other way, twisting the tissue paper until it looks like a straight piece of string. Now fold it into two and tightly twist it together again, making a fatter piece of string. Try pulling it apart now. You may well find it impossible to tear it in half.

The simple act of twisting creates enormous tensile strength (resistance to pulling) from potentially very weak substances. The cause of the strength is friction. Imagine two parallel conga lines of people, each person holding on to her companion's waist in front of her. The strengths of the conga lines are only as strong as the two weakest links—whoever has the weakest grip on her companions will break her line first. This is why tissue paper breaks so easily—it is nothing more than a sheet of parallel conga lines of plant fibers. Now imagine the two conga lines are rather more complicated: the person in the left line is holding on to the waist of the person ahead on the right, the person on the right holds on to the waist of the person ahead on the left. All the way up the two lines, each holds on to the person on the other side, all their arms crossing over. Now if one person loses her grip it doesn't matter so much, because everyone is still locked together by their crisscrossing arms. This is what twisting does to fabric. It winds the internal fibers around each other so much that even if a few individual fibers break, they are still locked by friction into the string and so they continue to provide strength. Twisting is so effective that it allows shorter fibers to become entwined together, locking them into strings of any length.

It should not be that surprising to discover that the friction of individual fibers can result in such strength. Every knot ever tied relies on exactly the same principle: the interlocking of individual strands into clever loops is designed to trap and squeeze two pieces of rope together. (You may have noticed that it's much harder to tie knots in really shiny, slippery cords, because there is not enough friction to keep the knots tight.) In most materials, all the tiny fibers have surfaces rougher than sandpaper when magnified, so when they are squeezed they become locked together by all their bumps, like pieces of a jigsaw puzzle. Friction caused by twisting can give immense strength, regardless of the individual strengths of the constituent fibers.

Every rope and string, and every thread made from many shorter fibers such as wool or cotton, is made in the same way. The process of creating threads from the shaven fluffy hair of sheep has been traditionally called "spinning" because that's exactly what it is. The separate strands of wool are twisted with more and more strands slowly introduced in order to lock them into the existing twisted structure. Today there is a real science behind the twisting. Careful calculations are made to figure out the amount of friction generated when certain fibers are locked together at different angles. From this we can figure out how many twists are needed to produce the strongest threads.

Twisting is not the only trick we use. Another is called weaving, and humans were certainly not the first animals to discover it. Birds commonly weave twigs and stems together to make intricately shaped nests, and beavers build huge dams by interlocking branches. The earliest example of woven cloth was discovered imprinted in clay by archeologists. These simple fabrics were made from the stems or internal veins of plants, resembling the texture of a burlap sack. They were more than 25,000 years old—much earlier than the discovery of metals. Some archeologists believe that Stone Age man may have learned to weave 40,000 years ago, and the technology might have been even more useful than the discovery of fire. It is possible that our view of the past has been distorted by the fact that stone survives so well over so many millennia, but cloth usually decays and vanishes in just a few months. Perhaps we should really call them cloth-age man, instead.

Those early cloths were woven using a method known as twining. The horizontal weft thread is passed over and under, over and under the parallel warp threads, then the next weft thread is entwined with the previous one, passed under and over, under and over both the warp threads and the weft thread below, and so on. The result is a weave a little like a net—it's very tough and holds itself together quite well even if damaged. The problem with twining is that it's very hard to automate with a machine as each new thread is entwined or sewn into the previous ones. Because of this, modern weaves are actually a little simpler.

The plain, or true, weave that is most commonly used in our fabrics follows a similar principle to twining. The first horizontal weft thread is also woven over and under, over and under the parallel warp threads. But the next weft thread is just placed on top of the first, woven under and over, under and over the same warp threads—it's not entwined with the previous weft. To automate the process you just need to lift all the odd-numbered warps with a stick and push the weft through, then for the next thread, lift all the even-numbered warps with another stick (called a heddle) and thread the weft back through again, pushing down (battening) the weft each time to make a nice dense weave. The other major kinds of weave are simply variations of the plain weave. Twill is made by weaving the weft over and under two or more warp threads at a time. Satin weave is made by weaving the weft under one and then over four or more warp threads at a time, making the weft "float" and giving it softness. By changing the types of threads used and sometimes looping in other short threads (as in a pile weave) or weaving together different types at the same time, all cloths are made.

Whether the woven material is cotton, silk, wool, or grasses, all are held together by friction. All those interlocking threads are enormously flexible, giving us soft and flowing cloths, but the only thing that stops them from unraveling into individual threads is the clever use of friction to lock the separate threads in place.

The whole idea of weaving fibers together to form a flexible and strong sheetlike material is so successful that amazingly it is used within our own skins. Collagen fibers (the same stuff that is removed and transformed by boiling to obtain gelatin and make jelly or gluey substances) are actually woven together within skin to provide its strength. Like the cloth we make, leather has a natural grain that follows the direction of the fibers. In leather, the grain is much more complex, often following the direction of the hair growth from the skin, but containing many fibers lying in other directions to give strength.

The grain of a woven cloth shows its biggest weakness. The weft and warp threads lie at right angles to each other, providing the direction of its grains. Try to rip a cloth diagonally, not with the grain, and the separate threads all work together, locking up with friction. If a thread made of cotton or wool is used, then the twists of the individual threads also add a huge amount to the strength of the cloth. But try to rip cloth with the grain and suddenly it's much easier. Because all the threads run parallel to each other, if you break the first weft thread between two warp threads, then you have another weft thread directly in line below, between the same two warp threads. Now the separate threads are not all pulling together—instead, the entire strength of the cloth relies only on the strength of the individual weft threads one under the other. Even worse, because the cloth is no longer flat, all the threads in the two pieces of the tearing cloth are now supporting each other with all their strength while giving no strength at all to the weak point that is ripping. So tearing cloth along its grain is easy. All you have to do is break one weft thread or one warp thread and keep pulling. With little assistance from friction, the other threads all break one after the other and you've torn the cloth in half.

The solution to the tearing problem is to use more complex cloths that comprise weaves with grains in many directions at once. Now any direction you try to tear will always have a few threads running in a similar direction, so any tears will be very short and won't run through the cloth like a ladder in a pair of tights. This is what nature tries to do in our skins, which is why skin is very hard to tear. It's also the solution used in materials such as carbon fiber or fiberglass (used, for example, to make lightweight but super-strong bodies for sports cars and boat hulls). The fibers are all randomly woven together to eliminate grain, and then coated with resin to hold them in place. Fiberglass will rip if enough force is generated, but tears are minimized by the random fiber arrangement. But making cloth with such complex weaves is very expensive, so most hard-wearing fabrics, such as denim or suit material, use twill weaves, with the diagonal pattern of weft threads providing more resistance to tears along the grain.

Even the best cloth will always be susceptible to sharp objects that can snag and break the individual threads of the weave. Once the break has occurred, there is no more friction to support the threads in that area. Add a little pressure and the cloth will probably tear. Your only solution is to restore the friction by sewing up the damage, clamping the damaged weave together with a new weave called stitches.

INFECTIOUS MESSAGES

You're surprised to see the guy from technical support sitting at your computer when you return to your desk a few minutes later. He scowls as you approach. You're still preoccupied with your ruined shirt and barely hear him telling you that you've caused a computer virus outbreak in the company. He's obviously mistaken. If anything, you probably saved the company from infection, because you remember receiving an e-mail yesterday from an old friend who had warned you about a computer worm called "I love you." Apparently, the program e-mailed people with fake messages and when they opened the mail it deleted a bunch of files and e-mailed itself out to new people. Your friend had mailed you instructions on how to remove the malicious program, although you couldn't seem to open the file he sent. What did you do that was so bad?

The IT person looks at you with disgust. The e-mail wasn't sent from your friend, he explains. It was a fake message sent by a new version of the worm itself. By clicking on the file you let the evil program install itself on your computer, and from there it had gone on to infect everyone on the network and everyone else in your address book. They'd had to shut down the whole system to remove the virus. Meetings had been canceled, hours of work lost. You are in trouble.

In 1970, the British comedy television show *Monty Python's Flying Circus* finished its final show of the season with a sketch featuring a couple in a restaurant asking what was on the menu. The chaotic answer (interrupted by a group of Vikings frequently bursting into song) was that the menu consisted of:

Egg and bacon

Egg, sausage, and bacon

Egg and spam

Egg, bacon, and spam

Egg, bacon, sausage, and spam

Spam, bacon, sausage, and spam

Spam, egg, spam, spam, bacon, and spam

Spam, spam, spam, egg, and spam

Spam, spam, spam, spam, spam, spam, baked beans, spam, spam, spam, and spam

Lobster thermidor aux crevettes with a Mornay sauce garnished with truffle paté, brandy, and with a fried egg on top and spam

When the end credits rolled, "spam" was inserted in most names. It was only a short skit, so the comedy team was no doubt surprised to discover that some 20 years later, their show had inspired the use of the word "spam" to mean unsolicited or junk e-mails.

E-mail is a wonderful invention—or at least it used to be.

When the World Wide Web was young (in the late 1980s and early 1990s), e-mail was a fast, reliable, and seemingly secure way to communicate using computers. In those days, the main users were university staff and students. There were no online stores or Internet banks. No downloadable music sites or social networking Web pages. The word *blog* was unheard of. But innovations move quickly in the world of technology. As the Internet was taken up for almost every conceivable type of information, e-mails got hijacked. Advertisements, then malicious programs and scams became hugely prolific. Just as the spam increased until it became overwhelming in the original Monty Python sketch, so e-mail spam is now one of the biggest problems for networked computers today. In 2006, 59 percent of all monitored e-mail traffic was spam.

More than half of all spam in that year was related to financial services. One common trick used by "cyber criminals" was to buy stock in a company, then send "dump and pump" e-mails to thousands of people with fake predictions that the stock will perform well. Enough people believe the e-mails for the price of the stock to be pushed higher, allowing the criminals to sell their stocks at a profit. Another trick is known as "phishing"— criminals send out e-mails that appear identical to legitimate e-mails sent from banks or online companies, asking you to confirm your security details or login information, or even just pretending to charge you for a fictional product and asking you to login to reply. Clicking on the link takes you to a Web page that also looks exactly the same as the one used by the bank or company, but in reality it's fake. When you type in your details, you are not able to proceed; instead, your information is sent to the fraudster, who uses it to access your bank accounts or steal your identity and perform criminal activities in your name. Other common examples of spam include messages that claim you have won the lottery, or that you can assist in the transfer of a huge inheritance and earn a percentage in the process. In the latter cases, those foolish enough to respond quickly find they have to pay "administration charges" of thousands of dollars before they can obtain their "huge payouts," which of course never arrive. Some people are even asked to fly to other countries to complete the transactions, where they have been kidnapped and ransomed back to their families. There are real criminals behind spam!

Other forms of spam are even more clever, and just as malicious. One nasty kind is the e-mail virus. Computer viruses have existed since the times of floppy disks. They are evil little programs that hide themselves inside ordinary programs (just as biological viruses hide inside cells) and are run invisibly whenever the legitimate programs are run. Instead of doing anything useful, viruses secretly copy themselves into other programs or onto disks so that they can infect other computers when the disk is read. Computer worms are similar except that they don't need to hide in other programs; they're full programs in their own right, and they'll just worm their way into the heart of the computer and run when the computer is booted. Viruses and worms used to be limited by having to be physically moved on floppy disks, but as e-mail became popular, it became a million times easier for viruses and worms to spread between computers. The problem was that files could be attached to e-mails, and those files could be viruses or worms. The trick was to fool the recipient of the e-mail with the attached virus or worm into accidentally running the program. A double-click with a mouse serves the dual purpose of opening a text or an image attachment and executing a program, so all that was needed was to disguise the program as a text or an image document and then write something in the e-mail to entice the recipient to look at the attachment.

In 2000, one of the most destructive e-mail worms used a little basic social engineering to achieve exactly this. The worm hijacked the address books of infected computers and sent a sweet little message to everyone. The subject line was "I love you" and the content of the message was simply, "Kindly check the attached love letter coming from me." The attachment looked like a text file, with the name "LOVE-LETTER-FOR-YOU.TXT.vbs," but in reality it was a program. Double-clicking on it ran the program and infected your computer. Because the message came from someone you knew (your e-mail was in the sender's address book), and because the content of the message was just too tempting to resist, millions of people fell for the trick. Once running on your computer, it copied itself to all the other computers it could find on the same local network, it overwrote image and audio files with copies of itself, it e-mailed the passwords from your computer to an address in the Philippines, and it mailed itself to everyone in your address book.

The "I love you" worm spread across the entire Internet in one day. It followed the rising sun, flowing around the planet and infecting each new country as people woke up and checked their e-mails. It has been estimated that 10 percent of all computers became infected with this worm, and the cost of repairing all the infected systems may have run into the billions in lost time for hundreds of companies and governments.

Because viruses and worms are so prevalent today, every

computer ships with antivirus software as a standard. This software runs quietly in the background as you use a computer, often monitoring the programs you download or run and checking their code against lists of known offenders. Viruses and worms have unique fingerprints (a pattern of binary 1s and 0s) or "signatures" that can be used as identification, so antivirus software ensures that the programs you download do not contain the fingerprints of any of the thousands of known viruses and worms. Researchers in computer science are attempting to develop artificial immune systems that would allow computers to detect harmful new programs that have never been seen before. But for now, current antivirus software must be updated with the fingerprints of new viruses. When the software is up-to-date, it is immune to the current viruses, just as your flu shot varies each year to protect you from the new strains of the virus. But just as biological viruses mutate and change themselves so that they can infect you again, so computer viruses and worms are altered and mutated to avoid detection by the antivirus software. (Some are even clever enough to mutate themselves.) For every new malicious program, many variants exist, each with its distinctive fingerprint.

The "I love you" worm was no exception. Some of its variants claimed to be invoices for hugely expensive Mother's Day gifts or flights. Some pretended to be jokes or anxious messages from friends. But the nastiest variants contained warnings about the "I love you" worm, with details about how harmful it was, and pretended to include a file with more details, or even include a program that would remove the worm. Because so many people had become infected with the original worm, many millions more fell for the trick of "curing" that worm, which allowed these variants to spread around the world all over again.

Until the computer scientists perfect their artificial immune systems, the only thing we can do is be vigilant and keep our antivirus software up-to-date. If you receive an e-mail from someone—even if it's someone you know—and the message seems a little strange, perhaps with a few weird spelling mistakes or capitalizations, do not open the attachment. No matter how curious you may be, just delete the e-mail. (Better still, don't even read the e-mail, because just the act of opening it may be enough to cause some viruses to run.) If you receive an e-mail from your bank or an online company that prompts you to click on a link in order to go straight to their Web page—don't click on it! Just go to your Web browser and find your own way to their Web page. If you're curious, you can use the right mouse button (ctrl-click for Macs) and copy the link in the e-mail, then paste it into Notepad or TextEdit. There you will see what the link really points to. If the address looks even the tiniest bit different from the genuine Web address, then the e-mail is fake and a criminal is phishing for your account details. Delete it! When browsing the Internet and a pop-up window suggests you should download a free program to speed up your computer, remove a virus, detect spyware, or almost anything else—don't do it. It will only infect your computer, and probably grab your passwords and mail them to a criminal somewhere.

The Internet used to be like a little country village where you could leave your doors unlocked and trust everyone around you. Today it is more like a big city—full of strangers who will deceive you or steal from you if you are not street-smart. You wouldn't leave your door unlocked in a city, or accept suspicious gifts from strangers, so don't do the same on your computer!

TIGHT SQUEEZE

The technical support guy takes hours. While he fixes the computer, you try to work at another desk. The tattered shoe and shirt are a constant distraction, but you are able to make some calls and ensure that your car is okay. By lunchtime you're still feeling rather self-conscious, so you decide just to grab a sandwich and a bottle of juice from the cafeteria. Taking the juice back to your desk, you realize there's really nothing to do while the computer is being repaired. You idly sit next to the technical support guy, pretending to go through some papers, drinking and nervously fidgeting with the glass bottle. Finally the tech support guy speaks to you. He's run a program to clean and optimize the remaining system. Apparently, the computer should be fine in 10 minutes. You start to thank him and hold out your hand to shake his. At the last moment you realize your finger is trapped inside the neck of the bottle. He walks away shaking his head, as you frantically try to wrench the bottle from your finger. It's stuck at the joint. No matter what you do, it doesn't move.

People are naturally curious creatures, and one of the most natural things we do is use the sensitive tips of our fingers to touch the world around us. The tongue is another sensitive area; babies often explore new objects by placing them in their mouths because they aren't yet able to move their fingers with precision. Most people absently play with objects around them even while in conversation, just as their eyes flick around to obtain more cues about the world. You might trace the pattern in a table, fidget with a pen, or unbend a paper clip. These are all subconscious activities that help your brain understand the feel of your environment.

Unfortunately, sometimes our curious fingers go places they shouldn't. Accidentally getting a finger stuck in a bottle, or a chain fence, or a drawer handle are common examples of this mishap (just search for "finger stuck" on YouTube if you want to enjoy one of these for yourself). Every day thousands of people manage to squeeze a ring onto a finger only to find that it does not come off again. But sometimes the mishaps are a little more humiliating. In 2007, a Wal-Mart employee in Lafayette, Colorado, made the news by getting his finger stuck in the surface of a cast-iron picnic table in front of his store. The fire department had to spend more than an hour cutting the table to pieces to free the embarrassed man, in front of an amused crowd. On another occasion, a professional bowler chose a bowling ball a little too small for his fingers and sent himself flying after his ball when his fingers became stuck. The game was aired on live television.

It seems somehow unfair that our fingers are able to become stuck so easily. Surely if they can be pushed into something, then they must be able to come out again? If only it were so simple. Our fingers are not perfect tubes. They're lumpy, fleshy things with innards that can be pushed around. Even worse, they can swell up and become bigger.

Our anatomy is partly the problem. Each finger has three visible joints (the thumb having two), with another within the wrist. The muscles that move the fingers are mostly wrapped around the forearm and attach to the joints of the fingers by tendons, like a string puppet moved by pulling its strings. We have some tendons running under the fingers so that we can clench them and grip things, and others running over the fingers, allowing us to unclench them. All are cleverly placed to give us amazing control, allowing us to spread the fingers wide, move each finger individually up and down, and move most of the joints independently from each other. The bones in fingers may be thinner than pencils, so to stop them from slipping or bending too freely like little snakes, the joints between the individual bones are enlarged. Each joint is carefully shaped to keep the bones locked together, with cartilage inserts to provide a smooth lubricated movement and ligaments to support the joints and stop them from moving too far. If you are double-jointed, this does not mean your joints are any different—it's simply that the ligaments that are supposed to limit the joint movements are a bit more elastic than they're supposed to be, allowing your joints to bend in directions that are not terribly useful.

Even the skin on fingers is special. On the fleshy underside of all the fingers and the palms, we have friction-ridge skin. This special skin is covered with unique patterns of raised ridges that allow us to grip almost any surface, just as the pattern of grip on shoes allows our feet to grip the ground better. The patterns are so unique (even between identical twins) that forensic scientists use fingerprint marks for identification of criminals. This skin also has far more eccrine (sweat) glands than other parts of the body, but not for keeping the hands cool. Water helps increase

Why Sh*t Happens

the friction by being attracted to hydrophilic surfaces (materials that like water and pull it toward themselves). So where dry skin might just slip over a surface, slightly damp skin can achieve a good grip. The skin also contains far more sensory nerves, allowing us to feel the detailed texture of surfaces in enormous detail. In contrast, the skin on the other side of the hand is completely different. It does not have friction ridges, it does not sweat much, and it does not have the same number of nerve cells. Instead, it is designed to cope with all the bending at the joints, so it has tough, wrinkled surfaces to protect the knobby parts from all the knocks they receive.

It's all a wonderful design, like everything else in our bodies. However, the anatomy of fingers does mean that they can become stuck in small places. Squeeze a finger through the small neck of a bottle and it may well fit. But now the circular ring of glass settles behind the second joint. At the sides, the wider bones cause a problem. At the top, the wrinkled skin bunches up behind the ring of glass. At the bottom, the friction-ridge skin and sweat grips the glass. The combined friction can be enough to stop the finger from coming back out.

But friction caused by your anatomy is only half of the problem. The other half is caused by your circulation. Like every part of your body, the cells in your fingers are living entities that require a supply of oxygen and nutrients for energy, and they require waste products, including carbon dioxide, to be removed. Our circulatory system takes care of this vital function. The heart pumps oxygenated blood from the lungs around the body. The oxygen seeps from the red blood cells in the arteries into the plasma, which seeps through the walls of the vessels to make up our interstitial fluid—the watery fluid that bathes all cells. From this our cells take up oxygen and nutrients, and release waste. The interstitial fluid then seeps back into veins and is pumped back with the blood to the lungs, where we breathe out the waste gases and breathe in more oxygen to enrich the blood cells again. There's another system of vessels known as the lymphatic system, which also helps suck up any leftover fluid and return it to the blood. It's also used by our immune cells to take a good look at anything nasty that might be trying to infect us.

We're watery creatures, and all the tubes and vessels within us need to be carefully controlled. There are valves in many of our major veins to prevent blood from falling back down in the wrong direction. If you have varicose veins, some of the valves have begun to leak and the blood is pooling within the veins, swelling them and making them discolored and painful. Remarkably, many of the blood vessels also have muscles woven into them, allowing our brain to dilate or contract them. If we're running fast, we need to dilate as many vessels as possible to allow a fast supply of oxygen-rich blood to circulate. If we're very cold, the vessels to nonessential extremities such as fingers and toes will contract. In extreme circumstances, your body may sacrifice parts of itself using this method. Mountaineers trying to survive in subzero conditions may lose their fingers, toes, and parts of their noses—their blood vessels constrict so much that the blood supply completely ceases in these areas. Any cells that do not receive a constant blood supply will quickly die. We call it frostbite, but the tissue may not be frozen—the body is simply making the judgment that it's better to keep organs such as the liver and kidneys alive, even if it means losing a few fingers.

Our blood supply changes depending on how much exercise

we get and how warm we are. The amount of leaky interstitial fluid also varies, especially if we're not moving around enough to help pump it back into the blood. Even gravity affects the amount of fluid present in different parts of the body. When in a very relaxed state, raise one hand above your head and let the other dangle down for 10 minutes, and you may well be able to see the difference in size between the two.

So if your finger is stuck inside a bottle, becoming hot and bothered is a natural reaction but unfortunately it's also the worst thing you can do. The increased blood supply will swell your finger even more, locking the bottle in place. Your second attempt may be to put the bottle between your knees in order to try and pull out the finger. But the lower your hand is, the more gravity will make the interstitial fluid pool in the fingers, and the more swollen they will be. If you become angry and still try and force it, then you may bruise yourself or even strain ligaments or crack a bone. You're really in trouble if that happens, because your finger will swell up to try and fix the damage, and may stay swollen for a long time.

The solution is to eliminate each of these problems. First, obtain something that will act like a lubricant—soap, oil, shampoo—and carefully work it under the rim of the bottle and ideally around that knob of the finger joint. Second, be calm, obtain some ice, and place it on the finger to fool your body into contracting the blood vessels. The colder you are, the better (within reason). Raising the hand high will also drain it of any extra interstitial fluid. Finally, don't just pull the bottle off—it may still be stuck on the bones or wrinkled skin and you do not want to hurt yourself. Slowly rotate the bottle around and ease it off gently. Eventually, what went in must come out!

FADING MEMORIES

Your finger is throbbing, but at least it's out of the bottle. Soap from the restroom and a painful struggle for half an hour did the trick. Sitting down again, you look at the computer. There is only a blank screen. Presumably, it's finished doing whatever it was supposed to do. Pressing buttons on the keyboard has no effect. You reach down and turn off the computer, wait 10 seconds, and turn it back on again. There's a strange whirring noise, and then a message appears in white letters against a black background: fixed disk failure.

Nothing else happens. You try turning the computer on and off again a few more times. All it does is make the same whirring noise and show the same message. Your computer is dead.

Computers are everywhere, but how many people really understand how they work—or how they don't work? When a computer dies, what goes wrong? Surely if they're made up of electronic chips, they can't wear out—so what makes a computer "break"?

Modern computers are mostly solid-state. That means that the majority of the clever work that gets done is within the hugely complex processor chips, which contain millions of microscopic transistors all directing electricity in intricate paths within them. There are often several computer processors within each computer—one or two that run your software, a few to manipulate graphics and produce the output on the screen, and yet more to handle inputs such as USB devices, keyboards, your disk drives, and mouse. There are more chips used to hold all the data (called memory chips) and yet more to transfer data between all of the processors and the memory on the "bus" (there are no wheels or fares on this bus, though).

The combination of electricity flowing through chips and the heat produced by that flow can and does slowly wear out the chips. There are three mechanisms that cause this. One is electromigration, which causes atoms in the metal that conduct the electricity to be swept along like pebbles in a streambed. If too many are swept away from one area and build up in another, then the chip may not conduct electricity in the way it was designed to and may fail. A second process is oxide breakdown, in which one of the special oxide layers that makes up a chip develops weak spots and melts away, causing tiny short circuits that destroy the chip. A third mechanism is hot-carrier interaction, where overenthusiastic electrons pushed by an electromagnetic field may punch through the oxide layer and help form cracks and imperfections. Older chips did not have such tiny internal components, and so had lifetimes of many decades. Modern super-miniaturized chips are now pushing the boundaries of physics, so they may last for only about 5 years of continuous use. Not quite as reliable as you thought, perhaps!

But computers don't just contain solid-state components— they also have a few moving parts. For example, when electricity flows through all the chips, some of it is turned into heat.

Modern computers can become very hot indeed, so most computers also contain a fan to cool them down. Some may have several fans: one for the internal power transformer that converts the main alternating current into direct current, and others that sit directly on the hot chips to cool them down. It's not uncommon to have a fan break down in a computer, and then for the chips to overheat and fail.

But that's not all. With current technology, we can make memory chips with huge capacities—more than enough to store the content of several encyclopedias. (To give you an idea of the scale of information, this entire book is about 600,000 bytes of information, where a byte can store one character, such as "a" or "!".) But the desire to store and manipulate more and more information means that even these chips are not enough. We now demand gigabytes of storage space, where each gigabyte is 1,000,000,000 bytes. For storing music and video, we need many terabytes of data (1,000,000,000,000 bytes). At the time of this writing, we could not make memory chips with these kinds of capacities, although this may well change within a few years. The solution is to use some form of physical storage device instead of an electronic one.

We've been using physical storage for as long as computers were invented. Before we even had memory chips, computer programs were stored on punch cards—literally pieces of card with holes punched into them. By the 1950s, computers began to make use of the new technology of magnetic tape, which allowed different parts of its surface to be magnetized in order to store information, and that magnetic polarity could be detected in order to read the information. In the old movies you still see the tall cabinets with reels of magnetic tape spooling back and forth—these were just used for storage, the computer was elsewhere. As you might imagine, they tended to break down frequently, making the computers very unreliable.

Some home computers continued to use tape for storage, but by the late 1970s and early 1980s, spinning magnetic disks had become recognized as a much better solution. Instead of spooling a tape back and forth to find the right information, a spinning disk only requires users to move a reading head from the edge to the middle. Data is recorded in a series of circles on the disk, by magnetizing little chunks of each circle. Just as you could skip to your favorite song by lifting the needle of a record player over the record, so a disk drive could skip to any chunk of data stored on the disk by moving its reading head. With some clever controllers, it could also keep track of any free space on the disk, wherever that might be, and fill it with new information to ensure the whole surface of the disk is used efficiently.

The designs of disk drives slowly improved. Initially the "floppy" magnetic disks were 8 inches across; after many years of development, they were able to store about 1 megabyte (1,000,000 bytes). They were bulky and unreliable, and so a smaller 5¼-inch "mini" floppy disk was seen as a big improvement. The reduction in size meant that the smaller disks only held a few hundred kilobytes of data, but capacities slowly increased. The next step was the 3½-inch "micro" floppy diskette, which introduced the sensible addition of a rigid plastic sleeve around the internal floppy disk to protect it.

Although floppy disks and their disk drives were hugely successful during the 1980s and 1990s, by the turn of this century, memory chips were able to offer more reliable solutions. The problem was that floppy disks tended to become dirty quite quickly. The disk drives would frequently pick up a lot of dust and dirt on their reading and writing heads, and so it was very common for disks to stop working and the data stored on them to be lost.

The problems had always been known, so in parallel to the development of floppy disks, hard disks were created. As you may guess from the name, hard disks are not floppy. They are rigid, nonremovable magnetic disks, mounted within a hard disk drive and sealed inside forever. Because there was no need to make them easy to handle, hard disk drives contain more than one disk inside them, one above the other. The original hard disk built in 1956 had 50 disks (platters), each 24 inches across (not a small device) and could store an amazing 5 megabytes. As the years went by, the technology improved and the disks became smaller and more precise. Soon 3½-inch drives became standard for desktop computers, and 2½-inch drives for laptops. Amazingly, drives only 1.8 inches across were developed for tiny portable MP3 players. Within them is the same technology: several tiny magnetic disks one above each other, all spinning at high speed, with microscopic reading and writing heads flicking back and forth, magnetizing the surfaces and reading the states. The technology is remarkable, because the tiny reading heads must float over the surface of the disks without touching them. To achieve this, they maintain their own internal air pressure, they have their own air filtration systems to prevent dirt from getting inside, and they have sensors to detect whether they're being bumped. If too big a jolt comes along, they'll park their heads out of the way. Modern hard disks can withstand unbelievable shocks—when switched off, you could play football with one and it would probably still work just fine. The precision and accuracy demonstrated when manufacturing a 1.8-inch hard disk would put the finest Swiss watch to shame.

However, hard disks are not everlasting. Many years of dramatic failures have resulted in extraordinary designs today, but any mechanical device will wear out eventually, and hard disks are no exception. One of the "classic" types of failure is known as a head crash. A sudden jolt while the drive is switched on, or a speck of dust in the wrong place, causes the read-write heads to hit the spinning surface of the disks and scratch them, or even become stuck. At best, the disk has lost the information around the scratched area, but more commonly, the whole disk will no longer work and may just lose the ability to read data, producing a repetitive clicking noise as the heads try to seek for the right information and fail, again and again. Sometimes the bearings fail in a hard disk, stopping it from spinning smoothly and producing dust, which then causes a head crash. Or the internal platters become misaligned and can no longer be reliably read. Sometimes excessive humidity can cause corrosion with similar results.

To the trained ear, it is possible to hear the death rattle of a hard disk as it prepares to give up. You may start to hear a rougher whine above the noise of the fans. You may even hear a noticeable scraping noise. Sometimes a period of heavy use over several hours can exacerbate the problem. If the computer can still read it, try a disk repair program, which should be able to tell you whether any parts are now unusable. If it has gone wrong, and your computer is now complaining that it cannot see a hard disk anymore, there are various things to try. Check the power and data cables to the drive—sometimes they come loose and the drive is fine. Try holding the computer at different angles—sounds crazy, but if the read heads are scraping a misaligned platter, it can enable you to access the disk just long enough to retrieve your data. And for the really desperate, some people have found that removing the drive, placing it in a freezer bag and leaving it in the freezer for 30 minutes can bring the drive back to life for a few minutes. The internal components shrink in the cold, freeing bearings and stuck heads. Some have even found that a little tap with a hammer is enough to free the internal stuck heads and allow you to access the drive briefly (although you may still need specialized software to retrieve your data). But these are all last resorts, likely to do more damage than good in the long term. If your hard disk has died and you have hugely important data on it, then the best solution is to send it to a specialist data retrieval company. They will open the hard disk in a clean room to avoid the tiniest speck of dust contaminating the platters, and they can then access the remaining data from each platter in turn. It's not cheap, and it's not something that can be done at home or even in a local repair shop.

Computers are just clever machines. We have to take our cars to the mechanic for regular service or they break down. Computer components such as processors and hard disks can't be maintained like car engines, but they can be replaced. The important thing to remember is that they will not last forever. If you want to keep your data, it's best to assume that it will all go wrong tomorrow and make sure it's backed up today!

SHATTERED HOPES

Perhaps more out of a sense of guilt than anything, when the techies return from their lunch break you insist on helping to carry the dead computer downstairs to the IT department. It's heavy, but you are determined to show that you can do something useful today. The room is in the basement, a windowless techno-laboratory filled with parts of computers and shelves stacked high with cables and monitors. As you set the machine down on the floor, the heavy fire door begins to swing shut behind you. The tech support guy is following with the monitor, so you reach out to catch the door to open it for him. It's a much heavier door than you expected and you don't catch it in time. There's a distinct crunch as your little finger is caught between the heavy door and the edge of the doorway.

Bones are not essential for strength, flexibility, and movement—the elephant has 40,000 muscles in its trunk and not a single bone. But bones do provide considerable advantages. A cage of bones helps support all the fleshy internal organs. A shell made of bone can support and protect the delicate brain from being squished. Stiff internal sticklike bones can be used like poles within our limbs to push against the ground, allowing us to move at speed.

But how could tough stick-like structures grow inside a living creature? Animal cells are naturally quite squishy, so they can't form hard substances on their own. Plants have rigid cell walls, so every cell provides its own support. But even rigid walls can be broken quite easily (we can cut plants with ease), and those that are really solid, such as trees, are not as good at repairing themselves because most of their solidity is created by the woody dead cells. We wouldn't want a series of new "shoots" springing from a broken bone in the way that new branches grow from a broken tree.

Animal cells don't have cell walls, so they can't grow themselves into treelike bones. Instead, they extrude various types of proteins, so our cells can knit together meshes of collagen and form cartilage (the stiff stuff that makes up your ears and nose). If the bodies of animals are supported by water, "bones" made only from cartilage can work quite well. Many ancient forms of fish (including sharks and rays) use cartilage for their bones with great success. But out of the water, cartilage is not quite strong enough. Cartilage leg bones are simply not tough enough to carry heavy organisms around. A new invention was needed.

The solution came from the answer to a completely different problem. Living organisms require a wide range of inorganic nutrients to enable their cells to grow and survive. Plants need calcium to build those strong cell walls. Animals need iron to enable their red blood cells to grab oxygen from the air; plants use iron to help make photosynthesis work and draw energy from sunlight. Both animals and plants need potassium, magnesium, sodium, sulfur, and countless other substances in order to stay alive. Our planet is abundant in all of these substances (which is no doubt why we all evolved to make use of them), so most are absorbed by plants from the soil, which are then eaten by animals, which are eaten by other animals, and so on. The problem was that sometimes there was actually too much of a particular substance in an animal. Excessive sodium can cause hypertension or affect your nervous system, making you twitch. Excessive iron can cause fatigue, weight loss, arthritis, and abdominal pain. Too much calcium in your blood and your kidneys may start to fail, and muscles such as your heart will not pump properly. The solution used for excessive iron is for certain cells (often around the heart and liver) to exploit a protein known as ferritin, which grabs hold of the iron and stores it out of the way. The solution used for calcium is to store excess amounts in little hard deposits, often around areas where there is cartilage.

Suddenly, we had a way to make really hard structures in exactly the shapes we wanted. We could grow scaffolding made of cartilage, eat lots of calcium, and then our cells could deposit hard calcium structures to replace the cartilage. The result would be superhard, inorganic structures that supported, strengthened, and protected us. This process is known as ossification. It's a little like fossilization, where organic structures are slowly replaced by stone. Inside us, cells carefully deposit substances such as calcium and remove the cartilage scaffolding as they go. As you might imagine, it's a long, long process that takes many years to complete. A newborn baby still has much of its bones made from cartilage—something quite obvious to see directly after birth, because the process of being born often squashes the whole head into a slightly strange shape for a few hours. It's much better to have a flexible baby than a brittle one. They don't call them bouncing babies for nothing.

The gradual process of ossification is also important for another reason. Our bones grow as we do. It would be a real challenge to have completely finished bones at the age of 5, for example, because many of them need to be more than twice that size in just a few years. (We grow as much as 8 inches per year during early childhood.) But at the same time, the bones need to be strong at the joints or else all the running and playing of childhood would just wear down the cartilage. So our bones have different regions of ossification: some at the ends to protect our joints, and some in the middle to provide overall structural strength. The partial ossification makes it easier to expand and grow bones, with cells dismantling and rebuilding the cartilage and the bone as the number of cells around them grow in the developing child. Small children only start developing bones in their kneecaps when they begin to walk. As we become older, the use of our bodies affects the growth of bones. Children who spend a significant amount of time training in gymnastics, for example, can place so much stress on their developing skeleton that their growth is measurably slowed, only to spurt quickly when training ceases. At puberty, the new hormones in our bodies cause the different areas of ossification to join up. Our bones are finished ossifying by the time we reach our mid-twenties.

Ossified bones are not just thick lumps of calcium phosphate. If our bones were solid all the way through, they would be much too heavy to move. Solid bones would have to be very, very thin—which wouldn't give us much protection—or we'd all need the muscles of a weight lifter just to be able to stand up. So our bones have a dense layer of solid bone on the outside, but are just a fine network of spongelike scaffolding inside. Like a modern skyscraper (which uses a metal skeleton with the rigid floors and walls put around the outside for strength), bones have a fine inner structure and a tough outer layer, making them both strong and lightweight.

Despite all the inorganic calcium, our bones are alive, packed full of cells. They have their own blood supplies, to keep all the cartilage and bone-building cells alive. They also have extensive links to our blood supply for another reason—bones are the organs that make all the cells in our blood. Within our long bones is a yellow jelly called marrow. Inside other bones, such as the skull, hips, breast, ribs, and shoulder blades, is a red marrow. The yellow marrow (or myeloid tissue) is made of millions of quickly reproducing generalist cells that are able to turn themselves into several varieties of the white blood cells used by our immune system; these help fight off nasty viruses and bacteria. The red marrow concentrates on making the red blood cells in our blood. When people suffer from leukemia, they have malfunctions or cancers in those generalist blood-making cells within their bone marrow. Because they cannot produce enough red blood cells (or because the red blood cells are not made properly and so are abnormal), they may become anemic, their blood may not clot properly, and they may become very weak. With insufficient white blood cells, their immune systems become depressed, making them more likely to become very ill from relatively harmless viruses or bacteria. Treatment for this disease often involves exposing patients to radiation and chemotherapy to kill the abnormal cells in the marrow. The rapidly dividing cells in the marrow are particularly susceptible to the effects of radiation; most of the nasty effects of radiation poisoning arise because the cells in our bone marrow are the first to die. Chemotherapy—a cocktail of toxic chemicals designed to attack and kill certain types of cells—is another way to kill cancerous cells. Once the malfunctioning cells are gone, donor cells from the marrow of a healthy person can be injected to enable new healthy marrow to grow again.

Bone- and cartilage-making cells never cease in their building work, even as they simultaneously make our blood. As quickly as some cells (osteoblasts) make new internal scaffolding, other cells (osteoclasts) absorb it again, so the insides and outsides of our bones are constantly being rebuilt throughout our lives. This process allows our bones to become stronger if we need to do more heavy lifting for a period of time. The extra forces pushing on the bones encourages the internal cells to build stronger internal support systems and thicker outer shells. If you were an astronaut, though, this mechanism would be a real problem. Those living in weightless conditions for several months have no forces pushing on their bones anymore, so the rebuilding cells have no encouragement to keep the bones strong. The cells that absorb existing internal supports continue to do their work, but with little being rebuilt, the bones of astronauts become lighter and more brittle. Astronauts in space for 6 months can lose as much as 10 to 15 percent of their bone mass, much of it around the joints, which are the areas that are normally under the most pressure. It's a real problem with no cure at present, although scientists are working on machines that might induce forces on joints by vibrating the bones while in space. Astronauts must go through weeks of recuperation after their missions in space, to enable their bones to rebuild themselves.

As we age, important hormones that regulate the balance between bone building and absorption may be low, so bones become thinner and weaker. There are also several diseases that affect the bone-building cells in similar ways. The resulting condition is called osteoporosis, and just like astronauts, sufferers lose bone mass, with the result that their bones become weak and brittle and fracture easily. (Also like astronauts, postmenopausal women are recommended to participate in exercise programs to reduce the effects of osteoporosis. Studies have shown that mixtures of strength and endurance training can prevent or reverse bone loss by up to 1 percent a year.)

Thankfully, most of the time our remarkable bone-absorbing and -rebuilding cells are in perfect balance, and so our bones are exactly as strong and light as we need them to be. Should we ever fracture a bone, the same cells play the very important role of knitting the broken pieces back together and depositing nice fresh bone to remove all signs of the damage. The only minor problem with the cells is that they don't actually know what shape the bones are supposed to be—they always followed the original cartilage scaffolding. So if you broke a bone but the fragments were left crooked, the osteoblasts will happily knit together the pieces into a solid, but rather crooked, new bone. That's why we put broken bones into solid plaster casts or use splints to lock the fragments into the correct alignment while new bone is built; we want them to lock them together perfectly. Children before puberty often have "greenstick fractures," where the bones partially bend and don't break all the way through (like a green stick of a tree). These heal especially quickly and well, because the bones of children are growing and being rebuilt at a fast rate anyway.

Bones are tough, but once ossification is complete it's not uncommon to crack them, especially by slamming fingers in doors. Sometimes cracked bones don't show up well on x-rays and so are very hard to diagnose. One approach used by some doctors is to touch a vibrating tuning fork to the bone. If you feel a sharp pain, it may well be because the cracked piece of bone is vibrating. Always go see a doctor if you think you have a broken bone—it is important that a medical professional checks it out. Often, a little crack may not even need a splint or cast, and as long as you don't put it under too much strain while it heals, new bone will grow to fix the problem in just a few weeks.

THAT SINKING FEELING

You're standing in front of your house again, exhausted. The taxi that dropped you off drives away. The nurse practitioner at work had assessed you and decided a trip to the hospital was not necessary. She splinted your injured finger to the one next to it, gave you a mild painkiller, and sent you home. You're left with a right hand that is clumsy and painful. It makes it difficult to fish your house keys out of your right pocket with your left hand, but after much scrabbling, you finally have them. Transferring them to the right hand, an involuntary clenching of the fingers sends a sharp pain shooting through the broken finger and you drop your keys. They tinkle when they hit the ground and then make a strange *ploink* noise. Looking down, you see why. They've dropped through a small sewer grate and fallen down the drain.

Why do things have to fall? Wouldn't it be great if, when you dropped things, they just hung in midair where you'd left them? Falling is a real pain in the butt, especially if that's where we land. But if nothing ever fell, if there were no up and no down, we would not exist. Nor would any of the planets and stars in the heavens above us.

The concepts of up and down are relative. The direction of

"up" in Europe is pretty much the same as the direction of "down" in Australia. On that side of the planet, objects fall up from the perspective of Europeans. Yet, if you go there, objects clearly fall down. This strange paradox points to the truth behind our perceptions of up and down. The word *up* really means "away from the center of the Earth" and the word *down* means "toward the center of the Earth." The force of gravity means everything nearby is pulled toward the Earth's core. The reason is simply that the Earth is a sphere (more or less), and so its center of mass is in its middle. If the Earth were bottle-shaped, then its center of mass would be toward the more massive base. Standing on the surface near the thinner neck would feel like standing on a slope; we would stand at a strange slant because we would be pulled at an angle toward the ground and not directly down into it.

The Earth does a lot more than pull us to its surface. It pulls all the separate rocks, metals, water, and everything else together. Gravitation caused the Earth to form in the first place, out of clouds of dusty debris left over from the explosions of previous stars. Earth's combined gravitational pull reaches far beyond our atmosphere—a layer of gases is also held in place by gravity. It catches stray meteors and asteroids and pulls them toward the Earth's surface. Gravitation even holds the moon in its circular orbit, like a whirling toy airplane on a string, preventing it from flying away into space.

But Earth is not so special. Although its mass holds the moon prisoner, the moon has its own gravitational force. As it whirls around us, its gravity tries to pull objects on the Earth toward it. The force is not strong enough to lift a feather, but it is strong enough to cause the water in our seas to bulge several feet toward it. (The molecules in water can move around more than those in a feather; when a vast enough number of water molecules have even a gentle pull on them, enough will move to cause a real overall effect.) As the Earth rotates around, day to night to day, and the moon orbits around the Earth, the bulges move across the oceans, making the water levels rise and fall against the shores, creating our tides. But the Earth and moon's gravitational pulls are miniscule compared to that of the sun. The sun is so massive that it holds many planets and whole ribbons of rocks in its grasp.

The same effect is evident on a much smaller scale when we drop objects on the ground. If you were to drop a child's marble and a cannonball from the same height, you'd find that they fall at the same speed and hit the ground together. Although the marble has its own microscopic gravitation that could pull the Earth toward it, and the cannonball has a slightly larger microscopic gravitational pull, the gravity of the Earth is vastly stronger than either of them, so their own tiny gravitational forces have no measurable effect. What counts is that the two objects are pulled by the same Earth gravity and so fall at the same rate.

Mass causes gravitation. The more mass an object has, the larger its gravitational field will be. Mass is simply how much there is of an object. It has nothing to do with size or weight. A large piece of balsa wood may have less mass than a much smaller piece of metal (such as a key). There are simply more atoms in the metal compared to the wood (which has a lot of air in it). The balsa wood will also weigh less than the metal—there are fewer atoms being pulled by the Earth's gravity in the wood than there are in the metal, so the combined force on the wood is less than that on the metal.

It took a genius named Albert Einstein to figure out why mass creates gravitation. He realized that space and time are flexible. Imagine that the universe is like the surface of a trampoline. Put a massive object—say, a bowling ball—onto a trampoline and its surface is bent by the mass. Now roll a smaller mass—say, a marble—toward the bowling ball, and you see its path is bent by the trampoline surface until it runs around and around the bowling ball. This is how the Earth forces the Moon to travel in circles around it. The mass of the Earth bends the space around it, forcing the Moon to "roll" around and around. Just as the trampoline surface farthest away from the mass is barely distorted, so the gravitational field generated by any mass has less effect the farther you are from that mass. Climb a high mountain and your weight will be slightly less, because you are farther from the Earth's center of mass (although this effect depends on the shape and composition of the mountain).

This flexible quality of space creates most of the effects we see in the night sky. It causes clouds of gases to spiral together and form spheres (stars and planets). It causes the stars to spiral together and form galaxies. Bizarrely, it's also the reason why all the galaxies seem to be flying away from each other at great speed.

At the beginning of the universe, every bit of mass, space, and time was contained in a miniscule point of energy. The "big bang" created our universe, exploding space and time outward from this tiny point, taking the mass with it. Draw dots on a balloon and blow air into it, and the dots seem to move apart from each other. Stretch space, and everything in it appears to fly apart. So that initial explosion is still expanding space itself, taking all the galaxies, stars, planets, and you and me with it. Outside our universe there is no space, no distance or position, so asking, "What is our universe expanding into?" does not have any meaning. If you had a computer program that modeled a galaxy being stretched, the question, "What is it expanding into?" also makes no sense in exactly the same way. There are no more things than there were before, so you don't need any more memory or a bigger computer. Neither the model, nor the real universe, is expanding into anything. It's just stretching.

Even light is affected by this phenomenon. If you were to take an astronomically long tape measure and extend it between our galaxy and another, it would always read the same distance, because it would be stretched as the space in which it is becomes stretched. The light traveling from a distant galaxy is stretched in exactly the same way. Its wavelength is stretched, shifting its color more toward a red hue. The "redshift" effect allows us to calculate how far away galaxies are from one another.

But light can be affected in even more extreme ways. Hugely massive objects may have so much gravity that they collapse and compress themselves into tiny spaces. The resulting "black holes" have such strong gravitational fields that they pull all matter into themselves, even light. If any light gets too close, it will be sucked down to the black hole's surface (which is why they are black). Light that is a little farther away will be bent as its path intersects the distortion in space, as if passing through a lens. So it is possible to detect a black hole by looking to see whether the light from other stars in the sky becomes strangely distorted by the gravitational lens of a black hole passing between the stars and us.

As bizarre as it sounds, time is as flexible as space. (They don't call time the fourth dimension for nothing.) For example, a massive object slows down time. The closer you are to the large mass, the more time is slowed. Go too near a black hole and time will become very slow for you. The same effect happens when you travel extremely fast—the closer you get to the speed of light, the more difficult it becomes to push yourself any faster, almost as though your mass increases. And just as if your mass were increasing, the closer you get to the speed of light, the slower time flows for you. It's why the speed of light is a fundamental limit in our universe, because to reach that speed you would have to push the equivalent of an infinite mass, which we can't do. If the whole thing sounds like science fiction, honestly, it's not. In 1971, two scientists named Hafele and Keating synchronized several cesium atomic beam clocks (the most accurate clocks available at the time), then placed some on board normal commercial passenger jet planes, flying around the world twice. When they came back and compared the clocks that had been speeding inside the planes with those on the ground, they found that, as predicted, a time dilation effect (increased by the speed and lessened by the greater distance from the Earth) had indeed made the clocks register different times. Today, the GPS (global positioning system), which consists of many satellites traveling at high speed some distance above us, only works because their clocks are constantly adjusted for the relativistic time dilation effects.

Thankfully, because we never really travel that fast and we never go too near objects the size of planets, our lives are only affected by the masses of the sun, moon, and, most of all, the Earth. All the different gravitational fields are overwhelmed by the gravitational field of the nearest massive object, our home planet. Time and space appear constant because the mass of the Earth is constant throughout our short lives. So when we drop something such as a bunch of keys, they are pulled "down" toward the Earth's center of mass, wherever we happen to be on the planet. There's nothing we can do about it, except hold on tighter or try not to drop small objects over drains. If the worst does happen and gravity grabs your precious keys from your fingers and shoves them through a grate, you can always try using a different type of attractive field that happens to be stronger than gravity over short distances. A magnet on the end of a string can work wonders.

Feel the Burn

The drain is not deep, so you decide to pull off the grating and reach down to retrieve the keys. It's tougher than you were expecting, especially using only your left hand. One almighty heave and the grating comes away. You lie down, reaching as far as you can, and manage to hook the key ring with your fingertips, then lift it up. But when you try to move the grating back, a sharp pain shoots through your arm, and you cannot find the strength to move the grating again. What have you done to yourself?

About one-third of an average female body, and up to half of an average male body, consists of muscle. Without all that muscle, we would not be able to move, but even more important, we would not be able to digest food, process nutrients and waste, and circulate blood around our bodies. Plants rely on osmosis to pump their water and nutrients from the soil (and can even move their leaves and stems around by pumping water in and out of different cells). Animals do not have that luxury; they must push, pull, and squeeze different organs and structures inside themselves day and night in order to stay alive.

We have three different types of muscle. One type is known as cardiac muscle. The cardiac muscle cells never stop pulsating;

although they are regulated by signals from the brain, a single cardiac muscle cell will happily pulsate on its own. This is important, because these muscle cells make up your heart, and it's fairly essential that it never stop beating. Cardiac muscle cells are designed to be powered by oxygen and to be immune to fatigue, because your heart may have to pulsate more than 2.7 billion times in your life without a single pause. Try clenching and unclenching your hand once a second for more than 5 minutes nonstop and you'll quickly realize how impressive your heart muscle is.

A second type of human muscle is known as smooth muscle. Like cardiac muscle cells, smooth muscle cells are involuntary—we cannot consciously control them. But smooth muscle is not designed to operate like the steady pump of your heart. Instead, it often forms sheets that are within your skin; the walls of your blood vessels; your reproductive, digestive, respiratory, and urinary tracts; and even in the irises of your eyes. Smooth muscle cells sometimes emit collagen to keep themselves together in a nice stretchy, woven matrix, and they help support and adjust the operation of our organs and vessels. Smooth muscles dilate the blood vessels around our bodies when we're working hard or we're warm, and they restrict them when we're cold. They squeeze our food and waste along the extensive tubes of our digestive systems, and they allow us to breathe by adjusting the passages into our lungs. Like the heart muscle, smooth muscle is designed to be used for long periods without becoming fatigued, and to recover very quickly if it is. Your brain does control many of the contractions of smooth muscles, but the control is totally unconscious. You will never be able to alter the way your stomach squelches your chewed-up food, or the way your iris changes size, in the same way that you can voluntarily control the movements of your fingers and toes.

The third kind of muscle is the type with which we're most familiar, because we can consciously control it. Skeletal muscle is the biggest and strongest variety of muscle. Lying in bundles woven around our bones, tendons attach one end of each muscle to a solid bone and attach the other end over a joint to the next bone. We have around 639 skeletal muscles (it's hard to count them exactly because some seem to be in groups with others). There are 30 muscles in your face alone, and huge numbers bundled in your forearms to operate your fingers and wrists. There are powerful muscles in the legs and arms to help us run, and delicate muscles in the tongue and eyelids to help us taste and see. Each and every skeletal muscle is wired to our brains in much the same way that a computer is wired to the motors of a robot. And just as the computer doesn't power the robot's motors—it sends a "move" signal—so, too, our brain does not power our muscles, but merely sends a "contract" signal. (Muscles also have spindle cells that sense movement and send signals back to the brain like the sensors of a robot, providing proprioceptive information.)

Muscles may be told to move in a similar way to the electric motors of a robot, but they are not powered by electricity. Motion is generated through chemistry. Inside each muscle cell (no matter which kind it is) there are strings (filaments) of proteins running from one end to the other. In skeletal muscle, these filaments are all lined up, giving them a striped appearance. The filaments are made from actin and myosin, but are normally kept from touching each other when in a relaxed state. If a signal is received from the brain, the tiny electrical pulse from the neuron causes a chain reaction, releasing calcium and causing the signal to pulse through all the muscle cells nearby. The calcium forces other insulating proteins to move out of the way, exposing the actin to the myosin. The myosin then binds to the actin filaments, grabbing on like people in a tug-of-war match planting their feet in the ground and pulling on a rope. The actin filaments are fixed at each end, so when the myosin pulls the actin toward the middle, the overall bundle of filaments contracts. Inside each skeletal muscle cell many sections of actin and myosin filaments are chained together, so when they pull at once, the typical result is that the filaments contract by a significant amount, shortening the overall length of the cell. When many cells contract at the same time, the result is a contracting muscle. To relax the muscle, the calcium is pumped away, the binding between the actin and the myosin filaments is broken, and the filaments separate and move apart again.

There are many different types of skeletal muscle cells because their chemical reactions are powered by different energy sources. Type I muscles (known as "slow twitch" muscles) are powered by oxygen and so have rich blood supplies and special internal mechanisms inside each cell to convert the oxygen into energy (organelles known as mitochondria and proteins called myoglobin hold on to the oxygen—these are what make these muscles red in color). Type I muscles are used during aerobic exercise; being powered by the air you breathe, they are able to work for long periods without fatigue.

Type II muscles are known as "fast twitch" muscles, and in

addition to using some oxygen, they also have a sugar-based power source called glycogen (and another called phosphocreatine) stored within the cells. There are several kinds of type II muscles. Type IIa is still mostly powered by oxygen and is used in vigorous aerobic exercise for several minutes. Type IIx is more powerful muscle, but relies on the glycogen and phosphocreatine much more than oxygen, so can only be used for 5 minutes or less, for example when running an 800-meter race. Type IIb cells mainly use phosphocreatine and are used for anaerobic exercise, because they need almost no oxygen. A 100-meter sprinter uses these ultra powerful muscles for short bursts of speed.

Unfortunately, although the anaerobic type II muscles are very powerful, the chemical reaction that is used to generate energy also creates lactic acid as a by-product in the absence of oxygen. Using these muscles for more than 2 or 3 minutes will cause the lactic acid to build up dramatically. Without rest to let the cells dispose of the acid, the pH of the muscle cells can become so low that their metabolism fails, causing us pain.

The muscle cells, or fibers, are so powerful that we almost never use them all at once. For most everyday uses, only a tiny percentage ever need to contract. When we heave with our muscles as hard as we possibly can, we're using about one-third of the fibers. If we used 100 percent of them, we would tear our own bodies apart, ripping the muscles from the bone or breaking our own joints. Nevertheless, it is common for muscles to become painful, and not just because of lactic acid buildup.

One symptom all but the laziest of us have experienced is the stiffness and soreness of our muscles 1 to 3 days after vigorous exercise. Contrary to popular belief, the pain is not a result of lactic acid buildup or glycogen depletion. Instead, the discomfort is caused by actin and myosin filaments that were ripped free from their normal positions within the cells by the intensive contraction of other filaments and other cells around them. If enough filaments are ripped free, the muscle cells die and the body must rebuild fresh muscle cells, usually with stronger internal filaments. This process is normal and takes a week or so to complete, although the stiffness may disappear sooner. The solution to muscle stiffness (formally called "Eccentric Exercise-Induced Muscle Damage") is simply to exercise regularly but not overdo it each time. Studies have shown that just one period of exercise a week is sufficient to maintain the muscles and avoid stiffness, though more frequent and regular exercise is of course the healthiest option.

For those who do exercise frequently, muscle cramps can be a problem. A cramp is the painful involuntary clenching of a muscle or group of muscles; it can occur around the site of an injury in order to stabilize it, after strenuous activity, or following a prolonged sedentary period. The exact cause of cramps is not always clear; it is possible that dehydration, or a deficiency in one of the essential muscle-related chemicals (calcium, potassium, sodium, and magnesium), may exacerbate the effect.

Every so often, you may overdo it all at once. Instead of stiffness a day later, or the painful weariness of lactic acid, or even the sore spasms of a cramped muscle, you may instead feel a sudden sharp pain in a muscle. Maybe you tried to lift a very heavy object, or you stretched a little too far when reaching for something. A "pulled muscle" is immediately painful, and you may also feel an immediate weakening of the muscle. The cause is normally that you've torn a significant number of muscle fibers. The muscle cells have been ripped from each other, damaging a small area of the muscle. Your body wisely makes that area painful to use for a few days, preventing you from further damaging the same muscle. While it rests, your body removes the torn and dead cells and replaces them with fresh, new, and hopefully stronger muscle cells. Depending on the severity of the pull, the repair may take 2 weeks or more to complete. As the muscle heals, the pain will slowly become duller and more like the stiffness of exercise-induced damage. You will recover just fine, and be strong again.

Muscles are amazing chemical-powered contracting organs, but like everything in the body, they can be damaged if you don't respect their limits and take care of them. Use them often, but not excessively, and they will stay happy, healthy, and pain-free.

KITCHEN FIREWORKS

You finally manage to limp into the kitchen, muscles aching. After the day you've experienced so far, you are ravenous. You throw open the cabinet drawers and freezer, looking for something—anything—that you can eat quickly. Everything needs to be cooked, but you feel like something quick and easy. Your eyes fall on a box of microwave pizzas. That will do the trick. Most of your usual plates are dirty, so you grab one from the back of the cupboard. It's a nice-looking plate with swirling gold patterns around the edges. You drop the pizzas onto their little cardboard stands, put them on the plate and into the microwave, and hit "start."

Rather than tidy up, you decide that you need a drink to relax a little, and grab a bottle of red wine off your rack. Corkscrew in, you heave out the cork, fully expecting the liquid inside to spill everywhere. But no, just a satisfying pop, and a healthy glug, glug, as you pour the wine into a glass. You suddenly notice that the microwave is making a strange crackling noise. As you turn to look at it, your smoke detector starts shrieking. You realize that there is smoke coming from the microwave, and sparks flashing from within, as though you have trapped your own evil thunderstorm inside it. You see another flash and realize the cardboard pizza box has caught on fire inside the microwave.

Most people know that metal and microwaves aren't a good combination. Far fewer people know why. When you think about it, the whole notion may sound like a myth. After all, microwaves are actually made of metal. Some even have metal grills inside them to help toast food. But it is no myth. If you're absentminded enough to place something containing even a tiny amount of metal into a microwave oven, you will probably see dangerous sparks flying from it. So why do these strange "microwaves" react so violently to metal, when the same substance is perfectly safe in a conventional oven? Why does metal in a microwave oven spark?

Microwave ovens rely on electromagnetic radiation—the same stuff used by cell phones to send signals, and the same stuff that is generated by lightning in the form of an electromagnetic pulse. The important thing about the waves of electromagnetic radiation used in ovens is their length. As you might guess from the name, microwave ovens use waves with a very small wavelength.

The origins of the microwave oven lie in the development of radar. In 1904, radar was first demonstrated, which proved that you could shoot a radio wave at an object and listen to its reflection. The idea is similar to sonar, which has been used by bats and dolphins for millions of years. These animals make very high-pitched noises and listen to the echoes. If there is no echo, there is no object in the sound's path. If there is an echo, then the closer that object is, the quicker the echo will come back. We can experience the same effect by shouting at a cliff side or large wall: the farther away we are, the longer the delay between our shout and the echo.

Sound travels in waves, or repeated compressions of air, caused, for example, by our larynxes (voice boxes) flapping and making ripples in the air. Long wavelengths are low sounds; short wavelengths correspond to higher sounds. Bats and dolphins use very high-pitched sounds, because the higher the sound, the shorter the wavelength; the shorter the wavelength, the smaller the objects that produce echoes. It's like needing a net with smaller holes to catch smaller objects. So if you want to see tiny things in the dark, you need to make very, very high-pitched noises. Some bats (who like to eat little moths) make noises so high-pitched that the wavelengths don't affect our ears, and we can't hear them at all.

The same principles apply to radar, except that radar doesn't use sound waves—it uses electromagnetic waves. These are the same waves that we see as light with our eyes and feel as heat with our skin, except that our eyes can only see a small range of wavelengths (and our skin feels even less). Visible electromagnetic waves have a wavelength between 400 nanometers (violet) and 700 nanometers (red), or 0.0004 millimeters to 0.0007 millimeters. Waves with even smaller wavelengths are called ultraviolet light, even smaller still are called X-rays, and really small ones are called gamma rays. Waves with longer lengths than red are called infrared (as used in infrared remote controls). All waves with lengths more than about 15 centimeters (6 inches) are called radio waves, so for example, a radio station with a frequency of 100 MHz has a wavelength of about 3 meters (3¼ yards).

Electromagnetic waves behave in much the same way, except that their different wavelengths allow them to pass through certain objects, be absorbed by some, and reflect off others. So when we're in a car listening to the radio and we go through a tunnel, we will lose reception because the radio waves cannot pass through the hill to reach us. If we're sitting by a hot fire, a simple screen will absorb the heat and prevent it from radiating onto our faces. And as I once found out when playing as a little boy, if you have a bright enough flashlight, you can light up the clouds in a dark night sky: the light travels all the way up and is reflected all the way back down to your eyes. The same principles also apply to sound waves, which is why moths are so hairy: they're trying to use the fuzz to absorb the sound of the bat's calls rather than reflect the noise back and give away their location. In general, if an object conducts waves well, it will also reflect them well. So a wooden floor conducts noise (put your ear to it and you will hear anything moving on it), and also reflects noise, producing good echoes. Similarly, a piece of metal conducts electricity and magnetism, and so also reflects electromagnetic waves extremely well.

Radar exploits these ideas. It simply makes use of radio waves that are broadcast out, with a corresponding receiver to listen for the reflections. Because metal and other electrically conductive materials are so good at reflecting radio waves back, it's an ideal method for detecting aircraft, submarines, or ships, all of which tend to be made from metal. By 1940, the British were in a hurry to improve this technology. In order to use radar to capture smaller objects, they needed to reduce the wavelength. So instead of using larger radio waves, they began to broadcast slightly smaller waves with lengths between about 1 millimeter and 15 centimeters ($\frac{1}{25}$ inch to 6 inches). These were called microwaves.

To produce these smaller waves, a new gadget was invented, called a magnetron. Although it sounds like a comic book superhero, this device is the key component in all radar systems and microwave ovens. It works by using a very high voltage (often more than 4,000 volts), which causes electrons to be fired out from a heated internal cathode. Instead of zipping straight across to the anode in a big spark, cleverly placed magnets force the electrons into a spin. As they zoom around, they pass by carefully placed metal vanes that begin to resonate at the right frequency. This electromagnetic resonation is then channeled down a little antenna and out of the magnetron as high-power microwaves. It's connected to the radar transmitter (or it's connected to the interior space of your microwave oven).

Once designed, the British gave the United States the plans for the magnetron and asked us to help develop and manufacture radar devices for the war effort. The Radiation Laboratory at MIT began work on the development of more efficient radar, which became the second most important military project at the time (the first was the Manhattan Project, which led to nuclear weapons). MIT asked the Raytheon company to develop a way to mass-produce the power tube of the magnetron. One of the chief engineers at Raytheon was a man named Percy Spencer.

One day, while working near a magnetron, Percy noticed that the candy bar in his pocket had melted. He soon discovered that he could cook popcorn by placing it in front of the microwave beam, and also that by directing the beam into a container, he could cook an egg. This discovery led to the development of the first microwave oven in 1947, which was called a Radarange. Its commercial viability was inhibited not only by its silly name, but also by the fact that it was a huge, water-cooled device that cost thousands of dollars. But by 1967, the company successfully developed the first low-cost, countertop microwave oven. It took only 8 more years before U.S. sales of microwaves were higher than sales of conventional gas ovens.

The design of the microwave oven has changed little since its invention. All microwaves use magnetrons to produce microwave energy (although modern designs are more efficient and more powerful), and all use a metal cage to trap the microwaves within the oven and force them to bounce around within the space without escaping. You will notice that your oven has metal walls and a metal grid in the door. Because the wavelength of microwaves used in ovens is 12.24 centimeters (about 4¾ inches) and the holes in the mesh are much smaller, the microwaves are simply reflected back inside. If your microwave has an internal electric grill attached to a wall, they'll bounce off that, too. The grill heats the food in the more traditional way.

Objects that do not reflect microwaves will absorb them. Anything that contains water tends to be pretty good at absorbing microwave energy. The electromagnetic waves grab the water molecules and twist them back and forth at enormous speed. It can do this because one end of every water molecule is positively charged and the other end is negatively charged, and the microwaves are producing an electric field that oscillates at a rate of 2.45 billion times per second. The field permeates the entire object, so all of the water molecules are grabbed and flipped at the same rate, vibrating one another and heating the object. This is why food cooks so much faster in a microwave oven—every part of the food is being cooked at once. In a conventional oven or on a grill, the heat gradually soaks through from the outside in.

There are some drawbacks to microwave cooking, however. Because the microwave energy is introduced to the oven in one place and it bounces around the inside, the waves can affect each other. Just like ripples in a bath, some waves may cancel each other out as they reflect from the edges, and others may reinforce each other. This can result in uneven cooking—the parts of your food that receive stronger microwaves will be hottest. To overcome this effect, most modern microwave ovens rotate the food, ensuring that, on average, each part receives the same waves. You may also notice that trying to defrost frozen food in a microwave can produce uneven effects. This is because ice does not have free water molecules, and the frozen ones will not be twisted and heated by the microwaves. So ice is not heated in a microwave, but water is. As soon as a few free water molecules are heated, they will melt neighboring molecules, which then heat up. So you may end up with some parts of the food that are cooked and while other parts are still frozen. The solution is to heat the food in short bursts, allowing it to rest for a few seconds and let melting occur before any hot spots are created.

Hot spots in food are one thing, but hot spots caused by unwanted fires are quite another, and if you want to avoid them, make sure you don't put any metal in your microwave. Metal reflects the microwaves, so aluminum foil would completely block the microwaves from heating your food. But even worse, metal conducts electricity very well. Inside the oven, where the electric field is oscillating at 2.45 billion times a second, anything that conducts electricity will have an electric charge pushed back and forth within it. In something like a spoon, this may be no problem. But if the object has sharp edges, then sparks may fly between them as the charge jumps between surfaces. Even worse, if it is a thin piece of metal, the charge can heat up the metal like the filament of a lightbulb, and you may see sparks or even a flame. So if you plan to dine with your favorite, gold-trimmed dinner plates, just don't put them in the microwave. Chances are very high that the pattern contains real metal, and that thin coating of metal is perfect for conducting electricity, heating up, and sparking. At best you may ruin your plate. At worst, if you've put something flammable such as cardboard next to it, you may just start a fire. Should that happen, stop the microwave, turn off the power, and, if necessary, use a fire extinguisher.

FINALLY CRACKED

Thankfully the sparks and fire went out immediately after you turned off the power to the microwave, leaving nothing but the blackened remains of your dinner and a kitchen full of smoke. You give up, and decide to call your favorite pizza place and have a pie delivered. Glass of wine in one hand, you go into the living room and pick up the phone. As you try not to move the broken finger on your right hand or use the pulled muscle in your left arm, you manage to drop the wineglass. In your panicking eyes it falls as though in slow motion, finally hitting the wooden floor just next to your rug and instantly shattering into a thousand pieces. Red wine splashes everywhere, but even worse, sparkling glass shards now cover the floor like glitter.

There's a popular myth about glass. Go on a guided tour around an old house in Europe, and you may notice that the centuries-old glass in the windows appears to be noticeably thicker at the bottom compared to the top. This, you will be told, is because glass is a super-cooled liquid and so over the centuries it continues to flow, falling under gravity and thickening the bottom of the glass. Sadly, no matter what the tour guide believes, this story is nothing more than a myth. It's the result of a misinterpretation of the evidence and a misunderstanding of the science. It turns out that window glass was sometimes made by blowing molten glass into a glass ball and then spinning the ball so that it flattened out like a plate with a knob in the middle. The outer pieces were cut to use as panes of glass, and because of the spinning process they were naturally fatter at one end and thinner at the other. The glass fitter would mount the glass with the fatter end at the bottom to make it stronger and look nicer. (Sometimes the central knob of glass was also used—you can still see this in the windows of some older buildings in the United Kingdom) We know that the glass did not flow, for now and again the glass fitters made a mistake and mounted the glass upside down, with the thin end at the bottom and the thicker part at the top. We also have examples of 2,000-year-old Roman glass that show no signs of flowing at all.

So if glass is not a strange, slow-flowing, super-cooled liquid after all, what is it? In reality, the material is a solid, but that solid is made by "super-cooling" a liquid extremely quickly. Glass is mostly made from silica, which is a molecule made from one silicon atom with two oxygen atoms stuck to it. Silica melts at a frighteningly high temperature of 3,133°F. If allowed to cool naturally, it will slowly crystallize, following the shape of its silicon-oxygen molecules. As it cools, silica naturally forms itself into hexagonal shapes. (Look at a lump of quartz or amethyst to see this effect, or indeed look at the sand on most beaches, which is made from tiny crystals of quartz.) But if molten silica is cooled down too rapidly (for example, when molten silica lava from a volcano meets the cold water of the ocean), its molecules do not have time to line up and form crystals. Instead, they are locked together in their chaotic, random patterns, to form obsidian, or "volcanic glass."

When we mimic the temperatures of a volcano by using a furnace, we can also melt silica and cool it in the same way. The result is glass: a transparent, brittle rock made from chaotic and randomly positioned silica molecules frozen in situ. Not a super-cooled liquid, glass is actually an "amorphous solid" (its molecules are not arranged in any regular order). Most modern glass also contains other substances added to make it melt at lower temperatures (sodium carbonate and calcium oxide, also known as soda and lime, and often magnesium oxide). Some glass also contains additives such as lead or flint to make the mixture more transparent. Other glass contains additives to give it color or to enable it to block certain types of light, such as UV light.

The molecular structure of glass makes it very special. In most solids, the atoms are nicely arranged in regular patterns like bricks in a house. There's no way for light to make its way through, so it is reflected or absorbed or converted into heat. In glass, all those randomly organized molecules are like the messy molecules of a liquid frozen in place, leaving more spaces for light to make its way through. Even better, the electrons belonging to the silica molecules are particularly bad at interfering with visible wavelengths of light. The electrons can convert some wavelengths into heat, and others they reflect. But the wavelengths that our eyes can detect are unaffected, and so are transmitted through the material. That's why glass is transparent to our eyes, even though it may absorb or reflect UV radiation.

The amorphous glass is also special for another reason. Unlike more structured materials, amorphous materials such as glass do not have a simple transition from solid to liquid when heated. Heat a metal and when its melting point is reached, the temperature of the solid will remain at the melting point while its molecules detach and form a hotter liquid. But heat glass and it continues to become hotter and hotter, until it first reaches its glass transition temperature, then reaches its melting point, and finally becomes a liquid.

Glass is not the only material to have this property; many polymers (such as plastics and rubbers) have the same characteristics. Unvulcanized rubber also has a glass transition temperature, below which it becomes a brittle solid not unlike glass. The glass transition temperature of rubber is much lower than that of everyday glass, so we are accustomed to seeing only the soft, flexible stage. Although its molecules are not really able to move past one another, they are able to move around, twist, and stretch. As rubber becomes warmer and warmer, its molecules move more and more, going from a bouncy rubbery texture to a gooey texture, before finally melting and turning into a liquid.

Glass does exactly the same thing, only at much higher temperatures. Above the transition temperature it moves from being a brittle solid to a gooey half-solid, half-liquid, before finally melting and becoming a real liquid. The glass transition is enormously useful when shaping the substance. Instead of heating glass to above 2,700°F and pouring it into very heat-resistant molds, it only needs to be heated to a few hundred degrees until it goes past its glass transition temperature and can be blown like a balloon, rolled, or pulled into different shapes. However, because even the glass transition temperature of all common forms of glass is beyond anything experienced outside a furnace, the glass around us is fixed and unflowing in its solid, brittle state.

We can change the toughness of the glass by how quickly we

cool it. One famous trick is to drip a blob of molten glass into a bucket of water. The sudden temperature change immediately solidifies the glass into a solid "drip" shape, with a bulbous blob tapering to a thin tail. The bulbous end is enormously strong and can withstand hits from a hammer. But use your fingers to break the smallest piece from the end of the thin tail and suddenly the entire glass structure—including that tough bulbous end—explodes into fine dust. The mysterious exploding glass drops fascinated King Charles II of England in 1661 after being presented with them by Prince Rupert of Bavaria. Now known as Prince Rupert's Drops, scientists have used slow-motion photography to film exactly what happens when the tail of a 2-inch drop made from ordinary soda-lime window glass is broken. A crack races at 4,000 miles an hour to the bulb and then spreads like the roots of a tree to encompass its entire surface, before the whole glass structure explodes outward. The cause of this extraordinary behavior is that initial rapid cooling. When the molten drop hits the water, its outer surface is instantly cooled, and it shrinks tightly around the still-molten inner core. Even when the entire structure is solidified, the tension remains like a balloon tightly filled with air. Breaking the tail breaks the tension just like popping the balloon, and the glass immediately tears itself apart. But unlike a rubber balloon, which might just tear itself into two pieces, the structure of glass is much more brittle. The molecular structure is haphazard, and there are many imperfections introduced by the other compounds. When under tension, just one crack is enough to trigger a catastrophic failure at countless points of internal imperfections, resulting in the whole structure turning to dust.

Toughened glass (or "safety glass") is made using the same process of rapid cooling to put the outer surface under tension. It makes the substance much harder than ordinary glass, but prone to the same kind of catastrophic failure. Shower doors, windows, and car windshields may be made of toughened glass. When damaged (perhaps by fatigue caused by heating and cooling in the shower, or by the impact of a stone or piece of gravel), the glass shatters completely into tiny pieces. Sometimes the larger pieces will continue to pop and break into smaller fragments for some minutes. It's almost like popcorn popping as the stored tension releases itself, creating new cracks and little explosions of glass. Most modern toughened glass is now laminated with a layer of plastic to prevent all the pieces from flying everywhere and harming us.

It's easy to prevent this from happening. Once formed, glass can be allowed to cool more slowly in special ovens so that all the tension is released in a process called annealing. The resulting glass will just crack or break into larger pieces when broken, but may not be as strong.

Drinking glasses and wineglasses obviously need to be both strong and safe. More expensive glasses may be made with glass that has expensive additives to make it stronger and shinier, and which is then annealed. Their rims may be cut with a hot blade or laser and then polished to remove all imperfections. It's an important step, because the slightest imperfection will turn into a crack that eventually will cause the whole glass to fail. Cheaper glasses may be made of several types of glass. Toughened glass may be used for the bases and stems and ordinary glass for the bowl. Rims may be "rolled," giving a slightly fatter edge that will resist chips and subsequent cracking.

Many glasses are designed to be tough enough to survive being dropped on a hard floor, but even the smallest chip will mean that they are weakened and ready to grow cracks. Few glasses survive being dropped regularly—unless you cover the floor of every room in your house with soft carpeting. If you do manage to break a glass, there's really nothing you can do but carefully pick up all the razor-sharp pieces and (ideally) take them to a recycling center. From there, they will be melted down and used to make new glasses, bottles, or windows. Who knows—in a couple of years you might even break the same glass again in another form.

A BLACK MARK

After placing a call to the pizzeria, your attention returns to the fragments of glass everywhere. For some reason, the base has shattered into tiny pieces, leaving the bowl as five or six jagged fragments. You find a paper bag and gloves and begin the work. Five minutes of careful cleaning and vacuuming later, and the pieces of glass are gone. In their place is a horrible red wine stain, soaked into the rug and beginning to dry. You vaguely remember hearing something about pouring white wine on red to make stains disappear, but what if it just wastes more wine and makes it worse? Why is red wine so hard to remove from carpets?

A weed is nothing more than a plant in the wrong place. Similarly, a stain is nothing more than a dye in the wrong place. Bright colors obtained from the juices of certain fruits and berries were once common ingredients in dyes for clothing and carpets. Every time we spill some juice, sauce, or wine, we reinvent another ancient dye.

On the surface, paints and dyes may seem to be very similar substances. They both change the color of materials when applied. The differences are clear when you look a little closer. Paints are like inks: they're colored glues designed to spread and then stick themselves to a surface. In contrast, dyes are designed to soak into a surface, fixing to each individual fiber of the material and changing its color by absorbing some wavelengths of visible light more than others. Different types of dyes use different chemical processes to attach themselves to fibers. Over the years, we've invented many types of fibers and equally many types of dye.

The oldest forms of dye were natural dyes, typically made from plant materials, and occasionally some minerals and animals. Several thousand years ago, most of our fabrics were made from animal hair such as wool, angora, mohair, cashmere, or threads extruded from insects, such as silk. These fibers are all made from protein. (It's the main kind of chemical used in living cells, so it's easy for them to extrude.) Natural dyes are typically acid dyes. The vinegarlike acids (a natural result of using berries or plant materials) enable the molecules of the mixture to attach themselves to protein molecules. They stick to the protein because they happen to have regions on their complicated molecules that have an affinity with the shape of the protein, enabling their individual atoms to form bonds, just like magnets of different polarities sticking together. The molecules also are attracted to water molecules in a similar way, making them soluble. So if you wanted to dye an animal-based fabric or silk, you simply had to soak the material in the water that contained the dye and wait for the molecules to form their bonds.

There are many different types of acid dyes today, some with stronger acids that produce a lovely even dye but that do not form very strong bonds with the fibers, meaning that they can be washed away (they're not colorfast). These are often used for carpets and rugs, which don't usually go through the washing machine. Others may be more colorfast, but because they bond so well to the fabric they may produce a less even color, with too many molecules binding to one area and not enough to another.

Food dyes are also a type of acid dye. Because protein is so common within cells, and because we tend to eat things made from cells (plants and animals), this kind of dye is ideal for changing the appearance of food. Today, most food dyes are artificial, made from ingredients as diverse as coal tar and mashed-up insects. Unfortunately, although they may provide vivid and appealing colors in foods (and cosmetics), many have been linked to cancers in more recent years and have been banned from use. There is no widespread international agreement about which food dyes are safe, with each country often regulating differently for their population. Colorings and dyes are still used in huge numbers of products, especially in products such as carbonated drinks, jams, and candies. It is known that some of the dyes in use today can cause allergies and behavioral problems in some children, so consumers are increasingly choosing "natural" products without colorings and dyes.

There are many other varieties of dye. Some are "fiber reactive," meaning they chemically bond to protein or cellulose molecules of fibers, linking so closely that they become a single colored molecule. Some require extra chemicals to be added to enable them to dissolve in water ("vat dyes," such as the ones used to dye denim). Some require chemicals to behave as a "mordant," fixing to the dye molecules and making them insoluble, and so preventing them from being washed away. Some rely on light to achieve this process, often showing a marked color change as they become fixed in the fabric. Many modern dyes are combinations of many different types of dye, enabling them to stain more than one type of fiber at the same time.

Dyes are not just used to make clothing, carpets, or foods look pretty. Much of modern biology and medicine relies on staining. If you've ever seen stained wood, you'll know that biological cells do not turn one even color in the same way that fibers within fabrics do. Stained wood is attractive because the stain brings out the grain of the wood, darkening some regions much more than others. Biological cells are not like the fibers in cloth. Different cell types have different functions, and cells of each type may produce different proteins inside and outside their cell walls. Fibers within cloth are all made from the same stuff. Use a dye that is attracted to a particular kind of protein, and if the fibers of the cloth are made from that protein, then they will all take on the color. But use the same dye on a group of cells, and only those cells that produce that protein will take on the color, and all the others will be unstained (or stained less). In wood this produces a lovely highlighting of the grain. In biological laboratories, it produces selective staining of certain cells, or even of certain structures inside the cells, depending on the stain. When you're using a microscope to identify how many cells of a particular type there are in a sample, the technique becomes absolutely indispensable. Often the difference may be completely impossible to detect with the naked eye, but by using "markers" to stain specific regions, it becomes possible to identify cell types and structures with ease. Today, robots do much of the staining, and computers are linked to the microscopes to count stained cells automatically, allowing scientists to analyze enormous quantities of microscopic biological features at high speed. The recent advances in DNA sequencing technology rely on staining the DNA molecules in order to analyze their structure and identify individual genes. During the development of new drugs, staining enables us to keep a close eye on different parts of cells to see exactly how the medicine affects them. Forensic scientists also use staining to identify blood or other bodily fluids at crime scenes.

Stains may be enormously valuable in many different areas of science, technology, and industry, but what about your own home? If you do spill red wine on a carpet or rug, what happens next depends on what the fibers of your carpet are made from. Grapes naturally contain tartaric acid (and some vintners—that's winemakers—may even add more tartaric acid if the wine is too sweet). Red wine also contains pigments called anthocyanins, and as the wine ages it develops larger molecules that may react to form colors such as browns, greens, and purples. Although the alcohol can inhibit the staining a little, all the other ingredients can combine to form a very nice natural acid dye that has a strong affinity to protein fibers such as wool and cellulose fibers such as cotton. So if your carpet is made from natural fibers, it will happily pick up the pigments and become stained by the wine. If your carpet is made from a synthetic material such as nylon or polyester, then it is much less likely to take up the stain, so water and soap should just wash it out.

For many years there has been a "home remedy" to remove stubborn red wine stains. Even recommended by wine experts, the trick is to put white wine over the red wine stain and rub it in before the red wine dries. According to those who recommend this solution, the result is that the red wine loses its ability to fix to the fibers and washes out easily. Others recommend adding salt, milk, soda water, vinegar, or detergent.

The difficulty with stain removal arises because the underlying chemistry is not identical. Each variety of wine tastes different because its chemical composition is slightly different—the grapes have grown in different soils and in different climates, and have been treated differently with different additives. Likewise, the fibers in each new rug or item of clothing may have undergone different treatments, including dyeing and bleaching. The result is that each variety of wine may have a slightly different affinity to the different fibers around you, and may react differently when other ingredients are added to try and remove the stain. So, depending on the wine and the fibers, sometimes any of the above remedies may work, and at other times none of them may work.

As a last resort, bleach may remove the pigmentation. Bleach does not wash away a stain; instead, it destroys the parts of the molecule that give the dye its color. The colorful regions of dye molecules are called chromophores and work because the shape of the molecule causes some of the electrons whizzing around the atoms of the molecule to become very excited by certain wavelengths of light. So a red chromophore absorbs all the visible wavelengths except those between about 625 and 750 nanometers, which we perceive as red when they're bounced from the surface and into our eyes. Bleach destroys some or all of those regions of the dye molecules, causing them to reflect more (or all) visible wavelengths and making bleached surfaces appear a different color (or white).

Thankfully, today we have some excellent products available

to avoid staining or to remove stains. Some enable you to shampoo an invisible mixture into the fibers of the carpet, which coats the fibers, keeping those natural proteins locked away from dyes ready to latch on to them. Others are specialized cleaning products designed specifically to break the molecular bonds between the stain and the fiber, while (hopefully) leaving the dye of the carpet untouched. Most of the products are pretty good, but every time you spill a liquid onto a new surface and then try to remove it, you are performing a unique chemistry experiment, with no guarantees that it will be successful. The only real way to avoid stains is simply to avoid spilling liquids of any kind. That's why there are a lot of stains in the world.

Hot and Bothered

You give up on the stain when you hear the doorbell. Looking back at the soapy rug, the stain seems to be gone, but the area you've been scrubbing looks suspiciously paler than the rest of the carpet. You bring the entire pizza, box and all, into the living room and grab a glass of water from the kitchen (opting this time for a plastic cup). On the spur of the moment you decide to spice up the pizza by chopping a couple of chili peppers and adding them to the top. Back in the living room you sprinkle them on, and then start eating the pizza with your fingers. Nice. You begin to relax, the exhaustion of the day hitting you. You tiredly rub your eyes, thinking that you should make it an early night. Suddenly your eyes are burning, feeling hotter and hotter. You didn't wash your hands after handling the chilies. Your eyes are on fire! How can a tiny amount of vegetable juice possibly do this?

Chilies are the fruit of a family of plants known as *capsicum*. Not all capsicum fruits are hot. The (sweet) bell pepper (also known as paprika, capsicum, or simply pepper) is a familiar red, green, yellow, or orange fruit. The color often depends on when it was harvested and how long it matured. A common ingredient in recipes across the globe, bell peppers are no spicier than potatoes. Their mildness is the work of a single gene that prevents the production of a substance called capsaicin in these varieties. In contrast, the spicy members of the family are often called "hot peppers." As well as being smaller, these peppers produce capsaicin, with the concentration of this irritant being highest in the pithy internal areas around the seeds.

Capsaicin (and five other very similar compounds with mostly unpronounceable names: dihydrocapsaicin, nordihydrocapsaicin, homodihydrocapsaicin, homocapsaicin, and nonivamide) is the substance that makes chilies "hot." In reality, chilies aren't at a higher temperature, nor do they increase the temperature of your mouth (eat something spicy and take your temperature, if you don't believe it). Chilies have a "hotness," or more properly, a "piquancy," because the compounds with those complicated names are especially designed to trigger the heat-sensitive cells in your mucous membranes.

In your mouth, eyes, nose, and stomach, and within most other mucus-producing membranes elsewhere, you have special sensory cells. These cells detect touch and temperature, and they send a pain signal to the brain if the heat is too intense. Capsaicin in chilies is designed to irritate those cells, fooling them into behaving as though they are being burned by something very hot. It's an evolutionary trick used by these fruits to prevent mammals from eating them and destroying their seeds. The digestive systems of birds do not affect the seeds, and by no coincidence, birds are immune to the compound and happily eat the fruit, spreading the seeds of chilies in their droppings.

Even cooking chili peppers will release enough capsaicin vapors to irritate the nose and cause sneezing and coughing.

But the piquancy or pungency of chilies is highly variable and depends on the type of chili. Each variety produces slightly different amounts of the five compounds, so some produce an instant irritation, some take several minutes for the irritation to build up to full strength, some are very mild, and some are completely unbearable. The "degree of hotness" was originally measured using something called the Scoville scale. Invented by American chemist Wilbur Scoville in 1912, the scale was based on the feeling experienced by tasters as they tried various dilutions of the chilies. The stronger the chili was, the more it had to be diluted until it no longer felt hot, so the "degree of hotness" was simply the level of dilution required. On this scale, the bell pepper had a score of zero, while pure capsaicin scored 15,000,000 to 17,000,000. Tabasco sauce (based on the tabasco pepper) scored 2,500 to 5,000. Jalapeño peppers scored 2,500 to 8,000. Thai peppers scored between 50,000 and 100,000. But the naga jolokia wins the prize. Also known as bhut jolokia, ghost chili, ghost pepper, or naga morich, it grows in northeast India and Bangladesh and is the hottest known pepper. It scores between 855,000 and 1,041,427. If chilies really did heat your mouth, these would make you breathe fire! Today, the Scoville scale has been replaced with more objective chemical analysis techniques to measure the exact amounts of capsaicin, instead of relying on human tasters.

Eating substances designed to cause pain may seem crazy. But while a European might be in agony after eating a curry containing the spicy naga jolokia, those who are used to the spices develop high tolerances. There is a real change to the sensitivity of the heat-sensitive cells in your mucous membranes if they come into contact with capsaicin regularly. So over the course of many years of eating hotter and hotter dishes every day, people in many countries lose the sensitivity to capsaicin in their mouths (and other regions) and can happily consume quantities that would make some of us cry in pain.

We've had a long time to become acclimatized to chili peppers. For 10,000 years, people in South America have cultivated different varieties and used them in their cooking. But surprisingly, even as recently as 500 years ago, most of the Asian countries that today are famous for their spicy food, such as Thailand, Korea, and India, did not use chilies at all. Europeans traders (who ironically use far fewer chilies in their foods), particularly the Portuguese and Spanish, introduced the fiery spices to Asia. There the climate was perfect for the farmers to grow their own chilies and produce their own fiery varieties, as you can taste for yourself today in any Indian or Thai curry. It has been suggested that chilies became popular in warm climates because the spices inhibited the growth of bacteria—or even disguised the taste of less-than-fresh meats. Although these may have been reasons in the past, in modern times most chilies are eaten because they are a traditional and greatly enjoyed ingredient.

The painful but temporary effect of chilies is so intense that capsaicin has become the active ingredient in "pepper spray." Sprayed directly into the eyes, it can incapacitate a person and is becoming popular with police forces around the world. The score of a pepper spray on the Scoville scale is 2,000,000 to 5,300,000. A tiny amount of capsaicin from relatively mild chilies accidentally rubbed into an eye can cause an unpleasant feeling of heat and pain, but the liquid from a pepper spray can be a thousand times worse. Victims feel intense pain, and may even lose their sight for 10 to 15 minutes. It often takes the body at least 45 minutes to flush the capsaicin (or artificial compound based on capsaicin) from the affected areas, with lots of tears. The symptoms are so intense that in rare cases when used on people with respiratory conditions such as asthma, pepper sprays have caused death—the irritated mucous membranes of the respiratory passages can become so swollen that they block the airway. The use of pepper sprays is heavily restricted in most countries of the world, and they're often classified as restricted weapons. In 1972, the use of pepper sprays was banned for warfare by the Biological Weapons Convention, but it remains legal for use in internal security. As horrible as the symptoms are, the effects are normally temporary and they are almost always less harmful than a bullet.

Thankfully, there may be rather more pleasant uses for capsaicin. Recent research has shown that the spicy compound may be the key to a new kind of anesthetic. Traditional anesthetics block a huge range of neurons, causing loss of pain but also numbness and a loss of feeling, movement, coordination, and mental alertness. The best kind of anesthetic would block only the neurons that are receptive to pain signals and nothing else. In 2007, scientists at Harvard announced that the combination of a compound called QX-314, which blocks electrical activity in neurons, with capsaicin, which opens up channels in the cell membranes of pain receptors, produces a targeted anesthetic that only switches off pain, and nothing else. The new combination of compounds may be the beginning of a revolution in anesthesia, allowing us to eradicate pain wherever it occurs, without the side effects of conventional painkillers.

Capsaicin and the related compounds produced by chilies are not soluble in water, but they do dissolve in oil. It's why you sometimes only feel your mouth heating up toward the end of a meal. While eating, the oils in the food were dissolving the capsaicin and carrying it to your stomach. Once finished, the oils are gone and water-based drinks will not have much affect on the remaining capsaicin inside your mouth. Research has been carried out to find the most effective way of removing the spicy heat from your mouth after a "curry overdose." One study found that although rinsing with water took 11 minutes to reduce the heat, and sugar water or fruit juice was 2 or 3 minutes faster, the outright winner was milk. It's thought that the combination of the protein casein and the fat breaks down the bonds between the capsaicin and the cells of your mouth, and helps flush them away. Milk chocolate and some beans and nuts also have a similar effect.

If you do accidentally chop some chilies and then rub your eyes, you basically have the same options as if you'd eaten something too spicy—the effect is the same for the mucous membranes in your eyes and in your mouth. The safest option, unfortunately, is to let your eyes flush themselves clean with tears. Although your eyes may become red and irritated, they are not being damaged by the capsaicin—they are simply being fooled into behaving as though they were being burned. If the pain is unbearable, flushing your eyes with cold water (keep your eyes open) may help speed up the process of capsaicin removal. If you have enough spare milk, you could even try flushing your eyes with this, although you should flush them with water afterward. Of course, the best remedy is not to rub your eyes with hot pepper juice. When handling any variety of hot pepper, always wash your hands thoroughly with soap and water (not just water, because capsaicin is not soluble in water), or wear gloves. Treat hot peppers as though they contain a dangerous chemical weapon—because they really do.

TAKING IT ALL IN

Your eyes have cleared a bit after being doused with cold water, and you return to the living room. The remains of your pizza are sitting on the wooden floor where you accidentally spilled them in your hurry to flush your eyes. At least you'd only just cleaned the floor. You pick up the pieces, and seeing nothing wrong with them—by some miracle the pieces landed dry side down—you dust them off and continue eating. As you begin the final piece you feel something strange in your mouth. A gritty kind of crunchy texture. You pick the gritty pieces from your mouth and discover they are tiny pieces of glass you must have missed earlier. Taking the slice of pizza closer to the light you realize it is covered in tiny fragments of glass, dust, and a few hairs. But if this piece is so dirty, how bad were the pieces you've just eaten? What happens if you accidentally eat dust, dirt, and glass?

Animals, fish, reptiles, insects, and indeed almost all multicellular animals are designed along very similar principles. We all have a mouth at one end, an anus at the other, and a windy internal tube linking the two. Our ancient predecessors were simple, wormlike organisms, and it shows. We're still nothing more than overcomplicated worms, our internal tubing ornamented with different limbs, organs, and skeletons.

In humans, our internal digestive tubing is anywhere from 16 to 39 feet in length. (The length often depends on the weight of the person rather than the height, with larger people having more tubing inside them to process more food.) All stretched out, we would be very long worms indeed. To make it all fit neatly inside our bodies, most of it is coiled up inside our lower abdomens.

When you consume food, the first thing you do is liquidize it in your mouth. Your teeth mash up as much of the solids as they can, and your saliva helps turn the result into a gloopy sludge. Saliva contains many proteins designed to break down carbohydrates in food, and digestion begins as soon as it comes into contact with the food. You produce around 1½ pints of saliva each day from three large glands (some the size of your nose) behind the throat and under the tongue; these glands squirt the fluid through little valves and into the mouth. You also have minor glands inside your mouth, at the back of your tongue, and even inside your lower lip (that's what the funny little lumps are that you can feel with your tongue). In addition to providing a good coating of mucus in your mouth and down your throat, saliva also contains many minerals and compounds designed to kill some types of bacteria, and even to reduce pain. (It's why we instinctively lick our wounds—our saliva may well clean, protect, reduce pain, and help the wound to heal.)

Once your mouthful of food has been turned into a nice slimy mush, your tongue gathers it together to form a little gooey ball called a bolus. It then pushes the bolus to the back of your throat, muscles close off the tubing to your nose (you don't want to push it up there if you can help it), and the tissues in your throat begin the process of squeezing the bolus down. Known as peristalsis, the smooth muscles in the lining of the tubular walls rhythmically contract, squeezing the food along just as we use our fingers to squeeze out the contents of a tube of toothpaste. Along the way, a flappy lid of cartilage tissue (the epiglottis) hinges down to cover the entrance to your airways (the trachea) and guides the bolus down the tube (the esophagus) toward your stomach. The impulse to breathe is temporarily halted as the food passes by. Then the smooth muscles of the esophagus squeeze the food all the way down. The squeezing process is so effective that it can even push pure liquids into your stomach when you are upside down—pretty important if you are bending down to drink from a stream. Normally it takes about 8 or 9 seconds for the bolus to reach the stomach. (If you pour liquid down your throat, gravity may take it there even faster, but peristalsis usually still takes about 8 or 9 seconds to catch up and let the liquid flow into the stomach.)

Next, a little valve opens (the lower esophageal sphincter, or cardiac sphincter, named because it is situated fairly near the heart) and the food is pushed inside the stomach. When things become a little messy and stomach acid accidentally spills up through this valve, we experience "heartburn"—the unpleasant feeling of stomach acid irritating the lower esophagus.

Inside the stomach, conditions are very different. Just the smell and anticipation of food on its way is enough to begin the secretion of gastric acid in the stomach. It's a highly acidic mix, mainly consisting of hydrochloric acid. Once food is within the stomach, acid production steps up further and the muscles of the stomach wall pulsate, slowly churning the contents like a cement mixer. The acid breaks down proteins in the food, and many other compounds assist in tearing the molecules apart. The acid also helps inhibit the growth of any bacteria or viruses that you have swallowed with the food. After anywhere from 40 minutes to a few hours (depending on what you've eaten), the stomach slowly releases the resulting fluid (known as chyme) into the outgoing tube, called the duodenum. (We don't normally get to see chyme, except when something makes us vomit, in which case the stomach convulsively squirts its contents up and out in an attempt to expel anything nasty that we ate accidentally.)

The duodenum, a tube between 10 and 12 inches long, receives the acidic chyme and triggers the gallbladder to excrete an alkali bile, and the pancreas to produce sodium bicarbonate, in order to neutralize the acid. The gloop is then pushed further along, mixing with yet more enzymes, which further break up the molecules into smaller pieces. Its next destination is the small intestine, a coiled and lengthy tube (several feet long) where nutrients are absorbed. Its wrinkled walls are covered in microscopic, fingerlike protuberances, which dramatically increase the surface area inside the tube. Water, vitamins, minerals, fats, sugars, and all the other useful nutrients are absorbed through the walls and into the blood supply. What's left is then pushed through into the large intestine, or colon, where more than 700 species of bacteria live and eat the gunk that comes through. Bacteria help break down the remaining undigested substances, such as fiber, and produce some vitamins for us in the process. The bacteria emit gas as they eat, which comprises nitrogen and carbon dioxide, with small amounts of methane, hydrogen sulfide, and hydrogen. So the gas you produce is all made by bacteria in your colon feasting on the remains of your food. The bacteria also play an important role in our immune systems. Because they are foreign organisms within us, our immune cells quickly learn to produce antibodies against them, and they prevent them from entering our bloodstream and harming us. There are so many types of bacteria in the colon under controlled conditions that our immune systems are given an excellent chance to learn what the latest designs of bacteria look like. So when a new and nastier variety tries to infect us, cross-reactive antibodies that were originally designed to control the harmless bacteria in our colons can be modified quickly and used to wipe out the new danger. Recent research suggests that the appendix, which is attached to the colon and was once thought to be a useless and vestigial structure, plays an important role here, because it is rich in immune cells. Some scientists have discovered that the appendix can also store a small supply of useful bacteria and help repopulate the colon after illness has flushed away the normal population.

Finally, the remaining vitamins and water are absorbed, and the brown sludge that we call fecal matter (or poop) is compacted over the next few hours. About 20 to 30 hours after eating, the solid waste is finally pushed from the opposite end of our bodies and the process is complete.

Our digestive system is remarkably adept at handling a huge variety of substances, and of course it needs to be. Only in the past few decades have we begun to understand that dirty food and contaminated water will make us ill. For most of the billions of years of our evolutionary history, we've eaten raw or badly cooked foods. We've eaten foods covered in dirt and gravel. We've eaten foods containing hair, feathers, bone, cartilage, seeds, bark, and everything else you can think of. So our bodies are designed to break down and absorb anything that will help keep us alive and simply expel from the other end anything that is indigestible. Eat tiny fragments of grit or glass, and as long as there is nothing sharp enough to perforate our internal tubing, it will just go straight through us. (Normally, if we are foolish enough to put something with sharp edges in our mouths we will feel it and spit it out long before swallowing.) Eat dust, which is likely to comprise fibers from clothing, dirt from outside, and dead skin cells, and what your body cannot absorb it will expel. If we were very unlucky, or very stupid, we could eat something poisonous. But we have excellent senses of taste and smell, and a vomit reflex for exactly this reason. Most common, naturally occurring poisons taste horrible and immediately make us want to spit them out or vomit.

Bacteria and viruses can cause us problems after we eat something dirty, however. These little "germs" are everywhere. They live on our skin, on our dishes, in our beds; they cover our homes (and indeed the world). Most are completely harmless. Many are extremely useful to us, such as the vast populations that live in our colons. And therein lies the problem. Humans and bacteria have evolved to cooperate. We need to be able to introduce useful bacteria into our colons to help us digest foods, so it is not in our interests for our digestive systems to kill all bacteria. A newborn baby must be able to introduce bacteria into its intestine, and adults benefit from replenishing their bacteria now and again, perhaps even deliberately with probiotic yogurts. Unfortunately, once in a while a new breed of bacteria or virus breaks the truce and tries to use the half-open door to infect us. Our colons (and sometimes even our stomachs) are lovely places for them to live, with lots of plentiful food and warmth. The colon even provides a nice passage through which some of the bacteria and viruses can escape, ready to infect another victim.

The result for us is typically a condition known as gastroenteritis. Our bodies react against the infection, increasing our temperature in order to kill off the invader and flushing the intestines with water to wash out the problem bacteria. The result is fever, diarrhea, and sometimes vomiting. If it lasts too long, it can become an extremely serious condition, as the intestine extrudes water instead of absorbing it. Sufferers become dehydrated very quickly, and depending on the severity of the condition, may not be able to absorb water properly by drinking, meaning that they require fluids from an intravenous drip in order to survive. Sufferers also lose essential salts and sugars. Gastroenteritis is highly contagious, and it is so easy for our internal tubes to become infected in this way that hundreds of millions of people worldwide suffer from the condition every year. Even today, the total number of people who die from the condition may be as many as 3 million each year.

Luckily, gastroenteritis is not a new condition, and our bodies are designed to recover quickly. As long as sufferers are kept hydrated and the missing salts and sugars are replenished, in just 2 to 6 days their bodies will have removed the unwelcome visitors from their colons and their amazing digestive systems will be back to normal. If you eat something questionable and experience alarming symptoms, always see a doctor. But remember, we are designed to eat a huge variety of things, including bacteria. The proper development of our immune systems relies on us being exposed to new bacteria every day. It is important that our foods and water supplies are kept entirely separate from and uncontaminated by waste that may have come from the colons of others, so wash your hands after using the bathroom. However, we'll usually be just fine after eating a bit of dusty or gritty food.

SHOCKING

The rain from earlier in the day has returned with a vengeance. You can hear torrential rain falling outside, and perhaps a distant rumble of thunder. Feeling better, even with dusty food in your stomach, you turn on the television to see whether there's anything worth watching. Flicking the channels, you're distracted by a bright flash outside. A loud rumble of thunder follows after less than a second. That sounded close. You look out of the window and another bright flash dazzles you, the thunder causing the windows to shake. At the same time, all the lights go out and the TV becomes black and silent. Heart pounding, you feel your way to a cupboard and find a flashlight, then locate your fuse box. A fuse has been blown. You flick it back on, and the lights come back. Back in the living room, the television remains dark and silent. No matter what you try—even changing the fuse in its plug—the TV set does not work. It's been killed by lightning. But how?

In the heart of a giant thunderstorm, the dazzling flashes of lightning and their accompanying crashes of thunder can be awe-inspiring and frightening natural phenomena. A bolt of lightning is pure electricity sparking across the sky. The power of that electricity may be as much as 120,000 amps at 3,000,000,000 volts, flowing for a few millionths of a second. It's enough power to run a 100-watt lightbulb day and night for several months. Because all that power is concentrated into a huge spark, its heat is hotter than the surface of the sun and is more than enough to turn sand into glass. As air is superheated and blown apart by the lightning, a shock wave expands from the electrical explosion. This wave of compressed air expands out like a ripple, moving at the speed of sound. If the lightning is many miles away, when the shock wave finally reaches our ears it has had a chance to bounce and echo off many other surfaces and so sounds like a long rumble of thunder. If the lightning is overhead, you hear the ear-splitting *crack!* of that initial fearsome electrical explosion followed by the rumble of its echoes coming back. (Another cause of the longer rumble is the fact that some bolts of lightning are several thousand feet long, so the noise from superheating more distant air takes longer to reach your ears than the noise from heating the closer air.) Either way, light travels much faster than sound does, so there's always a gap between seeing the flash and hearing it. The further away the lightning, the bigger the delay between flash and rumble.

At all times, day and night, somewhere on the Earth there is lightning ripping its way across the sky. The remarkable amounts of energy involved are generated inside clouds. There are no batteries or generators involved. All that energy originates from the sun and the rotation of the Earth. Evaporation of water from the oceans causes the formation of clouds—huge expanding bodies of floating water droplets swirling and rising through the atmosphere. As the droplets in the clouds move, some turning to ice, others combining to form larger droplets or breaking up into smaller droplets, something mysterious happens. Some of the particles become more positively charged and others negatively charged. The positively charged particles mostly cluster toward the top of the cloud, and the negatively charged ones gather at the bottom. The more of this charge separation that occurs, the more the cloud becomes charged like a giant battery, with the positive terminal at the top and the negative terminal at the bottom. At the same time, a large positive charge also develops on the ground, the force of the negative charge in the bottom of the cloud pushing away the extra electrons like magnets of the same pole repelling each other.

There are currently at least 12 different theories about why charge separation takes place within large clouds. The most commonly cited reason, that ice crystals rub against one another to create static electricity, may well be true (particles of dust in the cloud from an erupting volcano do exactly this), but it doesn't really explain why the whole cloud separates the charges. When static electricity builds up in a wool sweater, for example, the negative charge is fairly evenly distributed throughout the material. If you touch a door handle you may see a spark, like a little bolt of lightning. But if the sweater were like a cloud, it would be positively charged around your shoulders and negatively charged around your stomach. Every so often sparks would fly from shoulders to stomach. Clearly, that doesn't happen. (When you take off the sweater you may see lots of little sparks and crackles, but this is caused by slight, random variations in charge throughout the material, and charges combining in newly touching folds jumping to other regions with less charge. There is no clear separation of charge as in a cloud.) We're still trying to figure out why charge separation occurs. It seems likely that the cause is partly because smaller ice crystals are blown higher than larger ones, and the smaller ones may somehow have a positive charge. Unfortunately, scientists find it very hard to do experiments on anything as big as a thundercloud, so the phenomenon remains an unsolved mystery at present.

Charge separation creates an imbalance. When it occurs, there are water molecules at the top of the cloud with too few electrons and molecules at the bottom with too many electrons. If you fill a container with high-pressure (or low pressure) gas, beyond a certain pressure the container will fail and the pressure will equalize itself—the force of the higher pressure molecules will overcome the resistance of the container. Likewise, when the negative charge builds up enough in a cloud, eventually the pressure of the voltage becomes high enough to overcome the resistance of the air. When that happens, electrons start to force their way through the air, often proceeding downward in 55-yard steps toward the positively charged ground as they cut negatively charged channels through the air. These "leaders" are pushing electrons as they go, so they are significant electrical currents themselves. At the same time, electrons belonging to the atoms on the highest points on the ground (closest to the cloud) are pushed away, and positively charged "streamers" start to reach up through the air. These are fingers to the sky made from electrical current of many tens or hundreds of amps. When the negatively charged leader from the cloud makes contact with a positively charged streamer from the ground, the circuit is completed and all that pent-up electrical charge can flow in a bolt of lightning. The energy of this "return stroke" is so great that the air is superheated and produces a huge amount of heat and light. (Lightning also flies inside the cloud between the positive and negative regions following the same process.) Because the leader and streamers have carved their ionized channels through the air, it is common for four or five lightning strikes to occur in quick, flickering succession down the same paths. Lightning frequently strikes in the same place twice!

The formation of streamers from the ground is more likely to occur from higher objects (which are closer to the encroaching negative charge) and also from good conductors, such as metal objects (which have plenty of free electrons able to move easily). It's why golfers are frequently hit by lightning—their metal golf clubs or umbrellas may be the highest point in a large open golf course. It's also why you should not take shelter near a tall tree in an electrical storm. The height of a tree can make it more likely to create streamers and attract lightning, and when struck, its sap may explode and injure you. It's also why, if you find yourself in exposed conditions during an electrical storm, the recommended position to take is the "lightning crouch." You should crouch on the balls of your feet with your heels pressed together, preferably wearing rubber-soled shoes, and hug your knees. This way you are low down, but not touching too much of the ground, which might be about to conduct a great deal of electricity. If you feel a tingling sensation and your hairs are standing up, then take the position immediately, because you are in a large electric field and in immediate danger. Otherwise, the best solution is to jump in your car. If struck, the metal body of the car conducts the electricity straight past you to the ground, and you will be fine. (Of course, if you have a convertible or a carbon-fiber sports car, it won't work quite as well.)

The powerful blast of electromagnetic radiation from lightning does more than create a flash and a crack of thunder. It also radiates a quick but very intense electromagnetic field. Just as a radio antenna in an electromagnetic field (radio wave) has an electric current induced in it (which is how radios turn the invisible signal into audible sound), so, too, the electromagnetic burst from lightning can induce significant electric currents in metal objects or wires that are nearby. So although a direct strike from lightning on a power line may produce a significant surge of power, even a lightning strike nearby is enough to induce a power surge because of the electromagnetic field.

Most of our technology is designed to cope with the effects of lightning, with built-in protective circuit breakers designed to "trip" if they detect excessive surges of power. But the behavior of lightning can be unusual. In 5 percent of lightning strikes, the positively charged top of the cloud is blown forward and overhangs the ground. In that case, negative streamers rise from the ground, and positive leaders creep down, until a positive lightning strike occurs. Having much farther to travel to reach the ground, the charge has to build up much more, so positive lightning is five or six times more powerful than ordinary negative lightning. It can also sometimes seem like a "bolt from the blue" because the main bulk of the storm cloud may be some distance away and the skies might appear fairly clear. All that extra power produces a huge electromagnetic pulse, or EMP, which can be strong enough to induce excessive electrical currents to flow in electronic equipment nearby, melting their components and destroying them.

EMPs are more commonly associated with nuclear weapons. The blast from a nuclear detonation produces a huge emission of electromagnetic radiation called gamma rays. These are strong enough to knock electrons from air molecules and cause a large pulse of electricity to travel through any nearby electronic equipment. The cause is slightly different, but the effect is the same— your electronics are fried. The military has developed nuclear weapons for exactly this purpose, which would be deliberately set off in the atmosphere to cause the effect. Special "EMP-hardened" electronics, which use shielding to redirect the induced current away from the delicate components, are now standard for all military applications.

At home, we don't have expensive EMP-shielded electronics. At most, our gadgets have shielding to prevent them from emitting too much radiation so they avoid interfering with other gadgets. Although they may have fuses and circuit breakers to stop the power from entering their components through the wall outlet, they have little or no protection from the EMP of a nearby positive lightning strike. Thankfully, these occurrences are very rare. Modern buildings have lightning conductors to keep the surge away from the interiors, so at home the most common causes of lightning damage are spikes or surges of power caused by a distant strike on a power line. The momentary increase of power is sometimes so quick and so great that before the circuit breakers have a chance to cut the power, it's already made it to any electric device that is switched on—and fried its circuits. If lightning strikes your unprotected home or a tree right next to your home, it's also more likely that the current from the strike will find the power cable and run straight through the wiring of the house. Sometimes a strike this close will spark straight over the circuit breakers, blow all the bulbs from the ceiling, melt all the electrical sockets, and may well start an electrical fire. However, if you live next door to someone who just suffered a lightning strike like this, the EMP from the same strike may have invisibly fried the gadgets in your own home.

Lightning is still full of mysteries and surprises; although we don't know exactly how clouds can make it, we certainly know it's dangerous. Many people die every year from lightning strikes. Always try to avoid being in an exposed location during an electrical storm. When at home, if you are concerned about a fierce electrical storm nearby, power down and unplug important electronic items such as computers to protect them from power surges. If you're unlucky enough to have your equipment fried by an EMP, then your only choice is to replace it.

Pus in Boots

Your feet are tired, so you take off your shoes and socks and massage your toes. You decide to make a hot drink to help you relax. In the kitchen the stove seems fine—the gas lights without a problem—so you boil some water and add a packet of instant hot chocolate, stirring it well. You try to ignore the mess sitting in the sink; you can clean it up in the morning. While the hot chocolate cools down enough to drink, you return to the living room. Perhaps some music would be nice. You have a favorite CD somewhere. As you search for the disc, cup in the other hand, you inadvertently spill some of the hot liquid. It lands on your bare foot, scaldingly hot. Crying out in pain, you put down the cup and hop to the bathroom, putting your foot in the bath and pouring cold water over it. The pain dies down to a dull throbbing, but in minutes you can see the damage: A blister is rising on the skin where the liquid fell.

We have been drinking hot liquids for thousands of years. Tea was drunk in China more than 4,000 years ago, hot chocolate by Mayans more than 2,500 years ago, and coffee was discovered in Ethiopia 1,000 years ago. Apart from the stimulation provided by the ingredients, warm drinks have served several useful purposes. The process of boiling water kills off any harmful bacteria and parasites that might infect our digestive systems. The warm liquid literally heats us up from the inside, stimulating the dilation of blood vessels in the walls of the esophagus and stomach to carry the heat around our bodies, and making us feel more relaxed as a result. But there is also another, less-pleasant side effect of preparing and drinking hot liquids. Boiling water can burn us quite seriously if it touches our skin.

What happens when we're burned? When anything too hot touches our skin for too long, the membranes of the skin cells burst and the cells die. The stronger the heat and the longer it is exposed to our skin, the more it is conducted into our skin and the flesh below, and more cells die. Burns are measured using a scale. A first-degree burn is the mildest. Just the top layer of the outer skin (the epidermis) has been damaged. As those cells die, they release chemical messages that trigger dilation of nearby blood vessels and attract immune cells. The pain receptors in the skin also send their signals to the brain. The area becomes red, swollen, and painful; your body begins the process of cleaning up the dead cells to allow new ones to grow in their place, and also tries to teach your brain a lesson—don't do that again!

A second-degree burn is more serious. Now more cells of the epidermis are destroyed, and some cells in the top of the dermis are also killed. After a few minutes—or a few hours, depending on the severity of the burn—a void forms within the epidermis and lymphatic fluid (not pus) leaks into it. The result is a swelling like a balloon in the skin, which we call a blister, and usually enough pain to make us want to avoid letting anything touch the blistered skin.

Blisters are a design feature of our clever skin. They're an emergency response designed to provide a protective environment rich in immune cells for new skin cells to grow. Generally initiated when the upper layers of the epidermis fail, they protect against any infection that might try to take advantage of the dead outer layer and gain entry into us. Blisters do not separate the epidermis from the dermis; they actually occur within the epidermis itself. They form when a deep layer of the epidermis (known as the stratum spinosum) loses its ability to stick to the layer below, (known as the stratum germinativum, or basal cell layer). This may happen because the cells have become damaged or destroyed through excessive temperature.

A blister may also form when repetitive friction loads are placed on the skin—not just rubbing, but rubbing with pressure. The constant pressure causes tears to form in the stratum spinosum, which will open up to become a void in which lymphatic fluid pools, forming a blister. Just like the friction of your feet causing an old linoleum covering to separate from the floor in wrinkles or puckers, so, too, the friction of ill-fitting shoes can cause the upper layer of skin to tear away from the lower layer.

It's important that blisters occur above the basal cell layer, because this deepest layer of the epidermis is the one that contains all the fast-growing cells that make the layers above. So while the blister forms and provides a protective cushion, the basal cell layer underneath is stimulated into action. When blisters are the result of friction damage, instead of simply growing new layers of skin exactly as they were before, the basal cell layer is also stimulated to do a more thorough job. It grows a much thicker layer of skin, which we call a callus. The result, after about 28 days, when the whole area has regenerated, is a tougher, thicker area at exactly the place where the damage occurred. This is your body's way of protecting you from future harm. The next time the same friction load is experienced on that spot, your skin won't be damaged.

Blisters that form because of second-degree burns perform an important job, and they should be left alone. Many studies have investigated what happens to patients who have blisters that are left intact compared to those that have blisters lanced or drained with a needle. Generally, as soon as the seal of a blister is broken, the likelihood of infection increases, pain is worse, and often healing is slower. Of course, blisters frequently form in exactly the places most likely to receive friction loads or further accidental damage. It is quite common for them to pop, exposing the delicate inner layers of the skin and producing an open wound. Should this happen, it's very important to keep the area clean and preferably covered with a sterile bandage. A popped blister takes longer to heal, and an infected one takes a lot longer.

Third-degree burns are even more serious. Now the heat has been so intense for so long that the epidermis has been charred and destroyed. A blister cannot help here, because the basal cell layer has been killed and damage extends deep into the dermis. Pain may be much less than it would be for a second-degree burn, but this is only because the nerve cells that would send the signals to the brain have also been destroyed by the heat. Often second-degree burns occur around the edges of the third-degree wound, so the injury is far from painless. Blood naturally forms at the site of the wound, and all the body can do is form a scab over the area and try to rebuild the many layers of skin from scratch. Scarring is common after these types of burns, because the body simply creates a kind of generic skin covering to patch the hole. For more severe burns, it cannot match the pigmentation or hairs that should be there, because all those cells were destroyed. Sadly, the process of embryogenic development that made the skin and its follicles, pigments, and pores when we were in the womb is not switched back on again when we're adults, so many original characteristics are lost. This can be made worse if large areas of the skin are burned. Because blood may find it hard to reach the areas and feed the new skin cells as they try to grow, broad, thick, scabbed areas called *eschar* may grow. Sometimes surgery is needed to repair the skin, often utilizing grafts from other parts of the body (slices of skin epidermis taken from a healthy area and moved to cover the area with no skin).

Third-degree burns are often measured in terms of the percentage of the body surface area affected. For example, each leg including the foot counts as 18 percent, an arm counts as 9 percent, the front and back of the torso are each 18 percent, and the head and neck are 9 percent. Anyone with burns covering more than 10 percent (or less on sensitive areas such as the face, hands, or genitals) is considered critical. A large percentage means that the burn becomes more likely to be life threatening as the body's fluids simply leak from the open wounds. Infection is also exceedingly common. And some third-degree burns are worse still. Instead of just charred skin, the flesh below can be cooked or burned away. In devastating cases, even the bone may be charred.

There are many causes of burns. Scalding from hot water is

very common, whether from kettles, radiators, or even bathwater. Fires cause many third-degree burns, because the human body is made from plenty of flammable oils, fats, and proteins, despite the high water content. Breathing hot smoke can produce serious internal burns in the lungs. Acids can eat into our skin and cause chemical burns. Electricity can also cause severe burns as the high current heats up our tissues like the hot wire in a toaster. Those struck by lightning may have only minor burns visible on the surface of their skin, but internally they may have horrible burns following the path of the lightning within them.

Children are particularly susceptible to burns because their skin is more delicate. Just being exposed to water of 150°F for 2 seconds is enough to cause a nasty burn. Burns may also be produced by longer exposure to cooler temperatures; for example, 5 minutes at 120°F will also cause a burn.

If you have been burned, the first step is to remove the source of the burning. Get away from the hot water, put out the fire, and extinguish any smoldering clothes, but *never* remove clothing stuck to the burned skin or you'll simply peel off the skin as well. Wash off any chemicals causing a chemical burn and remove clothing that they may have soaked into. Put the burned area under cold water for long enough to cool it down, but no more. Take care; after a severe burn, even running water has enough force to wash away the skin. Never put butter or oils on a burn; this old "remedy" can be harmful because it traps heat and prevents oxygen from reaching the injury. Don't burst blisters, but try to bandage the area (over clothes, if necessary) with sterile gauze; don't use a Band-Aid, which will adhere to the skin and may tear it off when removed.

A minor first-degree burn will heal on its own. A minor

(coin-size) second-degree burn will also be fine if the blister is left alone. A larger second-degree burn or a third-degree burn requires immediate medical attention, especially if the victim is a child.

Burns will always be a serious danger. The Centers for Disease Control and Prevention report that burns and fires are the fourth most common cause of accidental death, with more than 4,500 of these tragedies occurring each year in the United States. Thankfully, the human body is an amazing piece of engineering, able to repair and regenerate itself, even after some unbelievably serious burns. Make sure all burns are cared for properly, and you'll heal and be as good as new again before you know it. Just leave those blisters alone.

JUMPING TUNES

After carefully applying a little antiseptic cream to your foot, you return to the living room and collapse onto the sofa. At least you found the CD you were looking for. It had been lying on a pile of others that you hadn't gotten around to putting away. You reach over and insert the CD into the machine, then lean back to listen. After 5 minutes of crystal-clear music, the sound suddenly deteriorates into a noise that sounds like hail falling on a tin roof. The music returns briefly, then skips 30 seconds ahead in the song. It then starts repeating the same split second of music continuously, a guitar machine gun with unlimited ammo. You eject the disc and take a look at it. As the light glints over its rainbow silver surface you see a few tiny scratches marring its shiny surface. Surely CDs are supposed to be indestructible. A few scratches shouldn't matter, should they?

The first optical storage discs were created in the early 1970s. Known as laser discs, they were 12 inches in diameter (about the size of vinyl records) and stored video as well as audio data. They went on sale in 1978 and were reasonably successful for the next 20 years, with millions of people worldwide using the read-only format. But their introduction was 2 years after VHS videocassettes, which were a cheaper and more flexible format, allowing consumers to record their own video, so laser discs never reached the same popularity or gained a significant market share. Four years after the laser disc came another competitor, the cheaper and smaller cousin known as the compact disc. It began life as a read-only, audio-only disc. Its small size and unrivaled clarity of sound made it a hit. Before long, CDs had made laser discs, audio cassettes, and vinyl obsolete.

The CD and its parent, the laser disc, both rely on many important inventions. Perhaps the most significant was the laser. Today a familiar part of our lives (laser printers, optical storage, fiber-optic telecommunications, laser pointers), lasers are incredibly important demonstrations of physics in action. A laser is simply a device that produces light. However, unlike an ordinary lightbulb that produces a wide range of different frequencies (which is why the light looks white to our eyes) and pushes light out in all directions (which is why we can light a whole room with a single bulb), a laser is much more specific. Laser light is normally just a single frequency of light, and it is normally pushed out in one focused line. The clue to how a laser works is in its name: Light Amplification by Stimulated Emission of Radiation. It relies on the behavior of atoms when stimulated.

Atoms are the extremely tiny particles that make up all molecules. Proteins, commonly used in living organisms, are comprised of a complex grouping of atoms that are wound up like a ball of string. Water, made from a combination of two hydrogen and one oxygen atom stuck together, has a very simple molecular composition. Substances known as "elements" are made from a single type of atom, such as hydrogen, oxygen, or carbon. Each atom is made up of many protons and neutrons, with electrons whizzing around them like planets orbiting the sun. Different elements simply have different numbers of protons in the middle. Hydrogen only has one; lead has 82. This is known as the atomic number of the element. All atoms of a certain element have the same number of protons, so carbon always has six. However, they may have different numbers of neutrons in the middle—these are known as "isotopes" of the element.

When we say that an atom is "excited," this means that energy has been transferred to the electrons whizzing around those internal protons and neutrons. An electrical charge or light (electromagnetic radiation) jolts the electrons and causes them to zip around with a bit more energy. If the electrons are jolted too hard, though, they'll simply fly away and join another atom, making the first atom more positively charged and the other atom more negatively charged. But if the electron is jolted just a little, it will be pulled away from its normal, comfortable place around the atom. When it bounces back to its normal orbit again, it generates electromagnetic radiation, or light.

The laser exploits these subatomic behaviors in a very precise way. Atoms of a special substance (the lasing medium) are "pumped" using flashes of bright light or electrical current. They then emit their own light at a frequency that depends on how excited they have become. This light is trapped between two little mirrors that bounce it back and forth, further triggering the atoms of the lasing medium to emit light at the same frequency and in the same direction. As more radiation is emitted in the right direction to bounce off the mirrors, the lasing medium produces more radiation in the right direction. Because one of the mirrors is only half silvered, when sufficient light bounces back and forth, it is strong enough to escape through the half-silvered mirror as a straight beam of one frequency of light. Out shines the straight laser light.

Anyone who has seen a CD before will know that the surface of the disc is a shiny silver color. It needs to be shiny because it is read by bouncing laser light from its surface. Information is stored on a compact disc in one very thin and surprisingly long spiral of bumps. If stretched out straight, the spiral on one little disc would be $3\frac{1}{2}$ miles long. The tiny trail of bumps is much too small to see with the naked eye (although it does produce a nice rainbow effect on the silvered aluminum surface). Lasers are essential for CD players because they allow a tiny beam of light to focus on the microscopic silver bumps and be read by a sensor. If the light were not focused in such a thin line, it would hit a larger area of the disc, making it impossible to detect bumps because light would reflect off of several bumps at once. With a laser, and an unbelievably precise motor that pushes the laser into the right place, a CD player can shine a point of light at a bumpy trail and detect each individual bump. When each bump is 0.0005 millimeters wide and each spiral only 0.0016 millimeters apart, you can understand why precision is essential. Even the speed of the disc is changed, slowing down from about 500 to 350 rpm as the laser moves toward the edge to ensure that the same number of bumps pass under the laser per second at all times.

CDs and vinyl records store information in a similar way: a spiral of undulations on a disc is read and turned into audio. The difference is that vinyl records use a wiggling groove cut into their surfaces. As a needle scratches over the surface, the wiggles vibrate the needle, and the vibrations are turned into a tiny electrical signal that is amplified into full-volume audio. So records store music very directly, as analog wiggles in their spiral tracks.

CDs also store information as spirals of undulations in their surfaces, but the information is not analog, it is digital. Instead of wiggles in the track corresponding to wiggles (compressions) in the air, the bumps and spaces on a CD spiral represent 1s and 0s in binary numbers. The audio on a CD is nothing more than millions of numbers, all written in binary (for example, 4 is written 00100000 and 37 is written 10100100 in binary). The numbers describe the shape of the sound wave every 0.000023 seconds (that's 44,100 samples each second for left and right channels). Those numbers are simply saying, "Up a bit, now down, now up a little more, now down a lot," which, when converted using a digital-to-analog converter, produces a nice wobbly waveform. This is amplified and pushed to your speakers or headphones, which then vibrate the air exactly according to that waveform and produce sound.

Using numbers to define waveforms is not perfect; it will only ever be an approximation. If there are not enough numbers to define a tiny change in the waveform, or if the sampling rate is too slow (if the waveform changes significantly in less than 0.000023 seconds), or if the "smoothing" process (to change the stepped wave defined by the numbers back into a smooth wave) introduces unwanted artifacts, the recorded sound will not be quite the same as the original. But you'd need some exceedingly good speakers and excellent hearing to detect the difference.

The binary numbers on a CD don't only define numbers.

Every number is stretched with extra binary 1s and 0s to ensure that there are never long gaps between bumps and to help the computer make sense of what it is seeing with its laser vision. The numbers are also interlaced out of order, so an entire revolution is read in order to figure out the next chunk of audio waveform. The interlacing makes sure that a scratch that is wide enough to distort the reading of many bumps in succession will not be disrupting several numbers in succession and causing an audible glitch. Instead, a series of numbers from completely different parts of the waveform will be disrupted, making the corruption inaudible to our ears. As if this weren't enough, there are also error correction components added to the numbers, which the computer uses to check that the numbers all make sense. One simple example of error correction would be to follow a number with a second number that says how many 1s there were supposed to be in the previous number. So 10100100 (37) would be followed by 110 (3). The error correction is sufficiently clever that the computer can figure out simple mistakes in reading and correct the numbers on the fly.

The result of the extraordinary precision of laser reading and error correcting digital-to-analog converters is pure crystal-clear sound at all frequencies audible to the human ear. But as good as the technology is, it can only cope with CDs that are well cared for. Those little bumps are read by bouncing light from them. Although a tough layer of clear plastic protects the aluminum surface, dirt, oil, scratches, or even dust will affect its optical characteristics. However, what most people don't realize is that the most delicate side of the CD is the side with the label. CDs are created from the back—the layer of bumpy aluminum is pressed onto the clear plastic, then a thin layer of acrylic is sprayed on, then the label is printed. Although scratches on the clear plastic side may distort the light from the laser, scratches on the label side can go through the layer of acrylic and actually damage the aluminum layer, destroying the little bumps that define those essential binary numbers.

If your CD is not playing correctly, this means that the laser vision of the reading computer can no longer make sense of what it sees. It may interpret some of the scratches as numbers and try to play them, resulting in hissing or crackling noises. The machine may even be fooled into reading the same circle of data over and over again instead of following the outward spiral, causing that familiar "skipping" sound.

CDs can become damaged when they're not kept in their protective cases, when they're carelessly handled, or when they're bounced around inside your car stereo. If minor scratches are visible on the clear plastic side, it is possible to polish them out using metal polish (always polish at right angles to the spiral, from the middle to the edge, to avoid creating your own confusing spiral pattern of polish). But if the scratch is on the label side, the CD is irretrievably ruined. You cannot put back the little bumps of aluminum once they've been scratched off.

Scratches can and do mess up CDs. Look at a CD jewel case and you'll see how it carefully holds the surface of the CD in the air and away from anything that might scratch it. You should try to do the same. Always hold a CD by its edges, and always keep it safe in its case. It will live as long as you do, if you take good care of it.

Chewing It Over

At times like this, there's only one solution. You return to the kitchen, open the fridge, and pull out a bakery box. You cut a generous slice of rich, gooey, chocolate cake and put it on a plate. It smells divine. To keep from making a mess with the creamy, runny chocolate, you find a fork to eat it with—no more spills today. You take a bite, letting the chocolate melt in your mouth. It's delicious. Each forkful is a delight. Before you know it, you're putting the last little piece in your mouth. Perhaps another slice. . . . But somehow you accidentally bite down on the fork. There's a horrible jarring feeling, a strange throbbing in your front tooth, and then your tongue feels something hard and sharp in your mouth. You look in the mirror. A piece of your front tooth has just broken off.

Humans are designed to be omnivores. Our digestive systems are well equipped to process plant material and meat. It's one reason why we are so successful and have spread across the face of the planet. We can eat a lot of the things that live around us. One important reason why we can eat and digest such a variety of foods is the range of teeth we have.

At the very front of our mouths we have flat cutting teeth called incisors, which move together a little like the flat blades of scissors to cut through larger foods and separate a bite-size chunk. We can also use these teeth a little like rodents and gnaw through tougher foods. Perhaps the most extreme adaptation of incisors is found in elephants, whose tusks are hugely overgrown and pointy incisors, and in narwhals, which have a single incisor adapted into a unicornlike horn.

On either side of our incisors we have canine teeth, named after dogs and their particularly good, long, pointy examples. In humans, these teeth have longer roots than the incisors, making them stronger, and they usually protrude slightly beyond the incisors. Canine teeth (also sometimes known as "eyeteeth" and "stomach teeth") are not meant for cutting; they are used to tear the flesh of animals. Carnivores, which eat only meat, normally have much more impressive canine teeth (or fangs) compared to their other teeth. One of the best examples of canines was in the now-extinct saber-toothed cat *Smilodon fatalis*, which had fangs the size of large kitchen knives. Research has shown that the cat probably killed its large prey with a quick tearing bite to the throat; surprisingly, its bite was much less powerful than the modern-day lion, which kills by grabbing the throat of its prey and holding on despite the struggling.

The next teeth along in our mouths are the premolars, followed by several sets of molars. These teeth are lumpy grinding teeth. The premolars resemble the canines a little more, and so they are able to help with some tearing, if necessary. The molars are designed to lock together with only small gaps between them when our jaws are closed. Their lumpy and sharp surfaces mash up all foods pushed between them by our tongues. (Even the English word *molar* derives from the Latin *mola*, meaning "millstone.") The chewing action is assisted by our jaws making slight circular motions instead of simply moving up and down, a process that grinds the food into tiny pieces that are then mushed together by our saliva and made ready to swallow. These teeth have to be firmly anchored into our jaws, because they must withstand the same kinds of forces that the jaws of pliers endure. To help them stay in place they have not one, but two or three long roots. (The roots of all teeth are long—typically twice as long as the length of the tooth visible in our mouths—but they are conical in shape, nothing like tree roots.) Molars are very common in animals that eat plant material, such as cows and horses. Elephants have extraordinary molars, many of which are bigger than a fist, which give them the ability to chew up bark and wood.

When biting, tearing, and chewing food, teeth must withstand tremendous pressure and cannot be worn down from chewing tough plant or bony materials. As our species evolved, we needed these amazingly well-shaped structures to be as hard as stone, and yet to be able to act like living structures. We needed them to grow from nothing, and to embed themselves securely in the bone of our jaws. We needed nerves within them so that we had some feeling of what we were chewing. Ideally, we would like them to repair themselves if damaged or even replace themselves. How could organisms create such a living stone inside themselves?

Astonishingly, evolution managed to figure it all out. Our teeth are indeed as hard as (some kinds of) stone. To be more precise, they're much harder than gold, silver, and copper, harder than most types of iron, and very nearly as hard as window glass and steel. Stones vary in hardness, depending on the minerals that comprise them. Hydroxylapatite (made from calcium and a few other elements) is one such mineral, naturally occurring as partially translucent crystals in rock. Hydroxylapatite is also the main component of tooth enamel, giving our teeth their hardness and brittleness. We really do have stones in our mouths.

But teeth are much more than solid lumps of rock. If they were, they would be so brittle that they would crack into pieces every time we bit down on something hard. So each tooth only has a couple of millimeters of enamel to provide the outer coating on the surface above the gum. Underneath is a softer layer called dentin, which provides a more resilient and shock-absorbing substance for the tooth. Unlike the superhard enamel, only 70 percent of dentin is hydroxylapatite; the rest is water and proteins (mostly collagen). Dentin has an amazingly complex structure, with trillions of tiny tubes radiating from the inner core out to reach the enamel. These help provide strength and conduct sensation inward toward the nerve. Within the gum, surrounding the dentin surface of the root, is a similar mixture known as cementum, which has a higher concentration of water and collagen. It provides an excellent surface from which collagen fibers tie the root of the tooth onto the nearby bone of the jaw. Although the fibers are very short, their natural elasticity provides a slight cushioning effect, allowing teeth to move slightly rather than break themselves or the jaw bone.

Within the core of the tooth is the pulp. It may just sound like a mess, but the tooth pulp is a complex organ in its own right, supplied by blood from a hole at the bottom of the root, and also filled with nerves and specialist cells for producing dentin.

There are also immune cells lying in wait, just in case the enamel and dentin above should fail and expose the pulp to bacterial infection.

Twenty of these amazing structures grow in our jaws, and then after a few years they are reabsorbed, discarding the outer enamel shells to leave room for up to 32 more to replace them. It's a sensible strategy from an evolutionary perspective. We spent most of our history without toothpaste, so it's a good idea to replace teeth after a while. But the second set of teeth only needed to last until we reached our thirties; a few thousand years ago, life expectancy was less than 40 years for most of us. One or two rotten teeth falling out didn't matter so much, and our diets contained few sugar-rich foods (unlike today), so our teeth lasted as long as we needed them to. There's no particular reason why we couldn't have more sets of teeth in our lives—other animals do. The incisors of rodents never stop growing, to compensate for the huge amount of wear caused by their constant gnawing. Sharks just keep growing row after row of new jagged teeth because their violent feeding often results in teeth being lost. Humans grow only two sets because that's all we ever used to need.

The ability to grow stone in our mouths is a remarkable feat, when you think about it. Cells in our jaws form tiny buds, which slowly grow bigger, building the different layers of the tooth and extruding the calcium-based minerals in exactly the right places. As they form, bone in the jaw forms around them and cartilage "ropes" linking bone to root slowly push the tooth upward. Even once a tooth is fully developed and surrounded by bone, it continues to develop and adjust itself. Place constant pressure on the tooth and the bone socket reshapes itself, absorbing anything in the way and developing new bone to fill any gaps. When braces are placed around teeth, this is exactly what happens. Your teeth are pushed into a different alignment and your jaw rebuilds the bone around them to lock them into place.

Even the stonelike substance of our teeth is under constant repair. New dentin is constantly produced from within, and the outer, superhard enamel layer is replaced as well. Within our saliva is exactly the right mix of calcium compounds to enable remineralization. So although acids may soften or even erode away the enamel, our saliva helps harden the surface and make new deposits. Our teeth can repair themselves!

It's a good thing, because in modern times our diets have become enormously high in sugars. There are always plenty of bacteria in our mouths ready to feast on the sugary residues left behind in the crevices of teeth and gums. Unfortunately, these bacteria (which form that white gooey coating that we call plaque) produce acidic waste products that eat away our precious enamel—and the dentin underneath. This can be a real problem, because once a cavity has formed in a tooth, it can become a comfortable hole in which bacteria can live. The longer they live there, the more their acid may tunnel deeper into the tooth, causing damage. Once a patch of enamel is removed to expose the dentin, you have "sensitive teeth." Those little tubes within the dentin are now exposed to the inside of your mouth and they conduct temperature all too efficiently into the nerves within the pulp. If enough dentin is eaten away, the nerves begin to feel pain. In the worst case, even the pulp may become infected and the entire tooth may need to be removed before it simply dies and disintegrates. It's not a pleasant feeling to have infected teeth. If you've ever had a toothache, you know exactly what it feels like when the nerves of a tooth become agitated.

Luckily, we have toothpastes to restore the balance. These gooey pastes comprise several useful ingredients: an abrasive powder to help scour away the bacteria, sometimes an antibacterial agent to kill some of the bacteria, perhaps a whitening agent to make the teeth appear whiter, and even some compounds designed to fill in the little tubes in exposed dentin and prevent the conduction of heat and cold to the nerves from being so intense. But the most important ingredient is fluoride—a compound that reacts with the calcium in saliva and helps remineralize enamel. It forms a slightly different compound called fluorapatite, instead of the natural hydroxylapatite, but this is a good thing. New enamel made from fluorapatite is just as tough, but it is slightly more resistant to erosion from acids. This is why all good toothpastes should contain fluoride—it helps our teeth rebuild themselves and makes them harder.

Because teeth are good at keeping themselves healthy, the best thing their owners can do is keep them clean, give them a nice dose of fluoride, and let them do the rest. Dentistry work is often damaging to teeth, involving significant drilling and loss of enamel and dentin; researchers recommend that restorative work (fillings) should only be performed on larger cavities. You may not always see the effects of remineralization on the surface of your teeth because it is slow and subtle, but if you have tartar or calculus deposits on your teeth, you are seeing one side effect of the process. Tartar is mineralized plaque—fossilized bacteria, if you like.

Our teeth become softer after eating sugary foods or drinking acidic juices and sodas. It is at these times that cleaning with an abrasive toothpaste may actually scrub away enamel rather than help rebuild it. Research has shown that after exposure to very acidic conditions it takes at least an hour for our saliva to partially harden the surface again and 6 hours for it to be back to full strength. But even when at maximum hardness, enamel is a naturally brittle substance, so it is possible to chip a piece off, or even break a tooth in half, if you are careless and bite too hard on something tougher than your tooth. A minor chip in the enamel will probably not hurt beyond a feeling of sensitivity because the dentin is exposed. It's not a serious injury, and a new layer of enamel will be deposited as long as you keep it clean. A more serious crack or split will require a trip to the dentist and may even result in a cap, a crown, or an extraction. Dentistry is very advanced these days and even a chip can be covered with special veneers to make the tooth look perfect again. But rather than relying on artificial fillings or substances glued onto the teeth, the best solution is to help them look after themselves. Flossing removes the bacteria between the teeth. Toothpaste with fluoride will keep them clean and allow them to remineralize. And watch what you bite into!

PATIENCE AND PAIN

It's been a long day and you still feel on edge. Perhaps a relaxing hot bath will help prepare you for sleep. You go to the bathroom and turn on the water, then leave it to fill the tub while you put your clothes in the hamper. After the day's events your outfit is in need of a serious cleaning, as are you. You sit on your bed for a few moments, recalling the litany of today's mishaps. The sounds of splashing snaps you out of your reverie—the water must have filled the bath by now. You make a quick dash to the bathroom, but in your haste you don't step very carefully. Your toe thuds against the side of the tub. For a split second you think it's fine, but then a sharp pain shoots up your leg. The sharp pain quickly fades, to be replaced by a throbbing ache, which slowly increases as though its volume is being turned up. It hurts enough to make you sit down. You're sure it's not broken, but why does it have to hurt like this?

It's hard to grow up without accidentally hitting an elbow, head, or toe against something now and again. The painful result is a reminder that we need to take more care to avoid damaging our bodies. Interestingly, there are some people who are born with a malfunction in a critical gene that prevents pain signals from ever reaching their brains. They grow up without any idea of the feeling of pain, and they often cause serious harm to themselves or even kill themselves accidentally.

The perception of pain is so fundamental to our survival that it affects our brains in profound ways. There is not one single pain center; instead, our entire brain lights up like a Christmas tree when pain is perceived. In the short term, we are immediately prompted to protect the painful area, to remove it from the source of the pain, and often to cease all use of the affected area while we examine it. In the longer term, our subconscious behavior is altered. If we hit our head on a specific low beam or handle, next time we'll remember to duck. An experience of pain that lasts for long, continuous periods (chronic pain) can even affect our emotions and attitudes. We may develop depression and become less active. Alternatively, a severe experience of pain, and a conscious awareness of exactly what led to that pain, may result in the development of an aversion to anything resembling the cause. We call that aversion fear. It may become a long-term subconscious memory that lasts far longer than our memory of the event that caused the aversion. You may no longer remember the time you fell off a high wall and painfully twisted your ankle as a child, but your fear of heights could still be with you.

We don't always perceive pain. Even when nerve cells send us pain signals, sometimes the larger priority is to run away from danger, rather than drop to the ground in agony. So there are regions of the brain that actively inhibit our perception of pain, sometimes for just a few minutes, sometimes for several days. But there are also areas of the brain that do the reverse, and make us hypersensitive to pain. When we're safe and recovering, such heightened sensations may, for example, encourage us to avoid using the painful part while it heals.

Astonishingly, there used to be considerable confusion about when we first begin to experience pain. A hundred years ago it was widely accepted that newborn babies simply did not perceive pain at all, because their brains had not yet developed sufficiently. Although it seems cruel by today's standards, for decades many "pinprick" experiments were conducted on sleeping infants in attempts to understand the onset of pain perception. Much confusion was caused in those early experiments by the seeming lack of sensitivity of babies right after birth—which turned out to be because the mothers had been given painkilling drugs while giving birth, and the babies received a dose via their umbilical cords. Today (as anyone with children can affirm), it is well understood that a baby in pain will show clear discomfort. Crying, wriggling, fisting, and large muscle movements, accompanied by clear respiratory and hormonal changes and erratic sleep, are all signs of pain. But those early scientifically flawed experiments sadly resulted in a culture that disregarded the pain of babies for much too long. Until recently, even major operations on premature babies were performed without any anesthetic at all. In 1985, a mother made headlines by explaining the routine operation that was performed in a specialized hospital in Washington, D.C., on her premature baby. He had incisions cut in both sides of his neck, another in his right chest, and another from his breastbone around to his backbone; his ribs were pried apart; and an extra artery near his heart was tied off. Another incision was cut in his left side for a chest tube. The baby was awake and conscious; the only drugs provided were to paralyze him. Although the little boy may not have remembered such experiences, the emotional traumas induced in his young brain were simply unknown. Thankfully, most modern medicine does now consider the perception of pain by babies, and this kind of treatment is a lesson from the history books.

Our brains experience pain throughout our lives, but despite its huge significance to us, its source is simply a few little signals from some tiny nerve cells. These cells are no more special than those that signal temperature or touch, but our brains are designed to treat them differently. Pain receptors, or nociceptors, may use fairly ordinary sensors, but they're wired up to the alarm bells in our heads.

The "wiring" in the human body is called the nervous system. Our brain and spinal column are known as the central nervous system. All the other nerves are known collectively as the peripheral nervous system. Like all cells, nerve cells (whether the neurons in our brain or the sensory nerves in our skin) are living chemical factories that are provided with energy by the blood supply and perform their specific jobs by producing the right kinds of proteins at the right times. Nerve cells make use of some pretty ingenious chemistry to alter their own electrostatic charge to produce little pulses of electricity. They sometimes have enormously long "wires" connected into them like the roots of a tree (dendrites) and a wire leading out (the axon). In the brain, a mixture of chemical and electrical signals produces all the thoughts and memories we will ever have. The output of little electrical pulses, through the spinal column and into our muscles, enables us to move. The input of little electrical pulses from the sensory nerves, through the spinal column, and into our brain enable us to sense everything.

To sense pain, we have nociceptors throughout our skin and

on the surfaces of ligaments, tendons, bones, blood vessels, and even other nerves. We also have some (but far fewer) pain receptors within body cavities and internal organs. The different numbers and locations of the receptors produce different feelings of pain. In the skin, where we have the highest density of receptors, we feel cutaneous pain—a sharp, immediate, and easy-to-locate sensation. In areas such as the blood vessels, tendons, and bones, we feel somatic pain—a longer-lasting dull pain that does not have such an obvious location. In the internal organs, we feel a visceral pain—an ache that is extremely hard to locate and is sometimes felt in a completely different area from where it actually originates.

There are no nociceptors at all in the brain, despite the fact that it is full of neurons. When you feel a headache, you're actually feeling the nociceptors in the membrane and blood vessels surrounding the brain, not within it. There is perhaps little reason to have pain receptors inside the brain—it's not something you can rest by using less, it doesn't really repair itself very well if damaged (in fact you'll probably die without medical attention), and the chances are that if your skull has been damaged enough to damage your brain, you're feeling more than enough pain already.

The nerve cells that respond to pain do not send signals if they are damaged themselves. They can't—they've been damaged. Instead, they have little sensors that respond to chemical signals produced by damaged tissue nearby. When other cells die unnaturally, they emit protein signals such as histamines and bradykinins, which trigger a chemical change in the pain receptor cells. Additionally, extreme temperatures or excessive forces (caused perhaps by tearing) trigger the cells. Like the neurons in our brains, the nerve cells then send a little electric signal up their long "wires."

Just like the wires in your home, the wiring of nerves is made from bundles of cables (axons) surrounded by a sleeve or sheath to insulate them. In your body that sheath is made from different substances, depending on the nerves. The fastest nerves are quick because they have a sheath made from myelin, which helps conduct the electrical pulse along at a much faster pace. Our best nerves can move the signal at about 400 feet a second, so our brain receives the first signal from a stubbed toe just over 100th of a second after the event. But some nerves, which don't have the special myelin sheath, respond much more slowly. Called C-fibers, these may propagate the signal at only 1½ feet a second (the electrical charge travels because of the movement of ions, not electrons). So a signal from our toe may take more than a second or two to reach our brain from these nerves!

This is the reason why stubbing your toe causes such a strange and noticeable delay between the damage and the sensation. In just over 100th of a second, you will feel the pressure of the impact and perhaps an initial sharp pain if you managed to damage the skin (perhaps by hitting the toenail). But then you may have a couple of seconds to wait before the aching pain from the internal blood vessels and bone reaches your brain. The damage was all done at the same time, but it just takes different amounts of time for the different nerves to tell your brain about it.

It all makes sense when you understand how you are wired inside. Many of the fastest-transmitting nerves are on the skin, to enable us to react very quickly before serious internal damage is done. Some nerves are even wired via the spinal column directly to certain muscles, bypassing our brain altogether. These give us superfast reflexes, making us snatch our hand away from fire before our brain even realizes what's going on. The slower, unmyelinated nerves are mostly reserved for those long-lasting, dull, aching pains. These receptors don't need to be fast, because the damage is clearly already done if we've hurt something inside ourselves. They provide a nice, long reminder that we're damaged, telling us to take it easy while our body repairs the mess.

It's not much comfort if you are suffering, but pain caused by tissue damage is there for a reason. Pain is a perception designed to be unpleasant. Without pain, we'd never learn how to take care of ourselves properly and would damage or kill ourselves far too easily. So we suffer now and again and, hopefully, learn because of it.

- 39 -

EUREKA!

Still sitting on the edge of the bath, you realize that the water level is now very high. You reach over and turn off the faucet. It's a tricky procedure with a a broken finger, a stubbed toe, a burned foot, and a pulled muscle in your arm. You feel as though you've fallen down the stairs. As you lean over you remember slipping on the tiled floor this morning. Perhaps it's déjà vu, for at that moment your hand slips and you fall back into the full bathtub. It's actually a nice feeling of warmth. You're floating in the deep water, feeling light and relaxed, a pleasant ending to an exhausting day. But when you look around, you see that water has overflowed all over the bathroom floor. Surely if you're floating, the level of the water in the tub shouldn't rise that dramatically—should it?

That famous moment, about 2,250 years ago, when Archimedes was taking a bath (and no doubt being anointed with oils by his servants) has become a legend. This eminent mathematician had been asked by Hiero II, the king of Syracuse, to figure out a way to detect whether a gold crown was pure or not. Archimedes realized while in the bath that his body was displacing an amount of water that corresponded to his volume. The larger the object immersed in the bath, the more the water level rose. Since the impure metal of the fake crown probably weighed less than one made of solid gold, he now had a method to determine the density of the metals. All he had to do was measure exactly how much water was displaced by the crown in question, and how heavy the crown was, and divide weight by volume to discover how dense the metal was (how much mass per unit volume). Then he could do the same with a lump of gold, dividing its weight by its volume to discover the density of the valuable metal. If the density of the crown differed from the density of the pure gold, then the crown could not be made from pure gold.

Archimedes was so excited by this revelation that he jumped from his bath and ran down the streets of Syracuse, shouting, "I've found it! I've found it!" which in ancient Greek sounded like, "Eureka! Eureka!"

It's a nice story, but it's highly unlikely to be true. Archimedes was an accomplished mathematician and inventor, who wrote many books (or parchments, as they were in those days) detailing his discoveries. He never wrote about this incident, nor did any other Roman writers who lived at the time. Instead, the story was first written 200 years after the death of Archimedes by a Roman architect called Vitruvius. Perhaps Vitruvius read the accounts about bathing written by of one of Archimedes' contemporaries, Plutarch:

> "Oftimes Archimedes' servants got him against his will
> to the baths, to wash and anoint him, and yet being
> there, he would ever be drawing out of the geometrical
> figures, even in the very embers of the chimney. And

while they were anointing of him with oils and sweet
savours, with his fingers he drew lines upon his naked
body, so far was he taken from himself, and brought into
ecstasy or trance, with the delight he had in the study of
geometry."

So it is clear that while Archimedes was a famous mathematician, he didn't actually like taking a bath very often, and probably never jumped out and ran around the streets of his home, shouting. Vitruvius almost certainly made the whole thing up.

Archimedes was unlikely to be so pleased with the idea of water displacement and density because he was a very practical early scientist. He probably knew that the displacement of water would indeed be the same volume as an object placed into the water, but if you tried to measure the displacement with enough precision to distinguish the densities of metals, the distortions caused by the surface tension of water made the computations very difficult. Light objects are partially supported by the surface tension; for heavy objects, the way the water sticks to the side of glass containers makes it hard to measure the tiny, tiny differences you'd need to find. Even measuring weights accurately enough would have been exceedingly difficult.

Archimedes probably knew these things because he'd written a two-volume book on buoyancy, and he was the first person ever to do so. Today, the Archimedes' Principle is named after him because of his important ancient work. Think of it like a law of nature that says: "When a solid body is partially or completely immersed in water, the apparent loss in weight will be equal to the weight of the displaced liquid." It's a hugely important principle, because it explains why things float (or sink) in liquids.

We know intuitively that some things float and others don't—push a light piece of foam under water and you can feel the force it exerts on your hands as it tries to rise back up to the surface. Hold a brick under water and you will feel that it wants to sink. Its weight exerts a downward force on your hands. But compare the weight of that brick when holding it in the air with its weight when holding it under water, and you will notice Archimedes' Principle: it does not feel quite so heavy when under water. Even though both the piece of foam and the brick are being pulled downward by the same gravitational force of the Earth, some-how their interaction with the water makes the foam rise in the opposite direction to gravity and the brick to have less force pulling it downward.

It all makes sense when you think about it on an atomic level. For its size, foam doesn't have many atoms. It's mostly made up of air trapped in bubbles. So foam is a little more dense than air, but much less dense than water. There are far more atoms in the same volume of water compared to the foam. When you push a piece of foam under water, all the atoms of the water are still being pulled downward by Earth's gravity. But there are more atoms in the water than there are in the foam, so the water experiences a stronger pull (it's heavier). As the atoms are being pulled downward and the foam experiences less of a pull (it's lighter), there is only one direction it can go: in the opposite direction of the water. (You'd see the same thing if you filled a cup with little polystyrene pieces and glass marbles, then shook it. All the marbles would sink to the bottom and the polystyrene pieces would be pushed to the top.) The force exerted by the heavier liquid on the lighter objects submerged in that liquid is known as buoyancy.

Place a heavier object, such as a brick, into water, and the reverse happens. Now there are more atoms in the same space compared to water, so the brick experiences more downward force than the water does (the brick is heavier). As it sinks, the water is forced out of the way and has to go upward. But forcing water upward takes some effort, because water has a significant weight itself. So the water atoms resist being pushed out of the way in proportion to how many of them are being pushed. As they resist, they push in the opposite direction of the falling motion of the brick, so they make the brick fall slower. In effect, the weight of the brick is reduced in proportion to the number of water atoms being displaced.

The same effect happens in air as well, but air happens to be much less dense than water. That's why water can only manage to float in air for short amounts of time as tiny droplets in clouds before turning into rain. It's also why the piece of foam may float to the surface of the water, but will not float beyond the water and up into the air—it's lighter than water but heavier than air.

We exploit the principles of buoyancy in every boat and ship ever made. Sometimes we use buoyancy to achieve the seemingly impossible. For example, some giant cruise ships weigh more than 50,000 tons. But that's nothing compared to the massive oil tankers that cross our seas every day. These can be as heavy as 650,000 tons when full of oil. Clearly, this much weight would sink like a stone if the density of the vessel were the same as a stone. So the trick is to make these ships *big*. The heaviest ship was also the largest ship, at 1,504 feet in length and 226 feet in width. Even though her hull was made of many layers of thick steel, the huge size meant that the average density was less than that of the seawater outside. That's all you need to create enough buoyancy to float, and so even these monsters of the seas float just as easily as a toy boat in your bathtub.

Buoyancy relies on enough volume to ensure that the average density is less than that of water. But problems arise if that volume changes. For example, if the pressure exerted on a submerged object is enough to crush the object and reduce its volume, then suddenly its average density increases, and its buoyancy is reduced. It's extremely important for a submarine to minimize this kind of compression of its hull, so its metal shape is made circular in cross-section to allow it to shrink a little but not bend and suddenly crush inward like a tin can. Submarines are perhaps the only form of boat that has complete control of its own buoyancy. Because they can't adjust their volumes, they adjust their average densities instead by storing compressed air. When they want more buoyancy, they release the pressurized air into special ballast tanks, forcing out the water in them. With more air in the same volume, the average density of the vessel is reduced, so the seawater pushes the submarine upward.

When the buoyancy of a submerged object exactly balances the force of gravity, the object is neutrally buoyant and floats exactly as if it were experiencing zero gravity. For this reason, special "neutral buoyancy facilities" are used to train astronauts before they go into space. Identical-looking and -behaving versions of their space suits and all equipment are constructed and carefully made neutrally buoyant. The astronauts then spend many hours submerged in the giant pools, learning how to operate the equipment and complete their missions.

The human body tends to be naturally quite buoyant, because the density of oils and fats is lower than the density of water, and we have fatty deposits under our skin. Those of us who possess a little more of that fat will float better for this reason. Water with more salt in it has a greater density, so we all float better in saltwater. We can also adjust our buoyancy by holding more or less air in our lungs, just like a submarine. When we swim, proper breathing helps power our movements, but also helps keep us buoyant. The whole idea of buoyancy and floating is so important that it's perhaps a little sad that Archimedes may be remembered more for something that never happened than for the Archimedes' Principle, which is as fundamental to science and technology today as it was more than 2,000 years ago. So the next time you float in a bath after a long and tiring day, spare this ancient scientist a thought.

Selected Bibliography

Note: For space considerations, this is an abridged version of the bibliography. Interested readers can download the complete bibliography from the author's Web site at www.peterjbentley.com

Chapter 1 (sleeping through alarm)

Blackmore, Susan. "Lucid Dreaming: Awake in Your Sleep?" *Skeptical Inquirer* 15 (1991): 362–70.

Crick, F., and G. Mitchinson. "The Function of Dream Sleep." *Nature* 304 (1983): 111–114.

Rock, Andrea. *The Mind at Night: The New Science of How and Why We Dream.* New York: Basic Books, 2004.

Van de Castle, Robert L. *Our Dreaming Mind.* New York: Ballantine Books, 1994.

Watanabe, Tsuneo. "Lucid Dreaming: Its Experimental Proof and Psychological Conditions." *Journal of International Society of Life Information Science* 21, no. 1 (2003): 159–62.

Chapter 2 (slipping on soap)

Butt, Hans-Jürgen, Karlheinz Graf, and Michael Kappl. *Physics and Chemistry of Interfaces.* Hoboken, NJ: John Wiley & Sons, 2006.

Journal of Synthetic Lubrication. Hoboken, NJ: John Wiley & Sons.

Chapter 3 (cutting yourself shaving)

Alberts, Bruce, ed. *Molecular Biology of the Cell.* Abingdon, UK: Garland Science, 2005.

Dowling, Tim. *Inventor of the Disposable Culture: King Camp Gillette 1855–1932*. London: Short Books, 2001.

Freinkel, R. K. *The Biology of the Skin*. London: Taylor & Francis Group, 2000.

Krumholz, Phillip. *A History of Shaving and Razors*. Adlibs Pub Co., 1987.

Lorenz, H. Peter, and Michael T. Longaker. *Wounds: Biology, Pathology, and Management*. Stanford: Stanford University Medical Center, 2003.

Romo, T., and L. A. McLaughlin. "Wound Healing, Skin." Emedicine.com, 2003. Accessed September 12, 2007.

Rosenberg, L., and J. de la Torre. "Wound Healing, Growth Factors." Emedicine.com, 2003. Accessed September 12, 2007.

Chapter 4 (toast on fire)

Drysdale, Dougal. *An Introduction to Fire Dynamics*, 2nd edition. Hoboken, NJ: John Wiley & Sons, 1998.

Jha, Alok. "Close Encounters. Special Report: Chemical World." *Guardian Unlimited*, May 22, 2004.

U.S. Department of Health and Human Services. *11th Report on Carcinogens*, 2005.

Chapter 5 (exploding liquid)

FDA US Food and Drug Administration. *Microwave Oven Radiation*, 2007.

Francis, T. J. R., and D. F. Gorman. "Pathogenesis of the Decompression Disorders." In *The Physiology and Medicine of Diving*, 4th edition, edited by P. B. Bennett and D. H. Elliott, 454–80. London: W. B. Saunders, 1993.

Hawkes, Nigel, et al. *The Worst Accident in the World: Chernobyl: The End of the Nuclear Dream*. New York: Macmillan, 1986.

Peplow, Mark. "Special Report: Counting the Dead." *Nature* 440 (2006): 982–83.

Chapter 6 (milk gone bad)

Adolfsson, O., et al. "Yogurt and Gut Function." *American Journal of Clinical Nutrition* 80:2 (2004): 245–56.

Carroll, Ricki. *Making Cheese, Butter, and Yogurt.* North Adams, MA: Storey Publishing, 2003.

Elli, Marina, et al. "Survival of Yogurt Bacteria in the Human Gut." *Applied Environmental Microbiology* 72, 7 (July 2006): 5,113–17.

Katz, Donald B., Miguel A. L. Nicolelis, and S. A. Simon. "Nutrient Tasting and Signaling Mechanisms in the Gut IV. There is more to taste than meets the tongue." *American Journal of Physiology: Gastrointestinal and Liver Physiology* 278 (2000): G6–G9.

Chapter 7 (wet MP3 player)

Adams, Charles K. *Nature's Electricity.* Blue Ridge Summit, PA: Tab Books, 1987.

Ozawa, Kazunori. *Lithium Ion Rechargeable Batteries: Materials, Technology, and Applications.* Hoboken, NJ: John Wiley & Sons, 2008.

Saslow, Wayne M. *Electricity, Magnetism, and Light.* Toronto: Thomson Learning, 2002.

Chapter 8 (bird droppings)

Blais, Jules M., et al. "Arctic Seabirds Transport Marine-Derived Contaminants." *Science* 15, Vol. 309, no. 5733 (2005): 445.

Croll, D. A., J. L. Maron, J. A. Estes, E. M. Danner, and G. V. Byrd. "Introduced Predators Transform Subarctic Islands from Grassland to Tundra." *Science* 25, Vol. 307, no. 5717 (2005): 1,959–61.

Sekercioglu, Cagan H. "Increasing Awareness of Acological Function." *Trends in Ecology and Evolution*, Vol. 21, no. 8 (August 2006): 464–71.

Skaggs, Jimmy M. *The Great Guano Rush*. New York: St. Martin's Press, 1994.

Chapter 9 (forgetting bag)

Baddeley, Alan D. *Essentials of Human Memory*. London: Psychology Press Ltd., 1999.

Boutla, M., T. Supalla, L. Newport, and D. Bavelier. "Short-Term Memory Span: Insights from Sign Language." *Nature Neuroscience* 7, 9 (2004): 1–6.

Martin, Randi C. "Components of Short-Term Memory and Their Relation to Language Processing: Evidence from Neuropsychology and Neuroimaging." *Current Directions in Psychological Science*, Vol. 14, no. 4 (2005): 204–208.

Poirier, M., and J. Saint-Aubin. "Immediate Serial Recall, Word Frequency, Item Identity, and Item Position." *Canadian Journal of Experimental Psychology*, 50 (1996): 408–12.

Tarnow, Eugen. "The Short-Term Memory Structure In State-of-the Art Recall/Recognition Experiments of Rubin, Hinton, and Wentzel." Eprints, 2005, http://cogprints.org/4670 accessed September 21, 2007.

Visscher, K. M., E. Kaplan, M. J. Kahana, and R. Sekuler. "Auditory Short-Term Memory Behaves Like Visual Short-Term Memory." *PLoS Biology,* vol. 5, No. 3, e56doi:10.1371/journal.pbio.0050056.

Chapter 10 (skidding on road)

Jurgen, Ron. *Electronic Braking, Traction, and Stability Controls (Progress in Technology)*. Society of Automotive Engineers, 1999.

Loadman, John. *Tears of the Tree: The Story of Rubber—A Modern Marvel*. Oxford: Oxford University Press, 2005.

Chapter 11 (diesel instead of gas)

MacKeand, Crawford. *Sparks and Flames: Ignition in Engines—An Historical Approach.* Montchanin, DE: Tyndar Press, 1997.

Chapter 12 (tripping on the curb)

Highstein, S. M., R. R. Fay, A. N. Popper, eds. *The Vestibular System.* Berlin: Springer, 2004.

Rabin, Ely, and Andrew M. Gordon. "Influence of Fingertip Contact on Illusory Arm Movements." *Journal of Applied Physiology* 96 (2003): 1555–60.

Robles-De-La-Torre, G., and V. Hayward. "Force Can Overcome Object Geometry in the Perception of Shape through Active Touch." *Nature* 412, 6845 (2001): 445–8.

Winter, David A. *A.B.C. (Anatomy, Biomechanics, Control) of Balance During Standing and Walking.* Waterloo, ON: Waterloo Biomechanics, 1995.

Chapter 13 (chewing gum in hair)

Redclift, Michael. *Chewing Gum.* New York: Routledge, 2004.

Chapter 14 (rain-soaked clothes)

Gomes, R., H. F. Levison, K. Tsiganis, and A. Morbidelli. "Origin of the Cataclysmic Late Heavy Bombardment Period of the Terrestrial Planets." *Nature* 435 (2005): 466–69.

Harman, Rebecca. *The Water Cycle.* Chicago: Heinemann Library, 2005.

Kasting, James. "How and When Did Water Come into Existence on Our Earth?" NASA Astrobiology Institute, 2002.

Chapter 15 (being lost)

Alerstam, T. "Detours in Bird Migration." *Journal of Theoretical Biology* 209 (2001): 319–31.

Berthold, Peter. *Bird Migration: A General Survey*, 2nd edition. Oxford: Oxford University Press, 2001.

Carrubba, S., C. Frilot, A. L. Chesson, and A. A. Marino. "Evidence of a Nonlinear Human Magnetic Sense." *Neuroscience* 144, 1 (2006): 356–67.

Dingle, Hugh. *Migration: The Biology of Life on the Move.* Oxford: Oxford University Press, 1996.

Chapter 16 (bee sting)

Meier, J., and J. White. *Clinical Toxicology of Animal Venoms and Poisons.* London: CRC Press, Inc., 1995.

Neugut, Alfred, Anita Ghatak, and Rachel Miller. "Anaphylaxis in the United States: An Investigation into Its Epidemiology." *Archives of Internal Medicine* 161, 108 (2001): 15–21.

Resiman, R. "Insect Stings." *New England Journal of Medicine* 26 (1994): 523–27.

Chapter 17 (sticking yourself with superglue)

Petrie, E. M. *Handbook of Adhesives and Sealants.* Columbus, OH: McGraw-Hill Professional, 2000.

Quinn, J., and J. Kissack. "Tissue Adhesives for Laceration Repair During Sporting Events." *Clinical Journal of Sports Medicine* Vol. 4, no. 4 (1994): 245.

Chapter 18 (electromagnetic interference from phone)

Agar, Jon. *Constant Touch: A Global History of the Mobile Phone.* London: Totem Books, 2005.

Chen, Zhi Ning Chen, ed. *Antennas for Portable Devices,* Hoboken, NJ: John Wiley & Sons, 2007.

Haykin, Simon. *Communication Systems,* 4th edition. Hoboken, NJ: John Wiley & Sons, 2001.

Hillebrand, Friedhelm, ed. *GSM and UMTS: The Creation of Global Mobile Communications*. Hoboken, NJ: John Wiley & Sons, 2002.

Chapter 19 (puncture)

Bastow, Donald, Geoffrey Howard, and John P. Whitehead. *Car Suspension and Handling*, 4th edition. Hoboken, NJ: John Wiley & Sons, 2004.

Turner, Ian. *Engineering Applications of Pneumatics and Hydraulics*. Chicago: Butterworth-Heinemann, 1995.

Chapter 20 (leaking pens)

Gostony, Henry, and Stuart Schneider. *The Incredible Ball Point Pen: A Comprehensive History and Price Guide*. Atglen, PA: Schiffer Publishing, 1998.

Nickell, Joe. *Pen, Ink, and Evidence: A Study of Writing and Writing Materials*. Lexington: University Press of Kentucky, 1990.

Chapter 21 (mistaken identity)

Bruce, V., and A. Young. *In the Eye of the Beholder: The Science of Face Perception*. Oxford: Oxford University Press, 2000.

Glennerster, A., et al. "Humans Ignore Motion and Stereo Cues in Favor of a Fictional Stable World." *Current Biology* 16, 4 (2006): 428–32.

Nelson, C. A. "The Development and Neural Bases of Face Recognition." Infant and Child Development 10, 1–2 (2001): 3–18.

Chapter 22 (torn clothing)

Hearle, John W. S., N. O'Hear, and H. A. McKenna. *Handbook of Fibre Rope Technology*. London: CRC Press, 2004.

Porwal, Pankaj K., Irene J. Beyerlein, and Stuart Leigh Phoenix. "Statistical Strength of Twisted Fiber Bundles with Loadsharing Controlled by Frictional Length Scales." *Journal of Mechanics of Materials and Structures* Vol. 2, 4 (2007) 773–791.

Chapter 23 (opening an e-mail virus)

Ollmann, Gunter. *The Phishing Guide: Understanding and Preventing Phishing Attacks*. Network Security Library: Phishing, 2005, WindowSecurity.com.

Tamimi, Zakiya M., and Javed I. Khan. "Model-Based Analysis of Two Fighting Worms." IEEE/IIU Proceedings of ICCCE, Vol. 1, Kuala Lumpur, Malaysia (May 2006): 157–63.

Chapter 24 (jammed finger)

Bergan, John J., ed. *The Vein Book*. New York: Academic Press, 2006.

Leggit, Jeffrey C., and Christian J. Meko. "Acute Finger Injuries: Part I. Tendons and Ligaments." *American Family Physician* Vol. 73 (2006): 5.

Walker, Pam, and Elaine Wood. *The Circulatory System (Understanding the Human Body)*. Farmington Hills, MI: Lucent Books, 2003.

Chapter 25 (computer hard disk failure)

Christou, Aris. *Electromigration and Electronic Device Degradation*. Hoboken, NJ: John Wiley & Sons, 1994.

Chapter 26 (broken finger)

Bain, Barbara, David M. Clark, Irvin A. Lampert, and Bridget S. Wilkins. *Bone Marrow Pathology*, 3rd edition. Boston, MA: Blackwell Science, 2001.

Orenstein, Beth W. "Lost in Space: Bone Mass." *Radiology Today* Vol. 5, no. 16 (2004): 10.

Wertza, Xavier, Damien Schoëvaërtb, Habibou Maitournamc, and Philippe Chassigneta. "The Effect of Hormones on Bone Growth Is Mediated through Mechanical Stress." *Comptes Rendus Biologies* Vol. 329, no. 2 (2006): 79–85.

Chapter 27 (dropping keys down drain)

Besson, Ugo. "How Does Weight Depend on Mountain Altitude?" *European Journal of Physics* 27 (2006): 743–53.

May, Brian, Sir Patrick Moore, and Chris Lintott. *Bang! The Complete History of the Universe.* London: Carlton Books, 2007.

Randall, Lisa. *Warped Passages: Unraveling the Universe's Hidden Dimensions.* New York: Ecco, 2005.

Chapter 28 (pulled muscle)

Byrne, C., and R. G. Eston. "Exercise, Muscle Damage, and Delayed Onset Muscle Soreness." *Sports Exercise and Injury* 4 (1998): 69–73.

Costill, David L., and Jack H. Wilmore. *Physiology of Sport and Exercise.* Champaign, IL: Human Kinetics, 2004.

Fox, E. L., R. W. Bowers, and M. L. Foss. *The Physiological Basis for Exercise and Sport,* 5th edition. Dubuque, IA: WC Brown, 1993.

Chapter 29 (sparking microwaves)

Bloomfield, Louis A. *How Everything Works: Making Physics Out of the Ordinary.* Hoboken, NJ: John Wiley & Sons, 2006.

Sarkar, Tapan K., Robert Mailloux, Arthur A. Oliner, Magdalena Salazar Palma, and Dipak L. Sengupta. *History of Wireless* (Wiley Series in Microwave and Optical Engineering). Hoboken, NJ: John Wiley & Sons, 2006.

Chapter 30 (broken glass)

Baeurle, S. A., A. Hotta, and A. A. Guse. "On the Glassy State of Multiphase and Pure Polymer Materials." *Polymer* 47 (2006): 6,243–53.

Chown, Marcus. "Why Do Teardrops Explode?" *New Scientist* (February 11, 1995) vol. 145, no. 164, 23.

Ellis, William. *Glass.* New York: Avon Books, 1988.

Johannsmanna, D. "The Glass Transition and Contact Mechanical Experiments on Polymer Surfaces. *European Journal of Physics* 8 (2002): 257–59.

Yamane, Masayuki, and Yoshiyuki Asahara. *Glasses for Photonics.* Cambridge: Cambridge University Press, 2005.

Chapter 31 (stains)

Druding, Susan. "Fiber-Reactive Dyes and Cibacron F in Particular." *Textile Artists' Newsletter,* Vol. III, no. 3 (1982).

Epp, Dianne N. *The Chemistry of Vat Dyes* (Palette of Color Series). Miami: Terrific Science Press, 1995.

Johnson, Julie. "Out, Out Damned Spot!" *New Scientist,* (December 24, 1994) vol. 144, no. 144, 29.

Chapter 32 (chile pepper in eye)

Barker, Catherine L. "Hot Pod: World's Hottest Chilies." *National Geographic Magazine* (May 2007): 21.

Billing, J., and P. W. Sherman. "Antimicrobial Functions of Spices: Why Some Like It Hot." *The Quarterly Review of Biology* 73, 1 (1998): 3–49.

Dewitt, Dave. *The Chile Pepper Encyclopedia: Everything You'll Ever Need to Know about Hot Peppers.* Darby, PA: Diane Publishing Co., 2003.

Perry, L., et al. "Starch Fossils and the Domestication and Dispersal of Chile Peppers (*Capsicum* spp. *L.*) in the Americas." *Science* 315 (2007): 986–88.

Rozin, Paul, and Deborah Schiller. "The Nature and Acquisition of a Preference for Chile Pepper by Humans." *Motivation and Emotion* 4, 1 (1980): 77–101.

Chapter 33 (food on the floor)

Guarner, F., G. Perdigon, G. Corthier, S. Salminen, B. Koletzko, and L. Morelli. "Should Yoghurt Cultures Be Considered Probiotic?" *British Journal of Nutrition* 93, 6 (June 2005): 783–86.

Salvatierra, M., A. Molina, M. Gamboa Mdel, and M. L. Arias. "Evaluation of the Effect of Probiotic Cultures on Two Different Yogurt Brands over a Known Population of *Staphylococcus aureus* and the Production of Thermonuclease." *Archives of Latinoam Nutrition* 54, 3 (Sep 2004): 298–302.

Chapter 34 (lightning kills the TV)

Adams, Charles K. *Nature's Electricity.* Blue Ridge Summit, PA: Tab Books, 1987.

Baba, Yoshihiro, and Vladimir A. Rakov. "Voltages Induced on an Overhead Wire by Lightning Strikes to a Nearby Tall Grounded Object." *IEEE Transactions on Electromagnetic Compatibility* Vol. 48, no. 1 (2006), 212–224.

Boccippio, D. J., et al. "Sprites, ELF Transients, and Positive Ground Strokes." *Science* 269 (1995): 1,088–91.

Shrope, Mark. "Lightning Research: The Bolt Catchers." *Nature* 431 (2004): 120–21.

Uman, Martin A. *All About Lightning.* Mineola, NY: Dover Publications, 1986.

Chapter 35 (burns and blisters)

Hanna, Tammy, and J. Martin Carlson. "Freedom from Friction." *OrthoKinetic Review,* vol. 4, No. 2 (March 2004), 34–35.

Hettiaratchy, Shehan, Remo Papini, and Peter Dziewulski, eds. *ABC of Burns.* Boston, MA: BMJ Books, 2002.

Knapik, J. J., K. L. Reynolds, K. L. Duplantis, and B. H. Jones. "Friction Blisters: Pathophysiology, Prevention, and Treatment." *Sports Medicine* 20, 3 (1996): 136–47.

Yasuhiko, Fukuya, Takano Kunio, Fujimaki Ayako, Noguchi Norio, Ganno Hideaki, and Miura Takako. "Clinical Comparison on Blister-burns: Preservation of Blister Liquid vs. Aspiration." *Japanese Journal of Burn Injuries* Vol. 28, 2 (2002): 80–86.

Chapter 36 (scratched CD)

Baert, Luc. *Digital Audio and Compact Disc Technology*, 3rd edition. Oxford: Focal Press, 1995.

Iga, Kenichi. "Surface-Emitting Laser—Its Birth and Generation of New Optoelectronics Field." *IEEE Journal of Selected Topics in Quantum Electronics* 6, 6 (2000): 1,201–15.

Chapter 37 (broken tooth)

Cheng, K. K., Iain Chalmers, and Trevor A. Sheldon. "Adding Fluoride to Water Supplies." *British Medical Journal* 335 (2007): 699–702.

Eisenburger, M., M. Addy, J. A. Hughes, and R. P. Shellis. "Effect of Time on the Remineralisation of Enamel by Synthetic Saliva after Citric Acid Erosion." *Caries Research* 35 (2001): 211–15.

Holloway, P. J. "The Role of Sugar in the Etiology of Dental Caries." *Journal of Dentistry* 11 (1983): 189–213.

Chapter 38 (stubbing toe)

Bear, M. F., B. W. Connors, and M. A. Paradiso. *Neuroscience: Exploring the Brain*. Baltimore: Lippincott, 2001.

Ranney, Don. "Anatomy of Pain." Ontario Inter-Urban Pain Conference, Waterloo, November 29, 1996.

Chapter 39 (overflowing bath)

Biello, David. "Fact or Fiction?: Archimedes Coined the Term 'Eureka!' in the Bath." *Scientific American* (December 8, 2006).

Jackson, Robert. *Liners, Tankers, Merchant Ships: 300 of the World's Greatest Commercial Vessels* (Expert Guide). Kent, UK: Grange Books, 2002.

Leslie, Mitch, ed. "The First Eureka Moment." *Science* 305 (2004): 1,219.

Tipler, Paul. *Physics for Scientists and Engineers: Mechanics, Oscillations, Waves, and Thermodynamics*, 5th edition. New York: W. H. Freeman, 2004.

ACKNOWLEDGMENTS

Thanks to:

Gordon Wise, Melissa Chinchillo, and Kate Cooper for the deals and advice.

My editor, Julie Will, for her enthusiasm and constructive criticism for this book.

Udi Schlessinger, Nguyet Ta, John Bentley, and David Turner for their feedback, proofreading, and fact-checking.

All the scientists and their efforts referenced in this book for their dedication and hard work in the quest to improve our understanding of the world around us.

You, my reader, for your curiosity. Be careful what you believe and never stop asking, *Why?*

And finally (as usual) I would like to thank the cruel and indifferent, yet astonishingly creative process of evolution for providing the inspiration for all of my work. Long may it continue to do so.

Science is an incremental process of improvement. If you spot something in this book you think is inaccurate, out of date, or wrong, feel free to get in touch at ithinkyourewrong@peterjbentley.com, and tell me about it. However, I'm afraid I will only believe you if you provide the evidence with a complete reference to the original source of your information, which should have been verified, preferably through peer review (a Web page address is not good enough, sorry). I can't promise to reply to all e-mails, but I will read them all! If you provide a valid amendment that is used in future editions, you will be acknowledged in the book.

INDEX

ABS, on cars, 67–69, 70, 125
AC, 22–23
Acid dyes, 215–16
Actin filaments, in skeletal muscle, 194–95, 197
Adrenalin, for treating bee sting allergy, 111
Agnosia, visual, 147
Air cushioning, in shoes, 128, 132–33
Airplanes
    braking of, 67
    cell phone interference with, 126
Air pressure
    effect on boiling water, 29–31
    effects on pilots, 33
Air springs, in vehicles, 132
Alarm clocks, types of, 7
Allergies
    bee sting, 111, 112
    from food dyes, 216
Alphabets, creation of, 135
Alternating current (AC), 22–23
Amnesia, types of, 60
Anaphylactic shock, from bee stings, 111
Anesthetic, capsaicin as, 225–26
Annealing, 212
Antennas, 123, 124, 125
Antilock brakes, 67–69, 70, 125
Antivirus software, 162, 163
Ants
    navigation of, 102, 103
    poisonous, 108
Appendix, immune function of, 232

Archimedes, 273–75, 279
Archimedes' Principle, 275–76, 279
Arms, for balancing, 85–86
Arthritis, bee venom treating, 111–12
Artificial immune systems, for detecting computer viruses, 162, 163
Astronauts
    bone loss in, 182–83
    neutral buoyancy facilities for, 278–79
Atoms
    floating and, 276–77
    heat and, 23–24
    lasers and, 252–54

Babies
    cartilage in, 179–80
    pain perception in, 268–69
Bacteria
    in bird droppings, 54–55
    in cheese and yogurt making, 36, 37, 39, 40
    in digestive system, 232, 233–34
    effect of temperature on, 39
    souring milk, 38
Balance, for controlling movement, 80, 83–84
Ballpoint Bic, 140
Ballpoint pens, 139–40, 141–42
Batteries
    car, 43–45
    effect of water on, 42–43, 45, 46–47

Batteries *(cont.)*
    invention of, 43
    lithium-ion, 46–47
    short-circuiting, 44–45,
        46–47
Becoming lost, 100, 105–6
Bee hives, 109
Bees, navigation of, 102, 103
Bee stings, 107–12
Bee venom
    as arthritis treatment, 111–12
    composition of, 110
Bell peppers, mildness of, 221–22
Benz, Karl, 74
Bich, Marcel, 140
Bic pens, 140
Bicycle tires, 66
Big bang, 188–89
Bird droppings, 49
    abundant production of,
        51–52
    composition of, 50
    illness from, 54–55
    property damage from, 53–54
    uses for, 50–51
Birds
    as honeyguides, 109
    migration of, 101, 102, 103,
        104, 105
    weaving by, 153
Biro, Ladislas and Georg, 140
Biro pen, 140
Black holes, 189–90
Bleach, for removing red wine
        stains, 219
Blisters
    from burns, 245–46, 247
    care of, 247, 249, 250
    from friction, 246–47
Boiling water, effect of pressure on,
        29–32
Bolus, digestion of, 229–30

Bone marrow
    function of, 181
    leukemia and, 181–82
Bones
    building and thinning of,
        182–83
    fractures of, 183–84
    function of, 177
    growth of, 178–80
    structure of, 181
Brain
    lack of pain receptors in, 270
    magnetic fields and, 104, 105
    memory and, 60–61
    movement controlled by, 79,
        81, 85, 86
    perception developed by,
        144–45
    skeletal muscles wired to, 194
Brain activity, during sleep, 2–4
Brain damage, affecting recognition,
        147, 148
Brakes, antilock, 67–69, 70, 125
Brick, sinking in water, 276, 277
Buoyancy, 277–79
Burned foods, cancer risk from, 26
Burned toast, 21, 26
Burns
    causes of, 248–49
    deaths from, 250
    degrees of, 245–48
    treatment of, 249–50
Butter, making of, 37
Butterflies, migration of, 101

Calcium
    in bone growth, 179, 181
    excessive, effects of, 179
    function of, 178
    in muscle movement, 195
Callus, formed after blister, 246–47

Cancer
     burned food increasing risk
          of, 26
     leukemia, 181–82
Canine teeth, 259
Capgras's syndrome, 148
Capillary action
     of ink, 138, 140
     of water, 97–98
Capsaicin
     as anesthetic, 225–26
     in chili peppers, 222
     developing tolerance to,
          223–24
     in pepper spray, 224–25
     reducing pain from, 226–27
Capsicum fruits, mild and hot
          varieties of, 221–22
Car batteries, 43–45
Carburetors, 74
Cardiac muscle, 192–93
Carriage springs, in early
          suspension systems, 128,
          130
Cars
     air springs in, 132
     antilock brakes on, 67–69, 70,
          125
     bird droppings on, 53–54
     cell phone interference with,
          125–26
     diesel engines in, 76
     disabling electronic support
          on, 71
     electronic stability control on,
          69–70
     limited slip differential on, 70
     putting wrong fuel in, 72–78
     shock absorbers in, 131, 132
     skidding of, 64–71
     tires on, 65–67, 70, 71
     traction control on, 70–71

Cartilage
     in marine animals, 178
     in newborns, 179–80
     ossification and, 179
Caterpillars, poisonous, 108
Cave writings, 135
Cavities, dental, 263
CDs
     information storage on,
          254–56
     introduction of, 252
     lasers and, 252–54
     scratched, 251, 256–57
Cell phones
     electromagnetic interference
          from, 120, 125–26
     functioning of, 120–23
Cells, staining, 217–18
Cementum, in gums, 261
Central nervous system, 269
Charcoal, for early writing, 136
Charge separation in clouds, 238–40
Cheese
     making of, 37
     raw milk, 39–40
Chemotherapy, for leukemia
          treatment, 181, 182
Chernobyl nuclear power accident,
          29
Chewing gum
     composition of, 89, 91
     for emergency repairs, 91
     origins of, 88–89
     stretchiness of, 89–90
     stuck in hair, 87, 90
          removing, 91–92
Chili peppers
     countries using, 224
     hotness of, 221, 222–23
     reducing pain from, 226–27
     rubbed in eye, 221, 226–27
Chyme, in digestion, 231

Circulatory system, function of, 167–69

Clay tablets, early writing on, 135

Cloth
    chewing gum stuck to, 90–91
    dyeing, 217
    strength of, 151–54
    tearing, 150, 155–56
    water absorbed by, 97–98

Clothing
    torn, 150, 155–56
    waterproof, 97, 98, 99

Clouds, charge separation in, 238–40

Coil springs, uses for, 130–31

Collagen
    cartilage and, 178
    in gums, 261
    in skin, 114–15, 154

Colon
    bacteria or virus infecting, 234
    in digestion, 231–32

Comets, water from, 94

Compact discs. *See* CDs

Compass, internal, for migration, 103–4

Compression
    for engine ignition, 74–75
    in shock absorbers, 131–32

Computer memory chips, capacity of, 172

Computer processor chips
    causes of damage to, 171–72
    types of, 171

Computers
    components of, 170–72
    hard disk failure in, 170, 175–76
    types of storage on, 172–75
    viruses and worms infecting, 157, 160–63

Contact adhesive, uses for, 116

Coover, Harry, 116

Corpses turned to soap, 10

Cramps, muscle, 197

Cutaneous pain, 270

Daimler, Gottlieb, 74

Darwin, Charles, 30–31

DC, 22

Decompression sickness, 32–33

Dentin, of teeth, 261, 262, 263, 264

Diesel, Rudolf, 75

Diesel engines, 72–73, 74–78

Digestion
    process of, 229–32
    teeth aiding in, 258

Digestive system
    bacteria in, 232, 233–34
    bad food handled by, 232–33, 235
    infection of, 234–35
    structure of, 228–29

Direct current (DC), 22

Disk drives, on computers, 173–76

Divers, decompression sickness in, 32–33

Dizziness, cause of, 84

Dreaming, 4–6

Dunlop, John Boyd, 66

Duodenum, in digestion, 231

Dyes
    vs. paints, 214–15
    types of, 215–17
    uses for, 217–18

Ear, inner, sense of balance from, 83–84

Earth
    gravitation and, 186, 187, 188, 191
    magnetic field of, 103–4

origin of, 94
origin of water on, 93–95
retention of water on, 95–97
Ecosystems, guano supporting, 53
Einstein, Albert, 188
Electrical current, types of, 22
Electrical fires, 25–26
Electric field, of electromagnetic
    waves, 123
Electricity
    batteries producing, 42–43, 44
    burns from, 249
    conductors of, 45–46
    in generation of heat, 22–23
    in lightning, 236–37
    magnetic fields and, 124
    static, 238
Electrolytes, 45
Electromagnetic interference from
    cell phones, 120, 125–26
Electromagnetic pulse (EMP),
    affecting electronic
    equipment, 241–42
Electromagnetic radiation
    from lightning, 241
    microwave ovens using, 200
    from nuclear weapons,
    241–42
Electromagnetic waves
    characteristics of, 202
    components of, 123–24
    radar and, 201
Electromigration, damaging
    computer processor chip,
    171
Electronic devices dropped in
    water, 42–48
Electronic equipment, lightning
    damaging, 236, 241,
    242–43
Electronic stability control (ESC),
    on cars, 69–70

Electrons, in generation of heat,
    22–23, 24
Electrostatic force, superglue and,
    117
E-mail
    early use of, 158–59
    spam, 158, 159–60
    viruses and worms from, 157,
    160–63
EMP-hardened electronics, 242
EMPs, affecting electronic
    equipment, 241–42
Enamel, of teeth, 261, 262, 264, 265
Engines
    diesel vs. petroleum gas, 72–78
    history of, 73–74
    steam, 73
Epiglottis, in digestion, 230
Equilibrioception, 83–84
ESC, on cars, 69–70
Esophagus, in digestion, 230
Evaporation, 95–96, 97
Exercise, muscle soreness after,
    196–97
Explosions
    battery, 43, 44–45
    steam, 27–29
Eye movements, sense of balance
    and, 84
Eyes, chili pepper rubbed in, 221,
    226–27

Fabric. *See* Cloth
Face recognition, 144–45, 147–48,
    149
Falling, 79–86
Falling objects, effect of gravitation
    on, 185, 187, 191
Faradaic reaction, 43
Fast twitch muscles, 195–96
Fecal matter. *See also* Bird droppings
    formation of, 232

Fertilizer, bird droppings as, 51, 52, 53
Fiberglass, as resistant to tearing, 156
Fiber reactive dyes, 216
Fingerprints, 118, 166
Finger(s)
    anatomy of, 166–67
    broken, 177
    stuck in bottle, 164–69
Fires
    burns from, 249
    chemical reaction causing, 24–25
    deaths from, 250
    electrical, 25–26
    in microwave oven, 200, 206
First-degree burns, 245, 249
Floating, 276–77, 279
Floppy disks, computer, 173–74
Fluoride, in toothpaste, 264, 265
Foam
    buoyancy of, 276–77
    for shoe cushioning, 133
Food dyes, 216
Forgetting, 56–63
Fossilization, 179
Fountain pens, 138–39
Fractured bones, 177, 183–84
Friction
    blisters from, 246–47
    fabric strength from, 152, 154, 155, 156
    slipperiness and, 12–13
Friction ridges, on fingers, 166, 167
Frostbite, 168
Fuel, diesel vs. petroleum gas, 72–78
Fuel-injection systems, on cars, 74

Gallbladder, in digestion, 231
Galvani, Luigi, 43

Gas, produced by digestion, 231–32
Gastroenteritis, 234–35
Gelatin, in glue, 114, 115
Gillette razors, 15–16
Glass
    annealed, 212
    broken, 207, 212–13
    changing toughness of, 210–12
    composition of, 208–9
    molecular structure of, 209
    myth about, 207–8
    transition temperature of, 209–10
Glues
    composition of, 114–15
    superglue, 113, 116–19
Goodyear, Charles, 66
GPS systems, 126, 190
Gravitation, 186–91, 276
Greenstick fractures, 183–84
Guano
    ecosystems and, 53
    islands made from, 52
Gum. See Chewing gum
Gunpowder, made from bird droppings, 51, 52
Gymnastics, growth slowed by, 180

Hair
    chewing gum stuck in, 87, 90
        removing, 91–92
    composition of, 16
Hair follicles, 16–17
Hair removal, history of, 14–15
Hard disks, computer
    design of, 174–75
    failure of, 170, 175–76
Heartburn, 230
Heat, generation of, 22–24
Helicopter landing pads, bird droppings ruining, 54
Henry's Law, 30, 32

Honey, creation of, 109
Honeybees
navigation of, 102, 103
stings from, 107–12
Horse-drawn carriages, suspension systems in, 128, 130
Hot-carrier interaction, damaging computer processor chip, 171
Hot liquids, benefits of, 244–45
Humpback whales, migration of, 102–3
Hydraulic systems, in shock absorbers, 131
Hydrochloric acid, in digestion, 230–31
Hydropneumatics, for suspension of vehicles, 132
Hymenoptera, venom of, 108
Hypnosis, false memories produced by, 59

Ice
for removing chewing gum from hair, 92
as source of water on Earth, 94–95
"I love you" worm, 157, 161, 162
Immune system, exposure to bacteria and, 232, 235
Incisors, 258–59, 262
Ink, development of, 136–37
Inner ear, sense of balance from, 83–84
Insects, navigation of, 102, 103, 104
Insect stings, 107–12
Insomnia, 6, 7
Internal combustion engines, 73–74
Internal compass, for migration, 103–4
Interstitial fluid, circulation affecting, 167, 168, 169

Iron
excessive, effects of, 179
function of, in plants and animals, 178

Jupiter, 94

Keys dropped down drain, 185, 191
Kinesthesia, 81–83

Lactic acid buildup, in muscles, 196, 197
Langerhans cells, 18
Large intestine. *See* Colon
Laser, atom behavior and, 252–54
Laser discs, introduction of, 251–52
Latex
in chewing gum, 89, 91
rubber made from, 65
Leaf springs, in suspension systems, 130
Leaking pens, 134, 141–42
Leather, strength of, 154–55
Lenoir, Jean Joseph Étienne, 74
Leukemia, 181–82
Light
black holes and, 189–90
stretching of, 189
Lightning, 236–43
burns from, 249
TV killed by, 236, 241–43
voltage of, 46
Limited slip differential, on cars, 70
Liquid, exploding, 27–29
Lithium-ion batteries, 46–47
London dispersion forces, superglue and, 117
Long-term memory, 58
Lost, becoming, 100, 105–6
Lower esophageal sphincter, 230
Lucid dreaming, 5
Lymphatic system, function of, 168

Magnetic fields
of electromagnetic waves,
123–24
as navigational aide, 104–5
Magnetic tape, for computer
storage, 172–73
Magnetron, in radar systems and
microwave ovens, 203–4
Mammals, migration of, 101, 102
Mars
asteroid belt and, 94
atmosphere of, 96
dryness of, 93
Mass, gravitation and, 187–88
Maybach, Wilhelm, 74
Memory(ies)
false, 59
long-term, 58
role of brain in, 60–61
short-term, 56–59
improving, 61–63
Metal springs, in suspension
systems, 128–31
Meteorites, water from, 94–95
Microwave ovens
design of, 204
drawbacks of cooking in, 205
electromagnetic radiation used
by, 200
functioning of, 204–5
origin of, 200, 203–4
sparking in, 199, 200, 205–6
steam explosions and, 27–29
Migratory creatures, 101–5
Milk
pasteurized, 39, 40
spoiled, 35, 37–38
preventing, 38–39
ultra-high temperature
(UHT), 39
Mistaken identity, 143–49
Molars, 259–60

Moon
gravitational force of, 186–87
lack of atmosphere on, 96
orbiting Earth, 187, 188
origin of craters on, 94
Mordant dyes, 216–17
Mountain climbers, water-boiling
difficulty of, 30–31, 32
Movement, human, complexity of,
79–86
MP3 player, wet, 42–48
Muscle activity, during dreaming, 4
Muscle cramps, 197
Muscles
function of, 192
pulled, 192, 197–98
soreness of, 196–97
types of, 192–94
Myosin filaments, in skeletal
muscle, 194–95, 197

Navigation aides, needed for
migration, 101–6
Nerve cells, as source of pain,
269–72
Nervous system, 269
Nike Air cushioning, 132
Nociceptors, 269–70
Nuclear weapons, electromagnetic
radiation from, 241–42

Oil, for removing chewing gum
from hair, 91–92
Oily skin, waterproof quality of,
98–99
Optical illusions, 146–47
Optical storage disks, introduction
of, 251–52
Ossification, 179–80, 184
Osteoblasts, 182, 183
Osteoclasts, 182
Osteoporosis, 183

Overflowing bath, 273
Oversleeping
    avoiding, 7
    reasons for, 6
Oxide breakdown, damaging
        computer processor chip,
        171

Pain
    delayed sensation of, 271–72
    different feelings of, 270
    nerve cells as source of,
        269–72
    perception of, 267–68
        in babies, 268–69
    purpose of, 272
Pain receptors, 269–70
Paints, vs. dyes, 214–15
Pancreas, in digestion, 231
Papyrus, for early writing, 136, 137
Parchment, for early writing, 136,
    137
Pasteur, Louis, 39
Pasteurization, 39, 40
Past experiences or lives, hypnosis
        producing, 59
Pens
    ballpoint, 139–40, 141–42
    fountain, 138–39
    leaking, 134, 141–42
Peppers
    bell, mildness of, 221–22
    chili
        countries using, 224
        hotness of, 221, 222–23
        reducing pain from, 226–27
        rubbed in eye, 221, 226–27
Pepper spray, 224–25
Perception
    development of, 144–45, 149
    of pain, 267–68
        in babies, 268–69

Peripheral nervous system, 269
Peristalsis, in digestion process,
    230
Petroleum gas engines, 72–73,
    75–76, 77, 78
Phishing schemes, 159–60
Phones, cell, electromagnetic
        interference from, 120,
        125–26
Pilots, decompression sickness in,
    32, 33
Pinocchio Illusion, 82–83
Pistons
    in engines, 74
    in shock absorbers, 131
Plants
    capillary action and, 98
    rigid cell walls of, 178
Plutarch, 274–75
Pneumatic shock absorbers,
    131–32
Pneumatic suspension systems, 132
Pneumatic tires, 66
Polarization, superglue and, 117
Pole-balancing problem, 80
Poop. *See also* Bird droppings
        formation of, 232
Potential energy, 129
Precipitation, 96
Premolars, 259
Pressure cookers, 31–32
Prince Rupert's Drops, 211
Probiotic yogurt, 233–34
Prosopagnosia, 147, 148
Pulled muscle, 192, 197–98
Pulp, tooth, 261
Punch cards, for computer storage,
    172
Punctures, in air-cushioned shoes,
    127, 133

Quills, as writing instrument, 138

Radar
    origin of microwave oven and,
        200, 201
    uses for, 202–3
Radar detector gadgets,
        interference from, 126
Radiation, for leukemia treatment,
        181–82
Radio waves, 123, 124–25
Rain-soaked clothes, 93, 97–99
Razor cuts
    bleeding from, 14, 18
    healing of, 19–20
Razors, invention of, 15–16
Red blood cells, leukemia affecting,
        181
Red wine stains, 214, 218
    removing, 218–20
REM sleep, 4, 5, 6
Rennet, in cheese making, 36–37
Rheumatoid arthritis, bee venom
        treating, 112
Robots
    limitations of, 80–81, 85
    motor control of, 194
    for staining cells, 217
Rodents, teeth of, 262
Rubber
    elasticity of, 89–90
    glass transition temperature
        of, 210
    for shoe soles, 114
    vulcanized, 65–66
Running, balance required for,
        79–80, 85

Safety glass, 212
Salmon, migration of, 101, 102, 103
Saponification, in soap making, 9–10
Satin weaves, 154
Scoville, Wilbur, 223
Scoville scale, 223

Seabirds, guano from, 51–53
Second-degree burns, 245–46, 247,
        249–50
Sensory feedback, required for
        movement, 81–83
Shampoos
    slipperiness of, 12, 13
    soap-based vs. synthetic, 11–12
Sharks, teeth of, 262
Shaving cuts. See Razor cuts
Ships, buoyancy of, 277–78
Shock absorbers, 131–32
Shoes
    air cushioning in, 128, 132–33
    construction of, 113–14, 115,
        116
Short-term memory, 56–59
    improving, 61–63
Sight, role of, in perception,
        143–44, 145–47
Silica, glass made from, 208–9
Singapore, chewing gum ban in,
        87–88
Skeletal muscle, 194–96
Skidding on the road, 64–71
Skin
    collagen in, 114–15, 154
    components and functions of,
        17–18
    fibers woven in, 154–55
    on fingers, 166–67
    oily, waterproof quality of,
        98–99
    pain felt by, 270
    superglue sticking to, 113,
        118–19
Sleep deprivation, prolonged, 6–7
Sleep disorders, 3
Sleeping through alarm, 1, 6–7
Sleep stages, 2–6
Sleep talking, 3
Sleepwalking, 3

Slipperiness, friction causing, 12–13
Slipping on shampoo, 8–13
Slow twitch muscles, 195
Small intestine, in digestion, 231
Smells, learned response to, 40–41
Smilodon fatalis, canine teeth of, 259
Smooth muscle, 193–94
Snoring, 2, 3, 6
Soap
        dirt-removing property of, 10–11
        recipe for, 9–10
        slipperiness of, 12
"Soap Woman and Soap Man," 10
Solid-state components, of computers, 170–71
Somatic pain, 270
Sonar, 200–201
Sound waves, 201, 202
Space, flexibility of, 188–90
Space pen, 141
Spam, e-mail, 158, 159–60
Spencer, Percy, 203–4
Spiders, venom of, 108
Spoiled milk, 35, 37–38
        preventing, 38–39
Springs, in suspension systems, 128–31, 132
Stained wood, 217
Stain removal products, 219–20
Stains
        red wine, 214, 218
                removing, 218–20
        uses for, in biology and medicine, 217–18
Standing upright
        balance required for, 79–80, 84
        sensory feedback required for, 81
Starlight, as navigation aide for migration, 103

Static electricity, 238
Steam engines, 73
Steam explosions, 27–29
Stings, bee, 107–12
Stomach, in digestion, 230–31
Stone carving, as early form of writing, 135
Stubbed toe, 266, 271
Submarines, buoyancy of, 278
Sunlight, as navigation aide for migration, 103
Superglue, 113, 116–19
Surfactants, 11, 12, 13
Suspension systems
        in early vehicles, 128, 130
        in modern vehicles, 131, 132
        pneumatic, 132

Tartar, dental, 264
Tastes, learned response to, 40–41
Teeth
        care of, 264–65
        damage to, 258, 263–64, 265
        growth of, 262–63
        hardness of, 260–61
        self-repair of, 263
        structure of, 261–62
        types of, 258–60
Third-degree burns, 247–48, 250
Thomson, Robert William, 66
Threads
        in ripped cloth, 155
        weaving of, in cloth making, 153–54
        wool, spinning of, 152
Tides, from gravitational forces, 187
Time, flexibility of, 190
Tires
        pneumatic, 66
        skidding, 64, 65, 67, 70
        vulcanized, 65–66
Titan, atmosphere of, 93, 97

Toasters
  fires in, 21, 24, 25–26
  heating of, 21–22, 23, 24
Toast on fire, 21, 26
Toe, stubbed, 266, 271
Toothpaste, protective ingredients
  in, 264, 265
Torn clothing, 150, 155–56
Toughened glass, 212
Trachea, in digestion, 230
Traction control, on cars, 70–71
Tripping on the curb, 79, 86
Turtles, migration of, 101, 102, 104
TV killed by lightning, 236,
  241–43
Twill weaves, 154, 156
Twining, as weaving method, 153
Twisting, strength from, 151–53
Type I and II muscles, 195–96

UHT milk. See Milk, ultra-high
  temperature, 39
Up and down, perceptions of,
  185–86

Van der Waals forces, superglue
  and, 117
Varicose veins, 168
Vat dyes, 216
Venus, atmosphere of, 96
VHS videocassettes, 251–52
Vinyl records, information storage
  on, 254–55
Viruses, e-mail, 157, 160–53
Visceral pain, 270
Visual agnosia, 147
Vitruvius, 274, 275
Voisin, Gabriel, 67
Volta, Alessandro, 43
Vulcanization, 65–66

Walking, balance required for,
  79–80, 84–85
Water
  boiling, effect of pressure on,
    29–32
  as conductor of electricity,
    45–46
  displacement of, 273–74,
    275–76
  effect on batteries, 42–43, 45,
    46–47
  in humans, 33–34
  origin of, on Earth, 93–95
  steam explosions and,
    27–29
  superglue interacting with,
    117–18
Water pressure, effect on divers,
  32–33
Waterproof clothes, 97, 98, 99
Wax, for early writing, 135, 136
Weaving, of cloth, 153–54
Whales, migration of, 102–3,
  104
White blood cells, leukemia
  affecting, 181
White wine, for removing red wine
  stains, 214, 218–19
Wildebeest, migration of, 101
Wine stains, 214, 218
  removing, 218–20
Wood, stained, 217
Worms, e-mail, 157, 160–53
Writing instruments
  for dispersing ink, 137–38
  history of, 135–41

Yogurt
  making of, 37
  probiotic, 233–34